THE SKULL OF YORICK

Also by Eric Larsen:

Homer for Real: A Reading of the Iliad (2009)

A Nation Gone Blind:
America in an Age of Simplification and Deceit (2006)

I Am Zoë Handke (a novel, 1994)

An American Memory (a novel), 1988

THE SKULL OF YORICK

**The Emptiness of American Thinking
at a Time of Grave Peril**

Studies in the Cover-Up of 9/11

BY

ERIC LARSEN

THE OLIVER ARTS & OPEN PRESS

From *A Writer at War: Vasily Grossman with the Red Army, 1941–1945 by
Vasily Grossman*, edited by Luba Vinogradova, translated by Antony Beevor,
copyright © 2005 by Ekaterina Vasilievna Korotkova-Grossman and Elena
Fedorovna Kozhichkina. Used by permission of Pantheon Books, a division of
Random House, Inc.

Excerpts from "Will the Real Economic Hit Men Please Stand Up?" used by
permission of Catherine Austin Fitts and Scoop Independent News
http://www.scoop.co.nz/stories/HL0503/S00090.htm

"How Republicans Created Executive Branch Hegemony" reproduced
by permission of Paul Craig Roberts

Excerpts from "Five Years Free: Why Haven't We Been Attacked Again?"
by permission of *Slate* magazine

Excerpts from "Enough of the 9/11 Conspiracies, Already" used
by permission of *The Progressive* magazine

Excerpts from "The Canon as Cannon," "Is Condi Hiding the Smoking Gun,"
"Delighted By the Joy Of Bad Things," and "The Clear Blue Sky"
by permission of the *New York Times*

Larsen, Eric,. 1941-
The Skull of Yorick:
The Emptiness of American Thinking
At a Time of Grave Peril

ISBN: 978-0-9819891-0-5
Library of Congress Control Number: 2010942592

The Oliver Arts & Open Press
2578 Broadway, Suite #102
New York, NY 10025
http://www.oliveropenpress.com

To our children
And to their children
And to their children after them.

Eric Larsen   *The Skull of Yorick*

HAMLET: Let me see. [Takes the skull.] Alas, poor Yorick! I knew him, Horatio, a fellow of infinite jest, of most excellent fancy. He hath borne me on his back a thousand times. And now how abhorred in my imagination it is! My gorge rises at it. Here hung those lips that I have kissed I know not how oft. Where be your gibes now? Your gambols, your songs, your flashes of merriment that were wont to set the table on a roar? Not one now to mock your own grinning? Quite chapfall'n? Now get you to my lady's chamber, and tell her, let her paint an inch thick, to this favor she must come. Make her laugh at that. Prithee, Horatio, tell me one thing.'

HORATIO: What's that, my lord?

HAMLET: Dost thou think Alexander looked o' this fashion i' th' earth?

HORATIO: E'en so.

HAMLET: And smelt so? Pah!

—*Hamlet*, V, I, 172-188

The obvious question is: How can we trust progressives when they are such reliable agents of the Police State?

—Paul Craig Roberts, "Progressives want 'direct action' but a disarmed public," *Online Journal,* June 22, 2010

CONTENTS

Author's Foreword xi

2006

1. Why Do You Suppose the *New York Times* (and *The Chicago Tribune,* and *The Wall Street Journal,* and the *Portland Oregonian*) Showed No Interest in Running this Piece? I

2. Walter Kirn and the *New York Times Book Review* Have Plenty to Account For... 5

3. Is America No Longer Just Blind, But Now Also *Insane*? 15

4. The Aftermath of the Crime of 9/11: America Aids in the Staging of Its Own Murder 19

5. Our Enemies the Left Gatekeepers, Pt. 1 29

6. Our Enemies the Left Gatekeepers, Pt. 2 .... 4I

7. Our Enemies the Left Gatekeepers, Pt. 3 .... 5I

2007

8. U.S.A.—Land of Liars 63

9. Amy Goodman: A Mind Prostituted 79

10. Poisoned Nation, Poisoned Truth 87

11. The Pernicious Hypocrisy of Frank Rich, Part 1 95

12. The Pernicious Hypocrisy of Frank Rich, Part 2 III

2008

13. The Premeditated Murder of the United States of
America 137

14. The "Debate" Over 9/11 157

15. Is Dwight Garner a Dissembler, Deceiver, and
Malefactor to His Nation? 181

16. Howard Zinn and the Tea Cozy 191

2009

17. Can the Literary Life Exist in a Post-1984 Nation? 205

18. Appendix 255

AUTHOR'S FOREWORD

1.

Naming things has never been easy for me, and finding a title for this book has been no exception. The book is a selection of relatively recent pieces on the subject of the American Collapse, or the Great American Hollowing Out, the Approaching Armageddon, or perhaps the Great American Cavitation. So shameless, so unadmirable, so loathsomely and horrifyingly ruinous—so *evil,* I believe it just to say—do I find the nature, culture, and behavior of "thinking" America, especially over the past two decades or so, that I gave serious thought to calling the book *Marching into Madness.* I tried an expansion (*Marching into Madness: Deception, Terror, and Loss*). I even tried *Abomination and Poison: American "Thinkers" Lie to Us and to Themselves.*

In the end, I came up with the long title you've already seen: *The Skull of Yorick: The Emptiness of American Thinking at a Time of Grave Peril.*

The title is long for a reason. Given the scope and purposes of the book, the title has to link together two things that normally (and often with immense snobbery) are kept apart, almost as if on opposite rims of a canyon, where they stare vacantly across at one another. For the moment, I am going to call those two things politics and literature.

Today's Americans are among the world's very worst thinkers—it was this conviction, among others, that led me to write *A Nation Gone Blind: America in an Age of Simplification and Deceit.*[1] And the same conviction, although the situation seems even more dreadful

---

[1] Shoemaker & Hoard, 2006.

now than it did four years ago, in 2006, is what leads me to gather up some of the pieces of what I've written since then and put them into this book.

Since at least the late nineteenth century, America has been bad at knowing how—or at learning how—to combine in a single mind what I'm calling the literary and the political. Europe has—or did have—a completely different tradition in this way than we did, and an earlier one. A person needs only a sprinkling of names—Turgenev, Tolstoy, Dostoevsky, Kafka, Gide, Mann, Koestler, Camus, Sartre—to make the point. In various important ways, such writers as those were literary *and* political. I'd happily try making similar arguments in the cases of George Eliot (especially the Eliot of *Adam Bede*), Dickens, and a few others among the English—Lawrence, conceivably, Orwell of course—but even in England (*and* in Ireland), literary intellectualism has had a different and frequently more subtle way than Europe's of combining the literary and the political. Joyce, for example, or Yeats.

Americans, on the other hand, have been especially bad in the matter of intellectual *wholeness*.[2] I talk about this subject at length in the second chapter of *A Nation Gone Blind* ("The Death of Literary Thinking in America"), and so I won't go through it again here. Still, however authentically rich the American literary tradition is, it's rich also in examples of the failure of the literary and the political to achieve a productive union in the individual mind—or in individual examples of literary art. When the political, or the cultural-political, consciousness has somehow been "joined" with a literary consciousness, the result has often been banality in the resulting *literary* qualities, however influential an individual work may have been—obvious examples being works like *Uncle Tom's Cabin* or Upton Sinclair's *The Jungle*. On the other hand, the "high art" of Henry James—whether it's to one's taste or not—offers literary splendor of an undeniably Olympian kind, though few would seek out either James or his books as guides to a political consciousness that's either particularly practical or very deep.

There are many examples of American writers who fail, overdose, or in some deleterious way fumble on one side or the other, the literary or the political, as if incapable of naturally incorporating the two. Hemingway, who was a true and nearly faultless literary genius early on, remained unsophisticated politically—and yet was unable

---

[2] In college, for a senior thesis, I wrote an essay called "Nathanial Hawthorne and the Puritan Allegorical Vision." It argued that Hawthorne was unable to write about immediate experience without the aid or platform of a prior idea *about* it. He lacked a natural blending of what I'm calling the literary and the political, no matter much he yearned for it, and no matter how much he struggled to bring the two together.

either to leave that unsophisticated side alone or to incorporate it into his aesthetic self. The "un-wholeness" of Hemingway's mind, the failure of the aesthetic and the social-political to find comfortable union there, may go a good distance toward helping explain the gradual but steady deterioration of the great writer's literary gifts. An example far removed in atmosphere, place, and time from Hemingway but not in kind is Grace Paley. Paley's high and subtle literary gifts, an American equivalent of Muriel Spark's, fell away to nothing as political compulsions and demands siphoned away the literary gifts instead of each kind enriching the other. On the other hand there are writers whose work dies—William Gass is an example—for an opposite reason, namely that it never really even *senses* the existence of the political where, seen or not, the political nevertheless dwells inside of life.

The point, though, isn't really to note this kind of bifurcated, half-unseeing, half-empty mind only in American writers and artists, but to note it in Americans in general—most notably in educated and influential ones. Take college presidents. Not since Laurence McKinley Gould left the presidency of Carleton College in 1962 have I myself met, known, or heard of another college president who has been what might be called *cultivated*. That doesn't mean they don't exist. It means I've never met, known, or heard of one.[3] There was a time when such figures rose to higher office or to higher levels of public or national service. Now, they are merely bureaucrats, species corporatus.

Such bifurcation, single-sidedness, or one-dimensionality of mind is doubtless caused partly by the strain of anti-intellectualism in American history—a strain well known, strong, widely written about, and just about never salutary. But we're looking at something now that's different from plain old anti-intellectualism. We're looking at something more subtle and insidious. We're looking at the manifestation of anti-intellectualism *by* intellectuals and *inside* of intellectuals themselves, a kind of self-imposed debility, disease, and handicap, even though at the same time this is something that the intellectuals themselves consider to be *good*.

I should explain that by "intellectual" I mean not only scholars, historians, philosophers or the like. I intend the word in a broader

---

3 "Cultivated" is a troubled word, but I've used it and I'll stick with it. According to thinkers like anthropologist, activist, and writer John Zerzan, humankind's most disastrous mistake was to leave hunting and gathering and turn to agriculture—or "cultivation." Only after that behavior-change, Zerzan (*Running on Emptiness: The Pathology of Civilization,* 2002) argues, did jealousy, oppression of women, disease, the concept of ownership, and war come into existence. "Cultivation" came at great cost both to humankind and to Earth itself. Now, many thousands of years later, the lack of it may very well return us (if we're very lucky) to hunting and gathering.

sense, as referring to writers, artists, creators, analysts, reporters, teachers, thinkers of almost every kind, people who've been to college, say, who should know *some*thing, and who hold employment that includes some kind of public responsibility. We are a nation, after all. Public responsibility of any kind that relies upon or requires the use of any significant element of intellectuality is by definition an important responsibility. But in our intellectuality we remain a nation of one-siders. If you were to imagine us, as a nation, as having only one big huge mind, it would be a mind with art and art-things all on one side, and politics and political things all on the other side. And nowhere would there be a whole, complete, integrated mind.

In *A Nation Gone Blind*, I chose, not altogether arbitrarily, the year 1947 as a marker of the beginning, or at least the newly intensified birthing, of what is now America's demonstrably perfected system of genuine mass media. The choice of that particular year means that since 1947 Americans have been steadily and purposively taught, encouraged, and indoctrinated to be more passive than active, more consumer than doer, and to see life and "reality" not as they actually are but as the mass media have already pre-defined and pre-packaged them. So expert and so all-encompassing is this system of mass media that not only has it created what Americans see and perceive as "real," but it has also trained and conditioned (or "cultivated") Americans to accept this pre-fabricated reality as something that they have both the *right* and the highly honorable *duty* to embrace and defend.

That was my very grim view of the American way of seeing and thinking when I finished writing *A Nation Gone Blind* in 2005. My view now is even more grim. I no longer think that an on-going process of conditioning, indoctrination, or habit-formation is necessary in order to make Americans continue to see a "false" reality in place of the real one. I now think that Americans *voluntarily* choose to do so. The metaphor of drugs is appropriate. With nothing more than a maintenance-regimen of the drug in question, Americans, without further aid or provocation, not only choose to see false reality as true or real reality, but they actually prefer, extol, and *defend* the false over the real.

It is difficult if not impossible to avoid concluding that Americans have degenerated to a rank among the least perceptive, informed, intelligent, or thoughtful people in the entire world. I passionately and devoutly wish that this weren't so. Nor, in the earlier parts of my life, could I have believed, ever, not in the remotest reaches of my imagination, that later in my life such a situation would have come so indisputably to be the case.

2.

I'm going to use the phrase "the skull of Yorick" as a way of help-ing to suggest the desirability of drawing together the two aspects of life now kept separate from one another, the ones I'm calling the "literary" and the "political."

Coming as he does from very possibly the greatest of Shakespeare's plays, Yorick is intended to evoke the literary side of things—or the literary part of our consciousness. That his skull is all that's left of him raises considerable ambiguities and not a few symbols. Human skulls, after all, are the cradles of our brains. And our brains are what we depend on for the creation of meaning. Yet when Hamlet peers into the empty skull of Yorick, what can he possibly find or see there except hollowness, absence, and nothingness?

Shakespeare is fully aware of this fact and knows very well exactly what he's doing at this point in the play. From beginning to end of the drama, after all, he has woven the greatest of all philosophic ques-tions, in ways large and small, throughout almost every scene. The question so woven is none other than the question of whether or not there is meaning to life.

At the moment when Hamlet peers into Yorick's skull, the an-swer would seem to be that, well, no, there isn't any meaning to life, this conclusion being reached on the grounds that there's nothing left of this once-brilliant court jester except nothingness. On the other hand, the equally-brilliant Prince Hamlet never stops poking and prodding at the question, often in some of the play's most memo-rable passages ("To be or not to be," for example, or "What is a man, / If his chief good and market of his time / Be but to sleep and feed? A beast, no more"). My own reading of the play is that the Prince does find his answer—but that he is prevented (whether by life, chance, or Shakespeare himself, I won't say) from telling what he has found:

> Had I but time (as this fell sergeant, Death,
> Is strict in his arrest), O, I could tell you—
> But let it be.—Horatio, I am dead.

Whatever the answer is or might be, we aren't going to hear it. "O, I could tell you," Hamlet says—but he doesn't tell us. Now, liter-ary people know and understand that the prince's failing to provide this "answer" is not a bad thing, but in fact a very good thing. Literary people know that the answer to a question is in a great many cases less important than the *asking* of it. In fact, the play *Hamlet* would doubtless be drained of the greatest part of its interest—and would never have endured as it has endured—if the prince were to give us the "answer" to the enormous question he has been pondering all the way from the opening scene to the closing one.

If the play were to provide an "answer," the whole drama would fall into insignificance and hold little of interest for anyone. Both the play and its greatness would disappear into near-nothingness—or, at best, into a slip of paper just large enough for an "answer" to be printed on it.

Now, two things need to be explained. One is exactly what I mean by a "literary person." And the other is why—and when, and how—a question is more significant than its answer.

Let's take the easier question first (partly because it will also help in tackling the second one). A fair number of readers may be angry at what I'm about to say, I expect, since I'm going to trample on something widely perceived by Americans to be a *right*, and one that, when it is taken as a right, is defended with great passion and adamance. Even so, here goes. The right I'm talking about is the "right" to be entertained. In light of this "right," the fact is that a person who may read all the time, book after book, throughout the year—the fact is that that person in great likelihood still won't be the least bit a *literary* one.

Here's why. The fact is that reading for entertainment, in whatever quantity, has little or nothing to do with whether or not such a reader is literary. This is less true of children and very young adults, whose often omnivorous reading for entertainment really *can* be a genuine step toward their becoming literary. Unfortunately, though, development in that direction is usually destroyed by the enormous pressure to simplify and adulterate oneself that comes with adolescence, especially in its commercialized or "mediated" form, almost the only form adolescence does come in now. Adolescent development toward becoming literary through reading is most commonly destroyed by conventional parents' powerful fear of having children who are in any significant ways different from all other children—meaning, for example, more sensitive, more thoughtful, more complex, more independent, more introverted, more discriminatory, and more fearless of the false judgments of their peers. Most of the intellectual and emotional destruction of all Americans takes place right around this point—adolescence. Only those infinitesimal few who for whatever reasons are able to escape that destruction will ever become, or stand even the faintest chance of being able to become, literary people.

I trust it's clear by now that I don't mean "literary" as a word suggesting the usual conventions, artsy people with their various affectations, tweed jackets with elbow patches, brier pipes, people who might gaze down their noses at you in disapproving ways through horn-rimmed or perhaps matronly glasses, or play the "poet" game of one-downmanship, seeing who can out-bedraggle, out-rag-and-patch, or out-slouch the next. All of that stuff has its place, and maybe even its fun, but I'm using the word "literary" to mean something different from bookstore, classroom, coffee bar, or library snobs. By my own meaning of the word, I fear that there are probably hardly more than a few handfuls of literary people left in all the humanities, English, and literature departments across the country. I base this dismal estimate on my own experience in a combined forty-five years as an academic. The last half-century's worth of dumbing down—witnessed by me—has known no social limitations and no professional barriers. I'd guess that by now, early in 2011, just about the same percentage of people in the academic and professional population is literary as is the percentage of the general population. My reasons for saying such a thing will become clearer as we go on.

We can conclude, in any case, that how much a person reads has nothing to do, generally, with whether or not that person is literary. More interesting still, we can conclude, that not even *what* a person reads has much of anything to do with whether that person is literary or not.

The real truth is that there's only one aspect of reading that has anything to do either with determining or revealing whether a person is a literary person or not. And that one thing is *how* a person reads.

I have referred elsewhere to something Marilynne Robinson said in an interview that ran in a University of Iowa Writers' Workshop newsletter. Robinson's remark has to do with writing, but here I'm going to show how it has just as much to do with reading as with writing.

Here is how I quoted Robinson in *A Nation Gone Blind* at a point where I was enumerating the qualities of serious writing:

> Serious writing must have the entirety of reality as its subject matter, and this subject matter must remain as whole as possible throughout the work if the work is to remain serious. This doesn't mean that every piece of writing must be about everything, but that serious writing must at every moment be as inclusive as is possible while still maintaining coherence. It must push the limit in this regard at every moment or lapse into the unserious. Marilynne Robinson, in an interview, expresses this idea as clearly and wonderfully as, say, Henry James might have a century ago: "Any writer," she says, "or any moment in writing, when the imagination seems to be *as alert as possible to everything that can be understood out of a moment or situation,* seems to me to be when that impulse is being made into art [emphasis mine]." [4]

---

[4] Quoted from *A Nation Gone Blind: America in an Age of Simplification and Deceit* (Shoemaker & Hoard, 2006), p. 141–142

Now let's take Marilynne Robinson's observation and apply it not to writing but to reading. It becomes the parallel, true, and important requisite that when a person is reading something—reading anything—they "be as alert as possible to everything that can be understood out of the moment or situation" both *in* the thing they are reading *and* in the act of their reading it. When *that* describes how a person reads, the person is a literary person, probably always has been, and almost certainly always will be.

It's a matter, above all, of being alert. It's a matter of being "as alert as possible to *everything* that can be understood out of a moment or situation"—in this case out of the moment and situation (and therefore the meanings) of *reading* something. This is what determines whether a person is an intellectual or not, is an artist or not, or is literary or not.

There. The cat is out of the bag. I've finally revealed what we've—I've—been talking about all along. Being "literary" means having the quality not just of being alert, but of being "as alert as possible to everything that can be understood out of a moment or situation"—and being this way *all the time.*

Not long ago, I wrote the third of a three-part essay taking up the question "Can the Literary Life Exist In a Post-*1984* Nation?" The title of that third part was "What Do Frank Rich, Dwight Garner, Rebecca Solnit, Don Delillo, and Thomas L. Friedman Reveal About This Immeasurably Important Question?" As it turned out, they revealed plenty, and they did so for this reason: That although all posed as such and perhaps believed themselves to be such, not a single one of them was an intellectual, an artist, or literary.

We're brought back again to the title I chose for this book, *"The Skull of Yorick."* In studying these people, in the essay just mentioned, what I learned was that every one of them—Rich, Garner, Solnit, Delillo, and Friedman—was *empty.*

How can this *be*? After all, these five people are prestigious, published, renowned. How can they be *empty*?

Let's take the matter step by step. For example, we might agree that the five aren't *completely* empty. We could be even more meliorative, in fact, and go on to say that they're only *half* empty. Another conciliatory step remains. Instead of using the negative to say they're half *empty*, we could use the positive to say they're half *full.* At least this way we make things sound more positive. Just imagine if these five figures, Rich, Garner, Solnit, Delillo, and Friedman, were *gas tanks.* How much better and more promising it would seem to know that they were half full rather than half empty.

But, unfortunately or fortunately, depending on you look at it, they're not gas tanks. Instead, they are writers, reviewers, novelists, columnists and analysts who are not only nationally but internationally known. They are people of considerable responsibility and no slight privilege. They hold positions of leadership, power, and influence. Therefore, they clearly must not be considered as gas tanks, while just as obviously they *must* be considered as intellectuals, artists, writers, and literary figures. That's how they are considered, after all, by those who *pay* them. That's how they are considered by those who *hire* them. That's how they are considered by those who *publish* them. And that's how they are considered by those who award them *prizes.*

Nevertheless, there remains a problem, and a great one. Two problems remain, in fact. Or three.

The first is the easiest to understand, and it can be understood through the asking of a simple question: At *half full,* are these people (or any others) going to be able to reach the level of consciousness identified by Marilynne Robinson as the level necessary if they are to create, think intellectually, or be *literary?* And the answer, of course, is that, no, they aren't going to be able. Not the half full, but only the full, those most entirely capable, most entirely equipped for it, can possibly be "as alert as possible to everything that can be understood out of a moment or situation" and be that alert *all the time.*

The problem, then, is that those who are only half full just can't do the job. But there's worse news. Even though we've chivalrously agreed to consider our representative group—Rich, Garner, Solnit, Delillo, and Friedman—as half full instead of empty, there's another matter to be faced. And that's the inescapable truth that if our representatives are half full—no matter how passionately mortal man might wish it otherwise—they are also, *half empty.*

So we've seen and named two of our three great problems: One, that our half-full group can't do the job required of them, and, two, that however meliorative the concept (or truth) of their half fullness may be, there's no escaping the concomitant truth that they're also half *empty.*

Things aren't looking very upbeat, but the worst of our problems is still to come. That worst problem comes clear with our next step—a step that thoroughness, responsibility, and honesty require we take. This step comes about thanks to the obligation we have to define precisely what we mean by a word, phrase, or concept once we've made use of it. We have concluded that our representatives are half full, and we can say now that what they are half full of is the ability to see, be alert, and so on. But if they are half full, they must also, as said, be half empty. And there's our third problem: How do you define the emptiness that makes up *half* of what each of our representatives is non-made of?

It's very bad, this required definition.

Again, we know that the concepts or powers of consciousness, seeing, perception, and awareness are the concepts or powers comprising the full half of our representatives. Logic and honesty, at this point, give us no leeway or escape. If the full half comprises what allows these people to *see,* then we have no choice but to define the empty half as being comprised of that which *prevents them* from seeing.

The empty half of them is blindness. The empty half of them is what keeps them in ignorance.

Being half blind, half ignorant, half in pitch blackness, they can't conceivably reach the levels and intensities of observation and understanding required to reach Marilynne Robinson's needed level of alertness.

It's as though our five subjects, Frank Rich, Dwight Garner, Rebecca Solnit, Don DeLillo, and Thomas L. Friedman, were walking around with their heads in sacks.

And here's the truly awful part about it: That *nothing*—no quality in American education, no quality in American media, no quality in American business, no quality in American literature or publishing, no quality in American academia, no quality in American art, no quality in American politics or American political thought, no quality in the American corporation—exists either *in order* to help (or that possesses the least ability to help) Rich, Garner, Solnit, DeLillo, or Friedman get their heads out of those black, thick, opaque, heavy sacks.

In fact, the opposite is true: Every quality in American education, every quality in American media, every quality in American business, every quality in American literature and publishing, every quality in American academia, every quality in American art, every quality in American politics and political thought, and every quality in the American corporation serves two purposes—one purpose being to encourage them to *keep* their heads in their sacks, the other being to make them as unaware as possible that their heads *are in the sacks at all.*

This book is a selection of essays describing and decrying this virulent and destructive American disease of *blindness that believes itself to be sightedness.* I don't have a better name for it—nothing, say, like the Houyhnhnms' definition of a "lie" as "the thing that was not." And nothing like Paul Levy's brilliant definition for the pathological yet ingeniously disguised cruelty of his own father, "malignant egophrenia."[5]

All I can call the thing I'm writing about, the thing that is destroying our nation and putting the entire world at risk—is *the disease of blindness that believes itself to be sightedness.*

---

5 Paul Levy (http://www.awakeninthedream.com/) is the author of *The Madness of George W. Bush* (2005) and a brilliant writer, artist, healer and independent researcher.

Aspects and manifestations of the disease are visible and abundant everywhere for anyone able to get out from under the edge of this disease's suffocating false-reality-blanket and *look*. The disease manifests itself in routine, omnipresent, and ever more crude propaganda of kinds that will work *only* on or with those who *already* suffer or are incapacitated by it—that number, unfortunately, comprising the very great majority of Americans.[6] The disease manifests itself in very large-scale things like the campaign and election of Barack Obama, who for two entire years told one untruth after another and yet was elected—by those suffering from the disease of blindness that believes itself to be sightedness. It manifests itself in a nation's tolerating the invasion and destruction of Iraq and its people on the basis of blatant lies and manipulations that could not *conceivably* have been taken as truth except by masses suffering from the blindness-as-sight disease in an extremely advanced form.

Other manifestations occur everywhere and all the time, in things and places great and small. If I were to continue citing and listing them, this "Author's Foreword" would itself quickly become the size of a book.

Still, the subject of the disease's manifestation in the realm of publishing and writing does deserve further note before we go on, since this will be the subject of not all but most of the essays that follow. Commercial publishing in the United States has become irreversibly depraved and monumentally false as the result of its own thorough infection with the disease of blindness that believes itself to be sightedness. In fiction, nothing but TV-on-the-page or movies-on-the-page is publishable.[7] The "subject matter" of such fiction must be innocuous by merit of the necessity that it fall only within the range of what is visible to the "half full" side of the American consciousness, while all that is invisible to the blind half must *remain* invisible. The governing rule in any institution, like the publishing institution, that is itself infected with the disease of blindness that believes itself to be sightedness, is that there *must be no growth or broadening in, on, or within that blind region.* Nor *can* there be any growth once those responsible—those in editorial and ownership positions, say—are themselves also inflicted with the disease. The system, once this happens, becomes self-regulating, those afflicted with the blind-

---

6 As an example of crudeness, consider the *New York Times* for June 4, 2010, where "Managing the News in China" tells us that "astronaut Yang Liwei was bloodied during re-entry in China's first space mission in 2003. The solution: clean him up and re-shoot the scene" (front page). Propaganda of this kind can work only on those blind to the equal or even greater use of "News Management" in America.

7 While in movies themselves propagandistic superficialities like *The Hurt Locker* win major awards.

ness making decisions suitable for others who are exactly as blind as themselves and just as certain that they are in fact sighted. Whole truth no longer plays a role and ceases entirely to be a valued concept or commodity. That is, the only truth that remains acceptable—the only truth *visible* to those existing in the "half full" side of conscious-ness—is truth that is already known and that has already been seen, with the consequence that it is at very best half-truth and is incapable of resulting in *change* of any significant kind at all.

The situation is somewhat different in the case of non-fiction, but only very slightly so, since in at least ninety-nine percent of cases, and very probably more, the only truth permissible as subject mat-ter is, again, truth already known and seen rather than truth previ-ously unseen or unknown. The book you now hold in your hands, for example, could not be published by any commercial or mainstream press in the nation, since its purpose is to cast light on things unseen and un-seeable by the blind half. That is why I created a press for the publication of it and of other books similar to it.

A last look at the book's title may be a help in drawing this preface to a close. As Hamlet peers into the skull of Yorick, it is empty, as we've said, even though it *once* served as the cradle and home not only of a human mind, but of a human mind capable of "infinite jest." Of the two words in that famous phrase, it's hard to say which is the more important. "Jest" can mean not only wit, humor, quickness, gift at repartee, but also simply *intelligence* itself. Knowing this, the read-er can hardly escape the huge significance of the word "infinite" as a modifier. No half-blind or half-seeing person was Yorick! No sufferer *he* from the disease of blindness that believes itself to be sightedness! From Hamlet himself comes the naming of Yorick's intelligence as "infinite," not only the highest of compliments from the most intel-lectual of princes, but an allusion also to the theme of thought and thinking that runs through the entire play and may even make up its central, fundamental subject—the subject of the human mind's role in determining (or in *creating*) the difference between being and nothingness, between meaning and meaninglessness.[8]

Americans, suffering today from their particular disease, can be compared, in this scene, both to Hamlet and to Yorick—or, more accurately, to Yorick's skull. Like the skull, they are empty (or half-empty) and blind (or half-blind). But they also *could* be like Hamlet—who, by looking directly and unflinchingly into that emptiness, finds a way to *think* about the meaning of the emptiness, which is another way of saying that he finds a way to "see" it, or even to see what the nature of that emptiness is. Once he understands the nature of the

---

[8] Notice the same word in Hamlet's "I could be bounded in a nutshell and count myself king of infinite space." (II, ii)

emptiness, one can very convincingly argue, it isn't any longer emptiness at all, but something else entirely, since it's now something that Hamlet *understands*. How can *that* be nothingness?

We don't need to settle such questions here and now, the sort of questions raised by this kind of conjecture. But I think that we do need to see how extremely clear the parallel is between Hamlet at that moment in the graveyard scene and Americans in general today. Like us today, Hamlet lived also in "a time of grave peril." A towering and wholly monstrous murder had been committed, poisoning the kingdom at its very heart, just as has happened with us. The kingdom of Denmark was poisoned, festering, on the brink of death, ruin, and collapse, exactly as is our own threatened, poisoned, and dying nation today. If we don't or can't begin immediately to see the truth of these facts, to see and understand the causes and truths and characteristics of them, in order to enable ourselves, like Hamlet, to *do something about it*—well, then, simply put, we're doomed. We're doomed to tyranny in place of freedom, chains in place of liberty, and, above all, to a cruel, demeaning, hollow, unforgiving, and empty imprisonment intellectually, emotionally, spiritually, and personally.

I referred to an essay asking two questions: "Can the Literary Life Exist In a Post-*1984* Nation? What Do Frank Rich, Rebecca Solnit, Don Delillo, and Thomas L. Friedman Reveal About This Immeasurably Important Question?" In that essay, I describe what it will soon be like for all of us if we Americans don't immediately—not soon, but immediately—find a means to heal ourselves of and then inoculate ourselves to the crippling, enervating, disempowering disease of the blindness that believes itself to be sightedness.

The following quotation from that essay is a description of what things will very, very soon be like if we fail to regain our sight, fail to look at the entirety of who we are, of where we are, of who our enemies are, and of what they have done and *are* doing to us. When the essay talks about there being no literary life, the reader should think of that phrase as meaning, equally, no intellectual life, no emotional life, and no spiritual life:

> It's not looking very good, is it. A nation composed entirely of liars on the one hand and, on the other, of the self-deluded who either believe the lies or accept them in an ever-expanding and endlessly adaptable ignorance— such a nation will never have a literature. How could it? None of the writers we've met in this essay [Frank Rich, Dwight Garner, Rebecca Solnit, Don Delillo, Thomas L. Friedman] would ever conceivably be able to provide even the barest rudiments of a literature. As for the "literary life," well, all that means is "literary person," isn't it? Same answer. So long as anyone is either lying to others or lying to him- or herself about the full and actual nature of the external reality they live within, such a person

can't possibly be literary. Sure, they can write poems, stories, and novels—but those will be (as most are already) empty ones, shells, imitations of pieces that once may have been written for *real*, but these copies will be nothing more than copies, lacking the wholeness, the purpose, and the aesthetic drive of the originals. These won't be aesthetically meaningful, nor will they be aesthetically complete, and these won't be *intellectually* meaningful, nor will they be *intellectually* complete, since not only will they be imitations but they'll furthermore be born out of a false-world, or at best a half-world, with half-emotions, half-knowledge, half-feelings— a distant cry from Marilynne Robinson's true and indispensible notion that the readiness for art comes only "when the imagination seems to be *as alert as possible to everything that can be understood out of a moment or situation.*" Ignorance, self-delusion, and a life's diet of falsehood are no recipe for this kind of wholeness and completeness.

As far as the nation's present path indicates, if we continue on it as we are now, we're destined to become a nation only more and more ignorant, more and more empty, more and more insane.

Can it be true? Can things be this bad? Well, let's start looking.

A NOTE ON CHRONOLOGY

The eighteen pieces that follow, dated from 2006 through 2009, are arranged in the same order they were written in. They have not been edited so as to make them seem to have been written for the purpose of filling a particular, planned volume. As a result, two things occur that should be mentioned here. The first is that references to the time passed since 9/11 will vary from piece to piece. In a piece from 2006, I will logically refer to 9/11 as having taken place five years earlier. In 2009, however, the reference will be eight years. For this reason—to help keep things clear—I have placed both at the beginning and at the end of each piece the date when it was written.

The second thing to mention is that the pieces, arranged here chronologically, also reflect changes in my own thinking. This is especially true in regard to 9/11 itself. I began reading seriously about 9/11 only in the summer of 2003 and understood quickly that the Muslim "attack" had in reality been a highly complex fraud planned and executed from the inside or from elements of the inside. This view became increasingly refined and more and more abundantly evidence-based as the years passed. The same evolution of thinking was true not only in regard to the perpetrators of the great crime but also in regard to what specific force or forces were the actual cause of the destruction of the World Trade Center buildings.

I initially believed the theory that the impact of airliners had caused "collapses." I soon read further and saw the absurdity of that notion—if only because it failed to explain Building 7, for example, also destroyed but never "hit" by a "plane." I later, for a short time, embraced Dr. Steven Jones's theory that the "planned demolition" of the buildings came about through the use of thermite or thermate—while now I consider Jones *and* his theory to be not only wrong but fraudulent, as I do also Richard Gage and his Architects and Engineers for 9/11 Truth with their own theory of "nano-thermite."

My view now—and the one I held by the time I wrote the final pieces in this book—is that there in fact were no airliners and was no demolition by means of conventional explosives of any kind, including mini-nuclear devices. The scholarship and research of Dr. Judy Wood, formerly of Clemson University, show irrefutably that the buildings were destroyed by directed energy weaponry and that they did not in fact "collapse" at all but were, instead, turned into dust long before they hit the ground or could have hit the ground, through molecular dissociation brought about by energy fields being directed in such ways as to interfere with one another at the locations where the buildings stood.

Dr. Wood's research, at the time of this writing, has not appeared in book form. I hope it will appear so soon, in spite of the obstructionism and opposition Dr. Wood has faced from virtually all sides in the so-called "9/11 truth movement," in spite of her irrefutable evidence and in spite of the complete solidity of both her research and her conclusions. Until such time as her book is published, readers must rely on Dr. Wood's web site, http://www.drjudywood.com/, where all of her research, evidence, and conclusions can be found, albeit not in the same clear, orderly, powerful, and narrative-driven form they take in her monumental book, clearly the most important book of the twenty-first century.

EL

As a courtesy to the reader, since many of the footnotes in this book contain URLs, we have created a webpage of all footnotes that contain links, so they are easily clickable. We hope this will make it easier for you to go to the referenced sources.

http://www.oliveropenpress.com/Oliver.009.02.Yorick.notes.pdf

THE SKULL OF YORICK

2006

1.

WHY DO YOU SUPPOSE THE *NEW YORK TIMES* (AND *THE CHICAGO TRIBUNE*, AND *THE WALL STREET JOURNAL*, AND *THE PORTLAND OREGONIAN*) SHOWED NO INTEREST IN RUNNING THIS PIECE?

To the Reader:

Early in 2006, I was urged to write op ed pieces as a way of drawing attention to my forthcoming book. Writing them was hard, publishing harder. This one (like the others) never did make it, so I published it on my web site as the piece you see here. It raises the question whether newspapers are interested in covering the truth—or not. Maybe they don't *believe* the truth? Or think that if they pay no attention, it will go away? Or maybe they really can't *see* it? The phrase "half-blind" comes into one's thoughts.

In early March 2006, I submitted the following op ed piece to the *Times* and never heard a peep. Now, I know perfectly well that that's the policy—if you don't hear within a week, they don't want the piece. Fair enough. But why do you suppose they weren't interested? Or why do you suppose *The Chicago Tribune* wasn't interested, or *The Wall Street Journal*, either, or *The Portland Oregonian*?

To me, that becomes an increasingly interesting question. For the sake of argument, let's assume that, at each newspaper, the piece really did get looked at and wasn't simply buried under thousands of other submissions of the kind that flood into the editors' offices. Let's assume that a staff member actually picked it up, read it, and made a reasoned decision not to run it.

What's interesting is: *Why* not run it?

Here's a kind of brain-exercise. Imagine that you were an op ed editor at the *Times, Tribune, Journal,* or *Oregonian*. What would you think about it? Would you hate the piece? Or would you like it, maybe even a lot, wish you could run it, but feel that you must not? And, of course, if you *must* not, then *why*?

Was there something unsound about it? Something lacking? Something untrue? Or—something *embarrassing*?

I first wrote and submitted the piece in response to a *Times* editorial (February 26, 2006) called "Proof of Learning at College." The question, raised by a then-current news item, was whether or not students really learn anything in college and, in order to find out, whether systems should be set up to measure whether they do or don't. The *Times* editorial concluded this way:

> Colleges and universities should join in the hunt for acceptable ways to measure student progress, rather than simply fighting the whole idea from the sidelines. Unless the higher education community wakes up to this problem—and resolves to do a better job—the movement aimed at regulating colleges and forcing them to demonstrate that students are actually learning will only keep growing.

Here's my piece:

COLLEGE IS TOO LATE

In a recent report, the Commission on the Future of Higher Education announced that "Too many Americans just aren't getting the education that they need" and that "many students who do earn degrees have not actually mastered the reading, writing, and thinking skills we expect of college graduates."

Near the same time, Margaret Spellings, the Bush administration's Education Secretary, was cited as holding the opinion that "The commission has made bold recommendations on improving the accessibility and affordability of higher education," recommendations that she intended to give "very serious consideration."

Well, I can speak to the validity of the Commission's findings. But I can also speak to the fallacy that any sort of cure will come about through "improving the accessibility and affordability of higher education."

I retired last February [2006] after 35 years as an English professor in a large public urban university, and it's no secret to anyone that over that span I was able to help only very, very few students in any significant way to improve their essential skills in reading, writing, or reasoning. When I began, in 1971, I saw quickly that any significant basic influence I was going to have on my students would be extremely slight. I saw this truth confirmed and reconfirmed semester after semester until 2006 rolled around.

The real truth, which any honest, independent, and well informed commission on "the future of higher education" would announce, is this: That unless students are educated in the basics before they leave high school, college is guaranteed, for all but the tiniest few, to be a great and expensive waste of effort. Basic preparation has got to occur *before* college, not in it.

Over my career, I typically taught two sections of composition a semester and two of a literature survey. Later, my load was reduced from eight courses a year to seven. And for the last decade or so, I taught only literature, no composition.

Multiplying the number of courses I taught by the average number of students in each, I find that I instructed approximately 9,873 students. I'll round up to 10,000.

Most of these students were considerate, polite, likeable, some even hard-working—yet they remained unreachable at the intellectual or educational levels that really mattered. Without practicing the least deception, I can place at a discomfiting 2%, conceivably 3%, the proportion of students who left any of my courses at a higher level of ability or achievement than they'd entered at. They may have read a book or two that they wouldn't otherwise have read, but their intellectual essence was unchanged, and certainly their basic skills were also. This meant that, for 9,800 of my 10,000 students, entering a course at F meant leaving at F; entering at C, leaving at C; B, B; and so on.

Well-intended as they were, my students remained essentially unreachable for the simple reason that by eighth grade, ninth at the latest, they had internalized the skills and concepts that would remain with them for life. Nothing I could possibly do would lead them to internalize new elements of structure or correctness in language, or make them more fully conscious of basic elements of logic, comparison, or analysis—the very motors and gears of thinking.

By freshman year in college, at age 17 or 18, they had learned everything they were ever going to learn of these things.

Helping two hundred out of 10,000 students gives me a job performance rating of 2%, not a number to please administrators, deans, or commissions on higher education. But I know with absolute certainty that nothing will change in academic stories like mine—or the nation's—until we make certain that the bedrock of education occurs at the only place it can: Early, in primary and middle school, at the brick-and-mortar foundations of lives.

2.

WALTER KIRN AND THE *NEW YORK TIMES BOOK REVIEW* HAVE PLENTY TO ACCOUNT FOR AUGUST 5, 2006

The essays in this book, as will become clear, all have to do with certain aspects of the truth—telling it, hiding it, distorting it, being blind to it. For the most part, the truth in question will be about 9/11. In the present case, however, that isn't so. Here, the subject—which may seem less important though it isn't—is *literary* truth, the telling, hiding, or distorting of it. Literary writing is a reliable and highly revealing barometer of the health of the society it's a part of. In this case, as you'll see, that barometer provides a reading so low as to suggest turbulent, stormy, unsettled weather—the kind of weather that no farmer or sailor would *ever* trust.

Over a period of two decades or so, I wrote four or five hundred reviews for a pre-publication book-review magazine. The magazine itself published approximately four thousand such reviews a year. Each was to come in at a length of 350 words, shorter if possible .

Reviewers working at this length sometimes said they were "the sonneteers of book reviewing," and I think they were right. The reviews required completeness within a very small space. There had to be integrity of movement from first line to last, with no sentence failing to carry the central burden and at the same time no sentence failing to advance the simultaneous description and judgment that were being made. Within the rigorous physical and rhetorical constraints of such brevity, there could above all be nothing unsound, nothing unsupported, nothing not based on evidence, if only because in so tiny a room there simply could be no furniture for hollow interlopers or empty guests to hide behind, with the result that such would be—and were—spotted immediately by the magazine's editor.

What I became practiced in, working with that editor, was how to hear, sense, and know the difference between a valid and solidly written *negative* review (in a flock of four thousand swans there hide a plentiful number of grackles and starlings) and a simply *bad* review, whether it be negative, positive, or neutral.

Simply put, a *bad* review is one that's not honest and not sound in the approach it makes to a book. And, further, not honest and not sound in its description and judgment *of* that book.

That kind of review, a *bad* one, is the kind Walter Kirn wrote on Cynthia Ozick's *The Din in the Head: Essays* in the *New York Times Book Review* for Sunday, July 2, 2006.[1]

The flavor—tone—of the review can be found in Kirn's opening words:

> Though few thinkers still bother to attack it, let alone go on proclaiming its death, the novel remains exceedingly well defended, commanding larger, more ferocious armies than such a modest institution requires. Indeed, protecting novels from all threats, real and imagined, seems at times to constitute a more vigorous cultural enterprise than the actual writing of the things.

Here are plentiful hints of trickery (*bad* reviewing) rather than of the candor and openness of good, even if negative, reviewing. From kickoff, we get an assiduously maintained tone of condescension, superiority, and superciliousness. This is a tone *not* making it clear that the writer feels a responsibility for doing a job well (that is, describing and reviewing a book that he's read and we haven't), but instead making it clear that he considers himself superior to the matter at hand—so much so that *that's* the first point to be made clear.

The diction, subtly but surely, reveals this tone, from the choice of the dismissive "bother" rather than "undertake" or "try" or "set out to," on to the intentionally overblown and therefore faintly sarcastic phrases "proclaiming its death" and "larger, more ferocious armies," on to the egregious and outright distasteful—in its sophomoric, nose-in-the air pooh-poohing of something actually far more vast and significant than *this* writer will allow—the phrase, that is, referring to the genre of the novel, "such a modest institution." Then, to round off this condemnation—by diminution of the subject and thereby suggesting superiority to it—Kirn has the pridefully mean-spirited gall to speak of novels as "things" in the pseudo-Wildean phrase, "the actual writing of the things."

Anyone who has studied, experienced, or come to know even a fair chunk of the tradition of the novel, say from Cervantes to Woolf to Faulkner (or to Ozick or, I shudder to add, to Kirn) knows per-

---

[1] http://www.nytimes.com/2006/07/02/books/review/02kirn.html?ex=1154491200&en=7c898f4a8997bc21&ei=5070

fectly well that these opening words can't be taken other than as the words of a poseur or a shallow thinker or, at the least, a person self-involved enough as to be unable to put aside his cocktail-party airs even for a moment.

Writing of this kind, especially as an opener, shows that we're in the hands not of a reviewer but of an essay-writing judgmental-ist, not an expert but a show-off. What are the chances of our getting from this person a good review, however negative? Very slim, one suspects. As I myself found out, they are in fact zero.

·

I know they're zero because Kirn's review set off so many alarm bells of falseness that it sent me straight to the book. I ordered it, received it, and have now finished reading it. I'm able to report that it's not even close to the same book that Kirn "reviewed."

Where to start? Well, perhaps on a note that's to some degree personal. As the author of a recently published, highly critical and deeply pessimistic book about American culture, I'd be dishonest if I didn't admit that Kirn's review brings me the joy and, simultaneously, the groaning sorrow of coming on still another piece of evidence that my book was right. Kirn, in short, provides a perfect example of an intellectual type that I wrote about in *A Nation Gone Blind: America in an Age of Simplification and Deceit*.[2] That type is one who *believes* him- or herself still to be an independently thinking intellectual and effectual intellectual judge of matters salient or germane—but who in fact is, instead, another half-seeing child of what I call the Age of Simplification. Kirn purports to be an intellectual. But in point of actuality he is one of the "simplifieds."

Everything he looks at in the review, he looks at wrongly by merit of looking at it *partially*. And, while he looks at it partially, he comports himself with the superiority and airy self-assuredness of one who firmly believes himself to be seeing all these things in their entirety and fullness.

These qualities of the simplified intellectual make of Kirn a habit-ual declarer of half truths that are taken by him as whole ones, and they make of him also an intellectual who is thin, testy, self-infatuat-ed, and, most important of all, *incapable of genuine seriousness,* very possibly because he himself is incapable of perceiving it.

The writer's supercilious tone, and his inability to get rid of it or find another one, reveals the presence of these thinned-out traits in

---

2 Shoemaker & Hoard, 2006.

one who believes firmly that he's seeing whole (though readers of Ozick's book will find *her* to be more greatly the whole-seer, Kirn the half). The review's second paragraph opens with snideness, again, as the half-seer mistakes style for substance: "The form's latest self-styled guardian is Cynthia Ozick," Kirn writes, and we ask: Why on earth the deprecating "self-styled"? The answer is that there's *no* reason, as Kirn himself reveals by tossing out a hypocritical crumb or two, calling Ozick "an accomplished novelist herself and a high-ranking literary critic," thereby leaving us to ponder how it is that she's both "high-ranking" and at the same time "self-styled."

That question won't be answered, as such questions are *never* answered by simplifieds like Kirn. Instead, he'll give us more conde-scension, half truths posing as whole, and more loaded words. Ozick, he says,

> along with so many other traditionalists, cherishes the belief, now quix-otic, that serious fiction and those who dream it up are still controversial enough to be embattled and "in danger of obsolescence."

Only Kirn and god know what he may mean by "serious fic-tion" or "dream it up," but we don't need god or anyone else to know that "cherishes" is a snide, condescending, and loaded word, or to know (as I know, having read the book) that Kirn is setting out to make Ozick sound like an obsessive, not an observer or thinker, and an obsessive, further, about something ridiculously *minor*—that is, ridiculously minor from the faux-Olympian view of the simplified.

It gets worse, if only by staying the same. After tossing out another handful of pseudo-reverential sops by naming some of the illustrious magazines Ozick has published these essays in, he writes that she

> sounds the latest of a million warnings about the oft postponed catastro-phe that only novelists still fear, despite their perennial attempts to make the public dread it, too.

And so Kirn, we realize, is never going to review this book and has no intention of doing so. Instead, he is going to trivialize its subject (as that subject appears to *him*), mock its author, and, as for himself, walk offstage to the applause of his like-minded and also-simplified friends, himself scot-free from harm, injury, or challenge for the very good reason that he has committed himself to nothing whatsoever, however much he may think and believe that he has stood up and spoken out for great and deep volumes of meaning.

In one moment of accuracy, he does quote Ozick directly:

"But if the novel were to wither—if, say, it metamorphosed altogether into a species of journalism or movies, as many popular novels already have—then the last trustworthy vessel of the inner life (aside from our heads) would crumble away."

As the author of "The Death of Literary Thinking in America: How It Happened and What It Means" (me, in *A Nation Gone Blind*), I can hardly deny that Ozick strikes in my own heart, unlike Kirn's, a sympathetic chord. I, in fact, see the situation as being even worse than Ozick does, as, too, I see more than merely the "popular" novels having already withered into something considerably worse than "a species of journalism or movies." But that's not the issue here. The issue isn't whether I happen to agree or disagree with Ozick's view. The issue isn't even whether *Kirn* agrees or disagrees with it. The issue is whether he shows not only any will but any *capacity* even to take the question seriously. In this single trait alone, clung to with a blind absoluteness, he proves himself a child of simplification.

The subject (the subject, that is, of greatest concern to *him;* anyone who reads Ozick will find that her book is broader and more wide-ranging than Kirn even remotely hints) is now out in the open, and Kirn follows the introduction of it by doing two things. First, he denigrates that subject through more insouciance; and, second, he misrepresents its actual role in Ozick's book.

The insouciance:

If novelists were all to go on strike someday, the world might finally understand that it can't live without them, as they [the novelists] insist, but since they can't seem to bear to drop their pens, society must rely on fuzzier evidence for the alleged necessity of their services.

And, in his next sentence, the misrepresentation:

In essay after essay, Ozick seeks to provide this evidence by praising her favorite fiction writers in ways that bring out both their virtues as individuals and their glories as a class.

Helen Keller as a "favorite fiction writer"? The poet Sylvia Plath? The poet Delmore Schwartz? The question, "What is a Jewish book?"? The essay on Trilling that's predominantly about how Trilling *wasn't* a fiction writer? The essay on Gershom Scholem, scholar and the founder of Hebrew University? Robert Alter and his translation into English of the Pentateuch? Obviously—*obviously*—Kirn either didn't read Ozick's book or he chose deliberately not to acknowledge the actual nature of its breadth, range, and often remarkable scholarship.

To lie, whether by omission or by commission, is deplorable and repugnant, and the result of doing so is also deplorable and repugnant. Kirn's review—yup, deplorable and repugnant—is also inexcusable, shameful, base, and unprofessional. Whether its presence in the pages of *The New York Times Book Review* says more about Kirn or about the *Times,* I don't know. In some terrible way, perhaps they're one and the same.

•

On the basis of his review, the only thing in the universe I'm able to imagine myself sharing with Walter Kirn is a dislike for John Updike. I indeed do dislike that famous writer, while, as it happens, Cynthia Ozick is filled with high admiration for him and sees his work as towering and deeply American. Maybe she's right, though my own tastes and judgment lead me to different conclusions. As, apparently, do Kirn's. But this—this distaste for a single writer in a single chapter out of the twenty that make up the book—*this* is no justification for hi-jacking an entire review and turning it into a kind of extended character assassination, first, and then diverting it into a wild-eyed rave about a subject that isn't even a part of the book's own immediate subject at all, *that* subject being "the canon," while the wild-eyed rave is Kirn's manic ad hominem attack on Ozick because *he* thinks she *must* be a defender of the "canon," a high-brow la-dee-dah member of the literati who even, god forbid, uses "long words."

The penury and malice of it, the narrowness posing as pride and righteousness—the *simplification* of a mind such as Kirn's, at least as it's exemplified here. He can't stand Ozick, Updike, or real intellectuals. And, by god, he's going to let all three of them have it.

He sets his primary victim up by quoting a line that does indeed express Ozick's high estimation of Updike, a line that, even for those who dislike that writer, may seem over-wrought:

> John Updike: the name is graven. It stands, by now, alongside Cather, Faulkner, Fitzgerald, those older masters who lay claim to territory previously untrafficked, and who make of it common American ground.

Kirn reveals his hatred of anything "elevated" by pronouncing that "The opening sentences of the book's fourth piece [the Updike one] are typical of Ozick's high-church manner, which sometimes seeks to persuade through extra syllables and weighty antiquarianism as much as through conventional argument." That Kirn's pronunciamento isn't true—the only truth revealed here is that he hates any style the least bit formal or unsimplified—doesn't much matter in a piece where the true and the false are already so inextricably mixed. What matters is that Kirn, in the power of his determination that everything be flip, simple, and supercilious, is himself unable to see the distinctions between what is false and what is true, and certainly not between what is serious and what isn't.

> Her point about Updike, once she gets around to making it and empties herself of incantations ("His effects are of sheen and shadow, color and form, spine and splay, hair and haunch"), is that he knows how to ground his large abstractions in small particulars.

This is typical of Kirn in its snideness, even though it's far from my own favorite Ozick sentence, either. This is partly because I find it impossible to imagine esteeming Updike—though what I've read of his fiction gives me an understanding of how well chosen her noun, "haunch," really is. I may not like Updike, but "hair and haunch" is about as accurate a pairing in evoking the Updikean mode and mood as I can imagine. Kirn, though, goes swirly-eyed with hate for it, as we'll see in a moment. More important, first, though, are his condescension, castigation, and scorn of Ozick for praising Updike by saying that "he knows how to ground his large abstractions in small particulars."

If Kirn were more fully apprised in the history of the novel, he would know how vitally central and immensely significant—though now all but lost—a quality in fictional narrative it is that he's excoriating here as trivial.

But the true depravities of his sustained ad hominem attack on Ozick and her presumed ilk, whom he despises equally, only now reach their full extent, as he departs altogether from the last vestiges of his duties and responsibilities as a reviewer—responsibility to talk, that is, about the book—and diverges onto a siding where he can hack and chop away at something he hates even more than he hates the mere Ms. Ozick. Here we go:

> A writer who opts for the feathered word "haunch" over its flightless synonyms, such as "thigh," who calls the speechlike prose of Philip Roth "a dazzling demotic voice," and who knows as though by instinct, that the proper term for something Saul Bellow-ish is "Bellovian" can be counted on to defend the Western canon—and to celebrate the idea of canons in general. For a civilization to be civilized it must have bars, Ozick asserts. Those bars must be placed high, and the rare minds who manage to vault over them must be regaled with anthems and medallions. In the nightmare of blurred distinctions, all will be lost, Ozick hints, and she means all—even our very lives, perhaps.

This is scandalous stuff. I, too, dislike Roth, but if you take out "dazzling" from the brew, what's left, the "demotic" part, is true enough.

That aside, I only wish Kirn would have *one* serious thought, give to *one* thing some serious intellectual attention, do *one* thing honestly, and for even *one* nano-second give up his prissy little "how dumb I am and therefore how cool I am" sophomore-level song and dance. For one thing, Ozick isn't a canon-defender, although she is an intellect-defender. Kirn seemingly wants *The Dunciad* to come true, the low to be the high, the dumb to be the smart. His little snit-words are unbearable and a bore, as in "the *rare* minds" and "*vault* over them" and "regaled with anthems and medallions." There are many words for this kind of writing, but one of them—or two—are "craven" and "bullshit."

What Ozick is really doing (though you'd never know it from Kirn's babblings) is simply talking about intellectual seriousness—and she's doing it, in this chapter, with the Jonathan Franzen/Oprah Winfrey fracas as a take-off point, when Franzen famously and self-damagingly remarked that "I feel. . . like I'm solidly in the high-art literary tradition." In the ensuing discussion, Kirn cites (or snipes at) what he wants to cite and snipe at and leaves out the rest. "Distinction-making, even distinction-discerning, is largely in decline," writes Ozick, unaware that she's touching the deepest nerve in Kirn's black and decayed "hey-this-dumbed-down-intellectual-world-is-great" tooth. He goes positively mad with rage:

> The canon [though in fact this subject has never been mentioned by Ozick] as cannon, holding off the savages. Like the rampant jihadists who frighten her [another figment of Kirn's imagination], she esteems the written word so highly [as Kirn, obviously, doesn't] that she equates its corruption with damnation. She's a bohemian fundamentalist, convinced that if literature should lose its special status as the final arbiter of humanness, the deity will unleash another Great Flood.

How about something that Ozick really does say? For example: "These observations [about general diminishment in literary interest] are hardly new, but familiarity does not lessen the shock and the ignominy of a pervasive indifference to serious critical writing."[3] *This* makes her "a bohemian fundamentalist," similar to a "rampant jihadist"? Something else she says—and she *really does* say it, though you'll find it nowhere in Kirn—is, as already mentioned, that "Distinction-making, even distinction-discerning, is largely in decline."[4] Ah ha! Now we *know* she's unleashed, a madwoman, a rabid antiquarian who wants to return to the calm certainties of, say, 1874. No, Kirn to the contrary, there's nothing whatsoever reaction-

---

[3] *The Din in the Head* (Houghton-Mifflin, 2006), p. 50 ("Highbrow Blues").
[4] p. 51.

ary here, nothing radical, nothing blinded by class superiority or by love of those "rare minds" that Kirn himself seems to be so jealous of or intimidated by that all he can do is mock them, never identify or define them. No, Ozick, not Kirn, is the one looking calmly and accurately at literary and social America today, with its "Distinction-making... in decline." Ozick is the one pointing to those losses that are indeed important losses—like the loss of being able to judge by distinction, a loss that, yes, perhaps more than any other, might allow America to be made a police state the day after tomorrow, if it hasn't already become one.

Leave it to Kirn to omit what Ozick *does* write in demonstration of her measured way of thinking, her practice of qualifying thoughts in the very ways that Kirn loudly declares she fails to do. "Writers," she says, "shouldn't be mistaken for priests, it goes without saying." These really are her words—unless, that is, Kirn has gotten into the printer's plates and scrubbed them out of every copy of the book except mine. But there's even worse trouble ahead—because Ozick is going to do that very thing so virulently despised by airs-but-no-airs Kirn: That is, *she's going to make distinctions*. What that means, in turn, is this: She's going to *think*. Here's the full paragraph, from her book:

> Writers shouldn't be mistaken for priests, it goes without saying; but neither should movie-script manufacturers be mistaken for writers. Readers are not the same as audiences, and the structure of a novel is not the same as the structure of a lingerie advertisement. Hierarchy, to be sure, is an off-putting notion, invoking high and low; and high smacks of snobbery and antiegalitarianism. But hierarchy also points to the recognition of distinctions, and—incontrovertibly—the life of intellect is perforce hierarchical: it insists that one thing is not the same as another thing. A novel concerned with English country-house romances is not the same as a tract on slavery in Antigua. A department of English is not the same as a Marxist tutorial. A rap CD is not the same as academic scholarship. A suicide bomber who blows up a pizzeria crowded with baby carriages is not the same as a nation-builder.

Is it the mention of the baby carriages that gives Kirn license to make the allegation—or utter the deception—that "rampant jihadists... frighten" Ozick? And what exactly is it in Ozick's list of things that aren't the same as other things that enrages him to say that her "Ciceronian crescendo," as he calls it, "rhetorically builds from a statement about aesthetics to an alarmist political manifesto"?

And if it *is* "a political manifesto" (it's not), what makes it "alarmist"? Kirn won't say, but instead he'll just toss a few more banana peels of innuendo and slur out onto the dance floor. He knows, I assume,

---

3 PP. 151–152.

that the very absence of distinction-making, hence the very absence of an intelligent *political* thinking that's capable of existing meaningfully with or alongside or within an intelligent *aesthetic* thinking—he must be aware, must he not, that this dumbed down situation, implied and deplored by Ozick, is one of the most powerful reasons for any thinking person to doubt strenuously "that America will ever again produce a literature beyond the sort it does now: a depleted, imitative, unimpassioned, unoriginal, essentially *unthinking* literature"?[6]

All right, so now I've quoted from the first page of my own book, though I must admit I'd rather quote from it than from Kirn. Only to the lazy or the philistine can it be mounted as a criticism that literary or aesthetic battles may be fought "with long words," and only the faithless to fact can either state or imply that Ozick's book is about so specific a subject as the "death of the novel," though her much, much broader book does indeed touch on that subject. Only the philistine, or the ignorant, or the affected, or the snob can allude to the massive and largely ruinous cultural changes of the past sixty years as "big issues that now feel small" and hope to get away without incurring if nothing else at least the white-hot wrath of guys like me, who feel pretty powerfully that if someone is going to drop a trendy little remark like that in a context more massive than, apparently, he can conceivably have the tiniest notion of—well, honor dictates either that he apologize for it or, another thing I'm pretty certain he's not capable of doing, explain why he feels so.

"Nothing gets old faster than an apocalypse that was scheduled for two days ago," concludes the eternally shallow Kirn, as if he knows the least thing about the apocalypse creeping up on us all. Never one to end on a glib note when there's a more glib one available, he adds that "If the novel did die a few years back, well, we survived, apparently."

I beg to disagree. Kirn's shallow, malignant, dishonest review of Ozick's book—his trashing of it in, oh, so glib and trendy language and through such hateful misrepresentations of it, a book far from perfect but infinitely more fine than his assassination of it would suggest; these things, not to mention that all of them are apparently perfectly agreeable and acceptable and fine in the eyes of the equally culpable editors of The New York Times Book Review— all of this being the truth of the matter, no, I won't agree with the likes of Kirn that we have survived, not at all, whether "apparently" or not.

Eric Larsen
August 5, 2006

---

[6] *A Nation Gone Blind*, p. 3.

3.

IS AMERICA NO LONGER
JUST BLIND, BUT NOW ALSO *INSANE*?
SEPTEMBER 30, 2006

To the Reader:

What are the motives for deceit? Self-gain, certainly, very possibly the central motive in the Kirn essay just discussed. Ignorance may be another motive for deceit, though it should probably be called a cause rather than a motive. And a third motive may be fear—or terror. When I wrote this next piece—on the occasion of the vote on the Military Commissions Act of 2006—it hadn't occurred to me yet that Congress-members would, could, or might act out of any other impulses than self-gain or ignorance. So it seemed to me that this insane thing—passing the Act—had been done only out of ignorance and self-interest. Then later I began to see the role that terror had played. I began to understand, with increasing clarity. that the powers running the highest levels of our own "government" were the true terrorist powers, and who they terrorized was us the people, including the pawns in Congress. As always, the pawns were self-interested and ignorant. But in addition, they were terrorized. So they did exactly as told and voted yet once more for the dismantling of the republic.

It's a serious question, whether America has gone insane.

My own answer is that, yes, it has gone insane.

Yesterday, September 29, 2006, Congress passed by generous majorities the so-called "compromise" version of the "Military Commissions Act of 2006." This act has to do, in great part, with the treatment of "enemy combatants," as they're known, who have been seized by the U.S.

And on that morning (when only the Senate had passed the bill, although it was correctly assumed that the House would follow suit), the *New York Times* wrote that the bill

would make illegal several broadly defined abuses of detainees, while leaving it to the president to establish specific permissible interrogation techniques. And it would strip detainees of a habeas corpus right to challenge their detentions in court.[7]

What this means is that now the President can himself decide in exactly what curious and interesting ways he may or may not choose to torture detainees. (Torture, by the way, is what we Americans are spoon-fed by the media to think of as "harsh treatment.") And the bill also means something more. It means that once they're seized, the detainees can sit in their cells and rot until the flesh falls from their bones and their eyes sink inward—forever, that is—all this time with no recourse whatsoever to means by which they might seek outside aid or find appeal through legal rights of any sort.

The United States can now legally toss *anyone it wants* into jail and forget about them forever.

Let me restate that. The United States is now legally entitled to declare anyone it wants an "enemy combatant." The United States is now legally entitled to throw those it so declares into cells, treating and torturing them in any way it chooses until they die in prolonged suffering, pain, agony, hopelessness, and terror.

In other words, as the *Times* said, the writ of habeas corpus will be "stripped" from them so that they will have no "right to challenge their detentions in court."

It needs no pointing out, but I am going to point it out anyway. This execrable, monstrous, inhumane situation has come about through the will of the Bush/Cheney administration, subsequently through the will of the United States Congress, and finally—it's a democracy, after all, isn't it?—through the will of the American people.

I will now ask three questions:

1. First, although the law is at present *intended* only for non-citizens of the U.S., what process or means will possibly be strong enough to impede or subvert the bill's enormous power of precedent, assuring that in future it not be imposed upon "enemy combatants" who are citizens of the U.S.? (In today's *Times*, in fact, Bruce Ackerman, "a professor of law and political science at Yale University," is cited as holding the view that the bill *already* "allows the administration to declare even an American citizen an unlawful combatant subject to indefinite detention.")[8,9]

---

[7] *The New York Times,* September 29, 2006, p. A-1.

[8] *The New York Times,* September 30, 2006, p. A-11.

[9] Also see Marjorie Cohn's "A Constitutional Shredding: Rounding Up U.S. Citizens," in *Counterpunch,* September 30–October 1, 2006: "Anyone who donates money to a charity that turns up on Bush's list of 'terrorist' organizations, or who speaks out against the government's policies could be declared an 'unlawful enemy combatant' and imprisoned indefinitely. That includes American citizens."

2. Second: Whoever you are, is your conscience clear, both as a human being *and* as a citizen of a putatively participatory republican democracy—is your conscience clear in regard to this fact of holding in your own hands and in your own heart the responsibility for such a foreboding, malicious, uncivilized bill's having come to pass?

I know that my own conscience is not clear. It is not clear at all. It is not clear by a long shot.

3. And third, back to where we started: Have we not, as a nation, gone mad? To this question, there's a corollary question. Isn't it a fact, with the passage of this bill, that the United States, by definition, has stopped being free and has become tyrannic?

•

Some, I know, will consider me naïve—those, for example, who will argue that "freedom" in the United States has already been lost for a very long time. My own views on the question of lost American freedoms is clear to any who might read *A Nation Gone Blind*. Even so, it seems to me that yesterday's relationship to liberty and freedom is significant in a new way. Yesterday was a new kind of marking point. That's because yesterday was the first time since 9/11 that a major law stripping away traditional—in fact ancient—human rights and freedoms has been passed by Congress not peremptorily, as with the so-called "Patriot Act," but *after full debate*.

9/11 was a trigger—our Reichstag fire—and, as a trigger, it quickly and easily shot out passage of the "Patriot Act," an act voted for overwhelmingly by a stunned, shocked, and awed Congress who hadn't read it.[10] Obviously, that massive piece of legislation had been prepared well in advance of its introduction to Congress, and just as obviously the pervasive atmosphere of fear at the time was in no way conducive to clear thought, extensive study, or the making of fine distinctions—all necessary in order for legislation to be passed responsibly, fairly, and meaningfully. If you do think of 9/11 as the trigger of a gun, it's perfectly reasonable to think of "The Patriot Act" as being the chief of the dum-dum bullets that came out of its muzzle.

Now, though, five years later, a bill has been passed that has the potential for even more damage to the republic, to human rights, and to freedom. And *this* bill has been produced by a majority of both houses after prolonged discussion, debate, thought, consideration, objection, and even some degree of compromise. The writ of habeas corpus goes back to Magna Carta—1215—and now, after eight

---

10 Update: I would now, of course, add "terrorized" to the three adjectives "stunned, shocked, and awed."

centuries of precedent, the Commissions bill strips it away. Same for the Geneva Conventions and same for torture. The Geneva Conventions don't go back eight centuries, but their significance for a liberal and civilized world and for human rights is and has been equal if not even greater.

The point? 9/11 was our Reichstag fire and, as such—as a "false flag operation," to give it its proper name—was the first major self-inflicted wound on the United States in the current calamity. But yesterday, the 29th of September, 2006, was the day marking the first fully debated, willfully considered, and *genuinely legislative* step to be taken in the United States' process of committing suicide. 9/11 as a self-imposed wound was *ill*egal. This self-imposed wound is perfectly legal. *This* self-imposed wound, in fact, is *itself* legality, is *itself* law.

And so we return again to our opening question. Can any nation, body, or person be considered sane if they write a binding law that initiates the process of its or their own suicide? I suppose the answer might possibly be yes, if the nation, body, or person did so unknowingly. And that leads us to a very, very interesting question.

Did the Congress *knowingly* enact this law? If so, it seems to me that its members, and therefore the nation itself that is represented by that Congress, must be declared insane. If anyone thinks that knowingly writing a law that requires *and* initiates your own suicide is *not* insane—well, let such a person go off and have that thought by himself or herself.

And what's the other possibility? Well, the other possibility, clearly, is that Congress wrote and enacted the law *un*knowingly, that is, *not* knowing what they were doing. Now, supposing this to be the case, what can possibly be said about them that's both true *and* that could shed light on what they've done?

The only thing both true and meaningful that could be said about them is this: *That they are blind.* That is, that they are blind to realities and consequences of what they're doing, and blind to the true nature of the world that they're doing it *in* and doing it *to.* They *can't see.*

That's the thesis of *A Nation Gone Blind.* Believe me, I take no joy in seeing my own book proven true in the context of this particularly horrific, overwhelming twist, or under these insurmountably dreadful, ugly, and despairing circumstances.

I am sorry. And afraid.

Eric Larsen
September 30, 2006

4.

THE AFTERMATH OF THE GREAT CRIME OF 9/11:
AMERICA AIDS IN THE STAGING
OF ITS OWN MURDER
NOVEMBER 5, 2006

To the Reader:
Without question, the most significant thing about
9/11 was what failed to happen *after* it. Americans
failed to see through it. Americans failed to doubt
and challenge the story fed to them by their government, an entity that had now become their enemy.
Long since conditioned into being blind to reality,
Americans accepted smoke and mirrors, accepted
the most ludicrous posturing and propaganda, as
constituting reality. Decoys, traitors, and disinformation agents infiltrated[11] every aspect and element of
American social, cultural, and economic institutions.
And Americans fell for it all. It was as though a con
artist had beguiled America into looking up at the
loveliness of the stars, the better to bare her throat to
the whistling approach of the scimitar.

1.

In light of the way things are going—the stripping of habeas corpus in the War Commissions Act of 2006, the "private" signing by
George W. Bush of a "revision" of the Insurrection Act that essentially neutralizes the Posse Comitatus Act and allows the Federal
government, at such time as it may wish, to turn U.S. troops against
U.S. citizens—all I can ask is this: How can there be so little response
to the police-state preparations being made by the government of our
dismal, ignorant, godforsaken, forlorn, fascism-teetering nation if it
isn't simply for the fact that the people who "live" in it really *have*

---

11 See Emanuel Sferios, "Five Years Later: What Have We Accomplished? An Assessment
of the 9/11 Truth Movement" (Sept. 11, 2006), available at: http://pilotsfor911truth.
org/forum/index.php?showtopic=1191

gone stark, staring blind, and for a good length of time *have been* as blind as bats, stones, fools, and anti-educated drones, as blind as those poor victims who now more than sixty years ago obediently boarded and rode the Nazi trains to Treblinka.

We're in very, very serious trouble, and the most absolutely astonishing thing about it is that, except for the small few who are trying desperately to broadcast the truth, nobody seems to be so much as noticing what's happening, on the one hand, or, on the other, to be doing anything other than smoothing out the road so that it *can* happen.

The absence of alarm or resistance, the absence in most of the population even of *awareness*—these absences come about in very great part as a result of our having been for so long a nation of non-readers. No one in America reads. No one in America *has* read for at least the past three decades and probably much longer. And no one in America is going to *start* reading. As a result, no one in the nation knows a pig from a poke or a fascist from filigree. I'm angry. I'm angrier than I've ever been in my life. I'm angry about things that I never, ever, not in my most distant predictions or dreams, thought I would see happening in my own lifetime—the step by step dismantling of the republic itself *and* the lack of resistance not just from the general population but also from the so-called intelligentsia.

I hear a chorus of rebuttal: "Americans do *too* read. More of them read more books now *than ever before in our history.*"

Maybe so. Americans may read, but most of what they read is lulling, familiar, soporific stuff, including what they're led to believe is "literary" or "quality" writing. And, really, what percentage of Americans read even *that* much? Take a look at *Reading at Risk: A Survey of Literary Reading in America* (the study put out by the NEA in 2004)[12] for a grim answer to that question. Or give a read, say, to the first chapter of *A Nation Gone Blind*. The truth is that almost all of America's "literary" writing today itself actually takes the form of lying, is comprised of lies, and that this is the case not most of the time but *all of the time,* quite entirely without the authors' knowledge of it—read Ben Marcus on the subject[13] in the now-diminishing and soon-to-die *Harper's.*

Well, I'd argue *that* point with you, a chorus of voices says, a chorus coming from highly comfortable and contented readers firm in their insistence that the literary world of today is perfectly fine, and even more firm in their contentedness with it, *and* with their regimen of a book-and-three-magazines a week, plus the *Times* every day.

---

[12] http://www.nea.gov/pub/ReadingAtRisk.pdf

[13] "Why experimental fiction threatens to destroy publishing, Jonathan Franzen, and life as we know it: A correction," Harper's Magazine, October 2005. http://www.harpers. org/WhyExperimentalFiction.html

And, the chorus asks, what about high-quality *non*-fiction, not only in books but in magazines? Tell us *that*! What about *The New Yorker*, for example? And *The Atlantic Monthly*? *The Nation*? And I: Oh, yes. Those. What about them indeed.

2.

The time for politeness, I am afraid, is past, the moment for good manners gone. The American media is a truth-barrier, not a truth-revealer, and that includes the genteel monthlies with their long and putatively respectable histories as well as it does the weeklies—*The Progressive, The New Republic, The Nation*—that once upon a time were the leaders of the pack in the business of truth-telling. No longer so. All gone, compromised to the point where their truth-zones are the size of pinheads. As for politeness, well, politeness is a great deadener, and if people—you and me, for example—can't find a way to start looking past it, and through it, and can't start seeing and *naming* the news for what it is—fascism, torture, murder, war profiteering, plunder, piracy, high criminality, treason, crimes against humanity, ecocide—well, then we're in it for good, beyond brake or redemption, and we're done for.

But what to do? And where find the means *to* do it? How do you wake up a country to the truth not only of what really happened on 9/11 but of what's now being prepared for every so-called citizen of a country where the elections are already rigged, fixed, bought, paid for, and meaningless and where 99% of the so-called citizens are paying no attention but are "consuming" in one way or another instead, wires stuck into their ears, beams aimed into their eyes, needles poked into their veins, eyes empty, mouths open, jaws slack?

I warned you that the time for politeness is past.

3.

Some will remember that a ways back I mentioned Treblinka, before we switched over to the subject of reading. Well, let's return. Not long ago, I read a wonderful and powerful book, *A Writer at War: Vasily Grossman with the Red Army, 1941–1945*.[15] Unable to meet the physical standards to qualify for military duty, Grossman managed to

---

15 *A Writer at War: Vasily Grossman with the Red Army 1941–1945*, edited and translated by Antony Beever and Luba Vinogradova (New York, 2005) http://www.amazon.com/Writer-War-Soviet-Journalist-1941-1945/dp/0307275337/ref=sr_1_1?s=books&ie=UTF8&qid=1284314311&sr=1-1

get himself attached to the Red Army as a journalist, writing for the newspaper *Krasnaya Zvezda* (*Red Star*). After writing his way through the battle of Stalingrad with all its incomprehensible suffering, he continued with the Russian army, writing the whole time, on its march all the way to Berlin, where he covered the end of WWII in Europe.

The paragraphs I'm about to cite have their origin in the summer of 1944, when the Red forces, pushing toward Poland and then Berlin, discovered the death camps first in Majdanek and then in Treblinka. Of the thousands upon thousands who were brought to their deaths at Treblinka or were forced into slavery there, only a tiny handful, forty terrified people hiding in the woods, had survived by the time the Red Army arrived. Grossman interviewed them, and he later wrote at very great length about Treblinka. Here, he has just described the horror of what it was like when sick and dying prisoners from within Germany were transported to Treblinka in cattle cars. We pick him up at a point of contrast:

> Trains from other European countries arrived at Treblinka in a very different manner. The people in them had never heard of Treblinka, and believed until the last minute that they were going there to work... [ellipsis in original] These trains from European countries arrived with no guards, and with the usual staff. There were sleeping cars and restaurant cars in them. Passengers had big trunks and suitcases, as well as substantial supplies of food. The passengers' children ran out at the stations they passed and asked whether it was still a long way to Ober-Maidan... [ellipsis in original]

> It is hard to tell whether it is less terrible to go towards one's own death in the state of terrible suffering, knowing that one was getting closer and closer to one's death, or to be absolutely unaware, glance from a window of a comfortable passenger car right at the moment when people from the station at Treblinka are telephoning the camp to pass on details about the train which has just arrived and the number of people in it.

> Apparently, in order to achieve the final deception for people arriving from Europe, the railroad dead-end siding was made to look like a passenger station. On the platform at which another twenty carriages would be unloaded stood a station building with a ticket office, baggage room and a restaurant hall. There were arrows everywhere, indicating 'To Bialystok', 'To Baranovichi', 'To Volokovysk', etc. By the time the train arrived, there would be a band playing in the station building, and all the musicians were dressed well. A porter in railway uniform took tickets from the passengers and let them pass on to the square.

> Three or four thousand people loaded with sacks and suitcases would go out into this square supporting the old and sick. Mothers were holding babies in their arms, older children kept close to their parents looking inquisitively at the square. There was something sinister and horrible in this square

whose earth had been trampled by millions of human feet. The strained eyes of the people were quick to catch alarming little things. There were some objects abandoned on the ground, which had been swept hastily, apparently a few minutes before the party emerged—a bundle of clothes, an open case, a shaving brush, enamel saucepans. How did they get here? And why, right where the platform ends, is there no more railway and only yellow grass growing behind a three-metre-high wire fence? Where is the railway leading to Bialystok, to Sedlez, Warsaw, Volokovysk? And the new guards grin in such a strange way surveying the men adjusting their ties, neat old ladies, boys wearing navy shirts, thin girls who had managed to keep their clothes tidy throughout this journey, young mothers adjusting lovingly the blankets in which their babies are wrapped, the babies who are wrinkling their faces... [ellipsis in original] What is there, behind this huge, six-metre-high wall, which is densely covered with yellowing pine branches and with bedding? These coverlets, too, are alarming: they are all different colours, padded, silk or satin. They are reminiscent of the eider-downs that they, the newcomers, have brought with them. How did this bedding get here? Who brought it with them? And where are their own-ers? Why don't they need them any longer? And who are these people with light blue armbands? One remembers all the thoughts that have come into one's head recently, all the fears, all the rumors that were told in a whisper. No, no, this can't be true. And one drives the terrible thoughts away.

People have a few moments to dwell on their fears in the square, until all the newcomers are assembled in it. There are always delays. In each trans-port there are the crippled, the limping, and the old and sick people, who can hardly move their feet. But finally everyone is in the square.

An SS *Unteroffizier* suggests in a loud and distinct voice that the newcom-ers leave their luggage in the square and go to the bathhouse, with just their personal documents, valuables and the smallest possible bags with what they need for washing. Dozens of questions appear immediately in the heads of people standing in the square: whether they can take fresh underwear with them, whether they can unpack their bundles, whether the luggage of different people piled in the square might get mixed up or lost? But some strange force makes them walk, hastily and silently, asking no questions, not looking back, to the gate in a six-metre-high wall of wire camouflaged with branches.

They pass anti-tank hedgehogs, the fence of barbed wire three times the height of a man, a three-metre-wide anti-tank moat, more wire, this time thin, thrown on the ground in concertina rolls, in which the feet of a runner would get struck like a fly's legs in a spiderweb, and another wall of barbed wire, many metres high. And a terrible feeling of doom, of being complete-ly helpless comes over them: it's impossible to run away, or turn back, or fight. The barrels of large-calibre machine guns are looking at them from the low, wooden towers. Call for help? But there are SS men and guards all round, with sub-machine guns, hand grenades and pistols. They are the power. In their hands are tanks and aircraft, lands, cities, the sky, railways, the law, newspapers, radio. The whole world is silent, suppressed, enslaved by a brown gang of bandits which has seized power. London is silent and New York, too. And only somewhere on a bank of the Volga, many thousands of kilometers away, the Soviet artillery is roaring.[16]

4.

"No, no, this can't be true." But it was true.

And the *coup d'état* that's happening in the United States today, the coup that has been happening since November 22, 1963, that sped up considerably during the 1990s and then more after January 2001, the coup that's been moving spectacularly fast since September 11, 2001—of it, too, people might say, *"No, no this can't be true."* But it is true, too.

I'm aware that I'll be reviled and calumniated for grave political incorrectness in comparing victims of the Nazi murder-machine to *us*; for implying that what those *total* victims suffered under the Nazis is in any way comparable to our oppression under the Bushiscti. It's necessary for me to say two things in clarification and defense.

First, I'm not saying that these two moments in history are the same. As of now, they are clearly not. I *am* saying that there are potential parallels between the Nazi genocide-machine and what the United States, now, may very easily become. A number of highly significant steps have been taken already—from the "Patriot Act" through the 2006 Military Commissions act—such that if the rounding up of masses of people; if the herding of them into camps; even if the murdering of them were to take place, those actions, right now, inside the United States, *would be legal.*

Consider where we've come. Torture is legal. The stripping of habeas corpus is legal, not just for outlanders but for citizens. With the Bushiscti's change of the Insurrection Act, and with that change's attendant weakening of Posse Comitatus—*Treblinka* would now be legal in America. Treblinka *is* now legal in America.

In our full-color, familiar-looking, and *seemingly* unchanged nation, our government has completed setting the stage for the legal arrest and incarceration of anyone it chooses without showing the least cause or justification whatsoever and without allowing the victim the right to any appeal. It has completed the process of legalization for that same government, should it choose, to turn guns or other military weaponry upon any citizens or any groups or on any categories of citizens or any categories of groups in the United States it may

---

[16] *A Writer at War* (New York, 2005), pp. 286–289.

choose. That is to say, it now has the *legal right* to arrest such people or groups, incarcerate them, torture them, starve them, kill them, ignore them, or do any combination of these things, or all of them.

And it's our fault. It's us, we're the ones who let it happen. We haven't been just blind, but we've been blinder than blind. We have been *insane* with blindness. We've been insane not to have seen from the start that 9/11 was the sheer fraud that it was, that it was a malicious, murderous, purposely self-inflicted wound delivered for the very purpose of scaring us mental defectives into total acquiescence—no, into total *eagerness*—as all the pre-existing plans for illegal invasion, murder, war crimes, and crimes against humanity were taken out of the category of plans and put into the category of *acts*. Illegal wars? *Eagerly* accepted. Massive stripping of civil and Constitutional rights through the fraudulently named "Patriot Act"? *Eagerly* accepted. Illegal spying on citizens? *No big deal.* Routine rigging and stealing of elections through "friendly" electronic voting machines that leave no paper trails? Another *no big deal.* And *now*? Well, what *of* torture? What *of* habeas corpus? What *of* Posse Comitatus? What *of* the Insurrection Act?

And it's been done on the basis of the biggest and most fraudulent lie of all. That's the stupid and obvious lie that "Al Qaeda" and a handful of ragamuffin and non-observant Muslim men hijacked *four* commercial airplanes *all by themselves,* and that—well, that *somehow* the entire military air-defense system of the most powerful nation in world history *happened* not to get any of its planes off the ground in time or at the right place in time to do any intercepting whatsoever for the entire hour and a half that was needed for the full plan of "attacks" to be implemented and brought to an end.

There's more. Book after book, article after article, scholar after scholar provide examples in abundance of the absurdity not only of the "official theory" itself of 9/11 but also of the "Kean Commission" report—and at the same time show the obviousness of 9/11 having been in fact a "false flag operation," a self-inflicted wound and self-generated "attack," whether planned and perpetrated by the Bushiscti themselves alone (probably not), or by what Webster Tarpley[17] calls the "oligarchy" or the "invisible" or "rogue" government that's actually in control of the nation—these questions are matters for scholarship, and they've been and are still being ever more deeply and accurately explored *through* scholarship.

But, setting the scholars aside for a moment, there's also all the rest of us, the population in general—everybody, the poverty-stricken and abandoned, the working class, the intellectual class, the profes-

---

17 Tarpley, Webster, *9/11 Synthetic Terror: Made in USA* (2005), http://www.amazon.com/11-Synthetic-Terror-Made-Fourth/dp/0930852370

sional class, the corporate rich, the old aristocracy, and so on. We—all of us—can be saved from tyranny, from fascism, even from the Nazi-style militarism that's already been more than half-way created—we can be saved from these, from permanent and total loss of a free republic, by only one means: The Bushiscti and whoever is ruling them can be stopped from wholesale plunder and destruction only by the free and clear exposure of the truth about 9/11, only by the acceptance of that truth by a sufficient part of the population, with the result that the perpetrators of one of the greatest of murderous and treasonable crimes ever committed can and will be brought to trial.

"Will never happen," says a cavalier and worldly voice from the other side of the room. "Too many in on it. Too big. Who's going to be the prosecution, for godsakes?"

Well, what about the people of the United States? Where are *they*?

Only exposure and trial could lance the boil whose toxin has leached everywhere already into the blood and tissue of the republic. Only exposure and trial could lance the flesh and release the purulent stench of the miasma of lies, fraud, cover-up, hypocrisy, and deceit lying beneath. Only exposure and trial could disinfect the secret corpo-military-intelligence gangsterism of murderers, thieves, killers, invaders, and high-level drug-runners that have come to constitute our so-called "government" by the invisible and the powerful, by the Trilateralists[18] and the Bilderbergers,[18] by the global hegemonists, by the profiteering, the cruel, the self-interested, the unfeeling, and the ruthless.

After all, that's who's in "charge" of America now, that's who is leading it ever more rapidly toward the tyranny that will serve their own interests alone with mountains of profit and power while destroying the liberties and wealth and lives of all the rest. Only by exposing the *one* most enormous crime of all their crimes, only by bringing *this* crime into the demystifying and sanitizing light of day and then by prosecuting those—no matter how many or how few—who committed the crime, and by convicting them: Only in this way can we regain the United States of America for its people, restore the nation's health, purge the purulent sickness and infection from the nation's blood.[20]

Why doesn't this happen? For one thing, there are millions of the genuinely blind, those so thoroughly deluded, having been kept in so

---

[18] http://en.wikipedia.org/wiki/Trilateral_Commission
[19] http://en.wikipedia.org/wiki/Bilderberg_Group
[20] Update: See Linh Dinh, "Collapsing America," Sept. 13, 2010: "As Americans, we need to get to the heart of this, because this madness and deceit are perpetuating themselves. If we don't have the courage and clarity to confront this evil, we won't regain our sanity or move forward. We might as well be dead. We're dying." http://onlinejournal.com/artman/publish/printer_6313.shtml

extreme a state of ignorance and often of poverty as well, that they can scarcely serve or save themselves, let alone serve or save their cruel and ruined nation. Then there are millions of others, the ones who are, or who *allowed* themselves to become, compromised and are now dependent upon the criminals for their livelihoods and for the livelihoods, safety, and wellbeing of their families, or who are dependent upon the *apparatus* of the criminals for those things, and, thus co-opted and intellectually ruined and depraved, will continue to do all in their power to keep secret the truth about 9/11. Among this group will be found members of high corporate leadership, members of the United States Congress, members of the Bush cabinet and others who serve near the center of that administration, while included also are thousands upon thousands of public figures who know the truth but in differing ways are self-interested enough to devote the entirety of their lives to suppression of that truth about 9/11. Salient among these are figures like Larry Silverstein, Rudolph Giuliani, Michael Bloomberg, Eliot Spitzer, Dick Cheney, George W. Bush, Condoleezza Rice, and Colin Powell, not to mention *every* publicly visible person in mainstream broadcasting or publishing throughout the nation.

That such people as those in the second category are traitors and should be treated as such is unarguable. But for those who make up another highly significant group, the question of treason is less clear cut: That is, America's intellectuals, the intelligentsia, if you wish. For purposes of clarity at this point in the discussion, I exclude the neocon intellectuals, some of whom *are* compromised, others less so, some not at all. Aside from the neoconservatives, though, I count as intellectuals those who are in academia, in journalism, in communications or the media, in publishing, and in the more sophisticated and substantive levels of the performing and creative arts.

This is the group that more than any other ought to be serving the nation most powerfully by exposing, describing, defining, and disseminating the truth, the whole truth, and nothing but the truth about 9/11. But *they're not doing it.* This is the greatest social and intellectual disaster of the present moment. These people are not doing the job they *should* be doing. They're *not* seeking, studying, describing, and displaying either the truth of 9/11 or the truth about our dying nation. Whether this makes them traitors also, or whether it does in some cases while it doesn't in others, and *why*—these are questions I'll take up a few steps down the road. There, we'll meet mainly *literary* people, those who, once upon a time and seemingly a world ago, were my own intellectual, artistic, and political companions—before they all went and died inner deaths on me, the outrageous, lamentable, and seemingly impossible event that's chronicled in *A Nation Gone Blind.*

One last matter remains before bringing this piece to a close. Let us return briefly to the quotation we saw earlier from *A Writer at War*. The relevant part is this, at the end of the quote:

> there are SS men and guards all round, with sub-machine guns, hand grenades and pistols. They are the power. In their hands are tanks and aircraft, lands, cities, the sky, railways, the law, newspapers, radio. The whole world is silent, suppressed, enslaved by a brown gang of bandits which has seized power. London is silent and New York, too. And only somewhere on a bank of the Volga, many thousands of kilometers away, the Soviet artillery is roaring.

There is no hope for those who will die in Treblinka, and yet there *is* a certain other kind of hope. The Red Army is coming. The Red Army *will* come and it *will* defeat the Nazis, even though not for two more years, maybe longer. *"And only somewhere on a bank of the Volga, many thousands of kilometers away, the Soviet artillery is roaring."*

But here and now, just exactly *who,* we must ask, just exactly *who* is coming now, from however far away, to save *us*? The answer is horrifying and profound. The answer is: *No one.* We are alone. We have cut ourselves off from the rest of the world. Our enemies and destroyers are among us, thick in our very midst. If anyone is going to save us, it's going to have to be us, we, alone, ourselves.

Eric Larsen
November 5, 2006

5.

OUR ENEMIES,
THE LEFT GATEKEEPERS, PT. 1
(IN WHICH ARIANNA HUFFINGTON TELLS THE
TRUTH—AND DOESN'T EVEN KNOW IT)
DECEMBER 2, 2006

To the Reader:
As I learned more about what 9/11 was and had been—a deliberate, highly complex, long-planned, self-inflicted, treasonous act of cold-blooded murder and destruction—my attention turned to what you might call a "secondary outrage." The vast conspiracy that brought about 9/11 was followed by the even more vast conspiracy to keep the truth of that heinous and ongoing[21] crime covered up. There was, by 2006, no longer any excuse for a plea of ignorance on the part of even the *most modestly* gifted, responsible, or in the least bit curious, intellectuals.[22] So it was that after 2006 my attention turned from 9/11 in and of itself and focused also on this second and arguably far more destructive crime and outrage: The crime of covering up the truth of the original treason, and therefore also, at the very least, of blunting opposition to the numerous criminal acts of war and human destruction, abroad *and* at home, that followed from the original atrocity.

1.

"The Face of Evil"

A person wonders—or I do—what Nicholas Lemann might have been thinking as he wrote "Paranoid Style: How conspiracy theories become news" for the October 16 issue of *The New Yorker.*

---

21 I say "ongoing" for the very simple reason that 9/11 has been—and remains still—the excuse for every war crime, crime against humanity, and crime against the Geneva Accords that the United States has committed, and goes on committing, since 2001.

22 See the appendix (p. 225) for a list of some of the 9/11 books I had read by the time I wrote the present essay.

I wonder if he was thinking, smugly, that he'd dangle right in front of us the real nuts and bolts of how the gate-keeper media go about doing their lying, omitting, distorting, suppressing, ridiculing, and covering-up of 9/11 truth in ways designed to make those media *look* as though they're truth-telling, honest, fair-minded, candid, thorough, and conscientious. I wonder, that is, whether he was thinking *so* highly of himself that here's what he was about to do: He was about to come right out and show us every last one of his magician's tricks—all the while knowing that his dumb readers would never "get" them anyway.

It's inconceivable—isn't it? No, it must be inconceivable. Of course it's inconceivable.

Or not. Either way, the next question is a corollary of the first. Which is worse, *knowing* or *not* knowing what it is you're actually doing when you make use of and demonstrate for your readers every last trick and deception, every last item in your magician's book of flip-flopping, tricking, conniving, slanting, omitting, suppressing, snipping, cutting, ignoring, distorting, and of making your audience look over *there* when what you're doing is over *here*: In a word, knowing or not knowing that you're engaging in the fraud in general that's attendant upon the pimping and whoring of what it means nowadays to "write" for publications like *The New York Times* or *The New Yorker*.

To write for those publications, that is, on certain subjects of utmost importance that nevertheless, by *diktat* of a pernicious corporate ownership, *must not* be written about truthfully. Like—let's just say—the subject of 9/11 truth. What does it mean for once-honorable and once-professional people and publications when, in place of telling the truth about 9/11, they instead distort, suppress, or ignore it; or when, instead of telling the truth about those who are *part* of the 9/11 truth movement, they choose to malign and calumniate them, cast aspersions on them, look down their noses at them, distort their aims, smear their character, or simply dismiss them—as Frank Rich himself did in the *Times*—as "conspiracy nuts."[23]

What it means is this: Either we are witnessing the most profound imaginable, the most unseeing and possibly even intentionally-maintained ignorance ever known among those thought of as our guides, leaders, and public intellectuals; or else—there being no other possibility—we are witnessing the intentional committing of acts and deeds—that is, varieties of lying—by these same people, acts and deeds that are among the most iniquitous and heinous, perfidious,

---

[23] See "The Longer the War, the Larger the Lies," Sept. 17, 2006: http://query.nytimes.com/gst/fullpage.html?res=9902EFDB1331F934A2575AC0A9609C8B63&scp=1&sq=the%20longer%20the%20war%20the%20larger%20the%20lies&st=cse

treacherous, shameful, dangerous, and unforgivable that may never have been seen on such a scale as this *or* over such a duration of time as this ever before.

Those in the left gatekeeper[24] media—from Frank Rich and the entirety of the *New York Times* to David Corn and the entirety of *The Nation*, from Amy Goodman and the entirety of Pacifica to Nicholas Lemann and the entirety of *The New Yorker* to Arianna Huffington and the entirety of *The Huffington Post*—every highly visible person among the left gatekeepers is either implausibly and totally ignorant, *or* each of them is in equal degree treacherous and iniquitous.

They are, my own judgment would lead me to say, quislings.

A powerful word, and so let's review it. An eponym, it derives, as many know, from the name of Vidkun Quisling, the infamous pro-Nazi Norwegian. It refers to a person, like him, "who betrays his or her own country by aiding an invading enemy, often serving later in a puppet government; fifth columnist."[25] Another definition is "A traitor who serves as the puppet of the enemy occupying his or her country."[26]

And exactly which "invading enemy" is it that our present left gatekeepers have chosen to serve, committing the betrayal of *us*, of America, in doing so? Those who have read the pieces preceding this one know at least in fairly clear outline who or what that enemy is, the enemy of America to whom the left gatekeepers have turned. And those readers know also that this enemy comes not from *outside* America, but from *inside*, which is why metaphors of poison, decay, and rot, of things destroying the body from within, are more appropriate and accurate here than are metaphors of invaders from outside or elsewhere.

And this basic fact, *this* essential truth, is what the left gatekeepers, at any and all costs, have chosen to suppress, falsify, ignore, to keep a secret known only to them and to our enemy.

I say these things for the simple reason that, as I write these words now, five years after the attacks of 2001, there is no longer any persuasive evidence whatsoever left to show that the attacks were *not* in fact a "false flag op," or, more simply, an "inside job." Scholars have produced volume upon volume of overwhelmingly persuasive evidence that this is so.[27]

Indeed, the "attacks" *were* a self-inflicted wound, an assault on America *by* America's military, intelligence, and oligarchic leaders. The attacks, in the interest of the very rich and powerful, and *only*

---

24 A term I am adopting from Barry Zwicker's use of it in *Towers of Deception: The Media Cover-Up of 9/11* (New Society Publishers, 2006).

25 *Random House Unabridged Dictionary*, 2006.

26 *American Heritage Dictionary of the English Language*, Fourth Edition , 2002.

27 Again, see the Appendix for a highly incomplete listing.

of the very rich and powerful, were repugnant, vile, opportunistic, cold-blooded, ruthless, murderous, unscrupulous—and treasonous. Many readers will remember the name Steven C. Vincent. Some may even remember the *Times* news article, by Anthony Ramirez, from August 4, 2005, that ran on page B1 under the headline "Slain Reporter Recalled as Intrepid in War." The lead paragraph went like this:

> Steven C. Vincent, a New York City journalist who was kidnapped and killed in Iraq on Tuesday, was described by friends and colleagues yesterday as an intrepid newsman roused by the attacks on Sept. 11, 2001, and committed to shoe-leather reporting, whatever the consequences.

Ramirez later comments that "Lisa R. Ramaci, 49, Mr. Vincent's wife, released a brief biographical sketch and a statement yesterday. She said her husband was 'a brave, honorable, decent and moral person who was murdered doing what he loved and thought was necessary.'" In Iraq, Vincent "[worked]on a shoestring budget... [and] did not have the money for a bulletproof vest or a Kevlar helmet, let alone the bodyguards large news organizations routinely provide for their reporters. Mr. Vincent and his interpreters took taxis wherever they went, instead of armored vehicles."

Vincent died in Basra, "shot three times in the chest," after having been kidnapped by "insurgents."

Something of greatest importance to the correct memory of Steven C. Vincent and to the correct judgment of his death is found in the article's second paragraph:

> For much of his career, Mr. Vincent, 49, a freelance writer, had covered the art world, including museums, auction houses and the antiquities trade. But in September 2001, when he scrambled to the roof of his apartment building in the East Village and saw the second airliner strike the World Trade Center, "I saw the face of evil in that moment," he later told a friend.

A "brave, honorable, decent and moral person," wrote Vincent's wife, "was murdered doing what he loved and thought what was necessary."

Yes, but murdered by *whom*? Literally, of course, people will say murdered by the "insurgent," or perhaps "insurgents," who pulled a trigger, or triggers, three times. But, no, that insurgent or those insurgents are not, and that insurgent or those insurgents *can* not be the real murderers.

On the morning of 9/11, Vincent said that when the second plane struck the south tower, he "saw the face of evil." And he did, it's true: That's exactly what he saw, the face of evil, purest evil. But the face he *thought* he saw wasn't the real one. The possessor or possessors of that one, the possessor or possessors of *that* face of evil, the *real* face of evil, the "face" that pulled off the job—some of them in the White House bunker, some in the Pentagon, some in the Booker Elementary School, some in the Air Force, some in the FBI, others in various military sites, stations, and intelligence units, groups, and offices—*that* "face" went totally unseen by Vincent just as it went unseen by almost everyone else. *That's* the face of those who, in cold blood, traitorously, in their own interests and *only* their own—murdered Steven C. Vincent.

He got murdered because he was idealistic, well-intended, and a sucker. We were *all* suckers[28] that morning—and many, many of us still are. Far worse than the real suckers, though, are those despicable figures of true iniquity, the gatekeepers, who know the truth and *still* keep it secret.

Poor Steven C. Vincent. Poor sucker, murdered not just because, like so many, he *was* a sucker—but murdered because, as a sucker, he was also an "honorable, decent and moral person."

For that's what they do, absolutely. That's what they do, not only our own quisling administration and our own quisling Congress but also our own quisling left gatekeepers: *They*—all of them—*they* routinely and regularly and consistently murder off the *best* people while busying their despicable minds with figuring out ways to keep the *worst*—that is, themselves—still alive and doing their wretchedly dirty work.

And so it is that Steven C. Vincent joined the company of all the others dead by murder, murder beginning with 9/11 itself, a company of dead whose number now, late in 2006, reaches toward a million.

2.

The "Pathological Refusal"

"Pathology" is another strong word, almost as strong as "quisling." It has to do with the study of disease and infection, and it can be made into an adjective, "pathological," in *that* form taking on the simple meaning of "sick" or "crazy," as in phrases like "pathological liar."

When Frank Rich, therefore, in the *New York Times* calls me or you or anyone else who studies 9/11 in order to find out the truth about it—when he calls you, me, or us "conspiracy nuts," what he basically means is that we're "crazy." He's saying we're "pathological."

---

[28] With certain and at times extremely important exceptions. Dr. Judy Wood, for example, knew from her first sight on television of the "collapse" of the south tower that she was witnessing an event not in conformity with any of the previously known or commonly understood laws of physics. (Source: Dr. Judy Wood in personal conversation with author. See http://www.drjudywood.com/).

Considering all this—the meanings and uses of words like these, along with the innuendo, calumniation, smear, and gutter-level name-calling that so often pop up when words like "pathological" are being thrown around—considering all this, it was particularly interesting to come upon a piece by Arianna Huffington in *The Huffington Post* for November 5, 2006.[29]

Huffington's piece is entitled "Haggard and the White House: Both Living in Denial," and her subject is the Bushiscti's "refusal to accept reality." In her lead paragraph, she writes that

> the Bush administration is sick. The fall of Ted Haggard[30] is just the latest manifestation of the central disease of President Bush and his cohorts: the pathological refusal to accept reality, and the delusion that reality can be changed by rhetoric.

A couple of sentences later, Huffington adds, with a possible nod to Oedipus the King (where the sickness of the King causes the sickness of the kingdom), that "while it's the administration that's sick, it's the whole country that's suffering." Then a list of some of the "denials of reality" that make the Bushiscti so "sick":

> The insurgency is in its "last throes," we've "turned the corner" in Iraq, gutting Social Security would "save" it, global warming doesn't exist, evolution is just "a theory," Rumsfeld and Cheney are "doing a fantastic job" . . .

•

Some clarification has to be made before we get to the matter of real importance and interest here. First, we all know that people in the Bush administration lie like rugs, and did lie like rugs even before the 2000 election.[31] And *lying* is a different matter indeed from "refusing to accept reality." A liar can be in perfectly good contact with reality and just be, well, a liar.

All right. That was pretty easy. But now we've got to figure out not only why there are so *many* lies but also why they've been going on so consistently and so plentifully and for so long. And the answer this time is: The lying is pervasive, necessary, *very* ineptly delivered and yet cornucopian in its abundance, for the simple but very important reason that the government that we *see* and are *aware* of is not in any way the government that's actually governing us or the country.

---

[29] http://www.huffingtonpost.com/arianna-huffington/haggard-and-the-white-hou_b_33324.html
[30] The widely known evangelical preacher exposed in late 2006 for a sexual affair with one Mike Jones.
[31] http://www.newamericancentury.org/aboutpnac.htm

Anyone who reacts to what I just said by thinking that I should be smeared and calumniated, à la Frank Rich, by being called a "conspiracy nut," is cordially invited to pick up a copy of Webster Griffin Tarpley's *9/11 Synthetic Terror: Made in USA*[32] and sit down for a good long read.

This "government," which Tarpley names our "rogue" or "invisible" government, is the composite power that pulls the strings. Some in the central parts of the Bush administration may be among those string-pullers, and these are the "moles" Tarpley identifies and describes for us, among them Cheney, Wolfowitz, and Tony Blair. Bush is a special case.

Most pathetic among all American presidents is George W. Bush—the biggest ninny of all presidents and the most left out. Badly educated, not smart, certainly not deep, he is the most obviously of all presidents since LBJ the string-jerked puppet of forces he himself can scarcely begin even to comprehend, let alone control.[33]

Bush, therefore, is insignificant in regard to Huffington's inquiry. Bush lies when and as he's told to. What else can he do, being a man of absolutely no resources of his own? And so every single lie from Bush, without exception, is nothing more than a brief diversion, the tugging of a tattered veil over the mass American eye, a temporary buying of time as the invisible government goes about the business of deciding its next step. A string is pulled—the hand rises. A string is loosened, the jaw drops. A button is pushed, out come certain words. Another button—other words.

But back to "reality" and being in touch with it. Very, very clearly, the true "Bush administration" (which is really just a way of referring indirectly to the "rogue" or "invisible" government) is as firmly "in touch with reality" as may be humanly possible. Many a quibble might justifiably arise at this point, not to mention some potentially very good counter-arguments—along *Dr. Strangelove* lines—suggesting that the invisible government itself can't be in touch with "reality" because its members are "pathological," their salient pathology being megalomania. Interesting as these arguments may be, even convincing as they may prove, they've still got to be set aside for the moment, since they'll take us away from our present subject.

Which is to say the present subject of "lying" and "reality," of doing the former and being out of touch with the latter. Now, the "reality" that the invisible government is firmly in touch with is what we'll call its *agenda*. For this invisible government does indeed have an agenda—and has had an agenda since well before November of

---

32 Tarpley, Webster, *9/11 Synthetic Terror: Made in USA* (2005), http://www.amazon.com/11-Synthetic-Terror-Made-Fourth/dp/0930852370

33 For any who find this an odd remark to be made about LBJ, I highly recommend *JFK and the Unspeakable: Why He Died and Why It Matters*, by James Douglass (2008)—EL, July 2010

2000.[34] And this agenda, in the invisible government's view (and in the invisible government's own interest), is not an agenda that's ours to know. Like all other elements of the invisible government's agenda, it is secret, precisely in the way it was made and kept a "secret" that the attacks of 9/11 were self-inflicted, that they were in fact the plan, product, and crime of the invisible government, with or without other helpers.

It's all perfectly logical, after all. The invisible government's agenda *must* remain secret because it's evil and if it becomes known ahead of time—known, that is, to brave, good, decent people, people like, say, Steven C. Vincent—those who have learned of it will resist, fight, rebel against it, expose it, and derail it.

The left gatekeepers, therefore, by definition, cannot be brave, good, decent people but must be the opposite of all of these.

The invisible government can make suckers of all of us, but only by keeping us in the dark.

And we aren't in the in the dark any longer. The truths of 9/11— and therefore the truths of the entire invisible government's agenda— are known and available, have been widely, deeply, responsibly, and plentifully researched, studied, and written about—but have never, ever been reviewed or described or revealed by the enemy gatekeeper media. These truths, even so, through the work of scholars and activists, have become widely known, made widely available, and remain widely respected. And so if any one of those whom we're now talking about—if Arianna Huffington, Frank Rich, Nicholas Lemann, Amy Goodman, David Corn—if *any* such people who are professional journalists and therefore intellectual leaders *don't* know about this massive literature on 9/11 truth—well, then they've failed to do their homework, they're failures at their occupations as investigators and reporters, they should be booted immediately from their jobs, and that's that.

On the other hand, if any one of these or others like them—Huffington, Rich, Lemann, Goodman, Corn—*if* any such people who are professional journalists and therefore intellectual leaders *have* done their homework, *do* know those widely-available and immeasurably important truths and yet purposely sit on them and keep them dark: *Then* such people as these aren't just crummy at their professions, and aren't just poor suckers like Steven C. Vincent, but they are, instead, every one, iniquitous, criminal, traitorous, monstrous quislings who should rot in hell and who are far, far, far beyond any *conceivable* pardon, ever.

---

[34] Read here about "The Project for the New American Century": http://www.newamericancentury.org/aboutpnac.htm

•

Let's see what Arianna Huffington has to say about them—and perhaps about herself, albeit in both cases inadvertently.

"Was Ted Haggard's absurd claim," asks Huffington, "that... he saw Mike Jones, but only for massages and that... he bought meth from Jones but never used it, really... different from Bush and Cheney and Rumsfeld continuing to claim we're winning in Iraq?"

We're back here to the subject of simple, old-fashioned hypocrisy and lies—in the case of the good reverend Haggard, certainly—while possibly, though not *surely*, "denial of reality" is involved in the Bush-Cheney-Rumsfeld reference. Either way, here's what's important, as Huffington—while adding Mark Foley into the soup—unknowingly blurts out the real, honest-to-god truth, as anyone who's read *Hamlet* or *Lear* or *Oedipus the King* or *The Oresteia* seriously knows very well:

Mark Foley and Ted Haggard are textbook examples of how the relentless denial of reality perverts judgment and rots the soul.

Now, just possibly, we may really be getting somewhere, though I doubt that Huffington knows it. The mishmash, the mix-up between simple lying versus actual denial of reality is still at work and still unclarified. But Huffington, knowingly or not (probably not) keeps pushing toward our real subject:

That both... claims were made with the expectation that the public would buy them shows what the chronic refusal to acknowledge reality does to one's judgment.

Well, maybe so. Whatever we're really talking about—plain lying or authentic reality-denial—at least a new spice has been added to the mix, and that spice is the subject of judgment being warped. And, *voilà*, things begin suddenly to sound very, very familiar to anyone who has been closely involved in the 9/11 truth movement *or* to anyone who has been closely involved in observing the work of the gatekeepers *of* 9/11 truth.

Let's read on, and, as we do, pay special attention to the word "but," where the emphasis added will be not Huffington's, but mine:

I have little doubt that Haggard's homophobia was real.... *But facts are stubborn things.* .... Haggard chose to deny them, suppress them and attack those who exposed them.

And so, here at last, though unbeknownst to the very person who has brought and guided us here, we've finally reached home. For what Huffington has done, and done perfectly, is provide us with a spot-on, absolutely accurate, bull's-eye descriptive definition of precisely what it is the left gatekeepers do, have done, and doubtless—unless they're exposed, punished, purged—will "choose" to go on doing without end: Namely, deny and suppress the "facts," and, as we've seen, "[attack] those who expose" them.

•

Arianna Huffington, in condemning others, has with absolute perfection and perfect ignorance put the finger on herself. She has put the finger on Frank Rich; put the finger on David Corn; on Amy Goodman; on Nicholas Lemann—*and* on all the editors of all those writers and on all the managers and directors in *charge* of those editors.

Huffington has, in other words, put the finger on *all* the left gate-keepers. She has put the finger on that kind of people who ruthlessly and relentlessly and cruelly or perhaps in cowardice continue to make it impossible that "brave, honorable, decent and moral" figures like the late Steven C. Vincent—and the three-quarters of a million others, or more, who, like him, are dead—will *ever* be allowed the dignity of the truth, will *ever* be allowed to be dignified *by* the truth.

He was a sucker. He took the bait, and because of it he died. People may think he was a martyr, but, no, he, like *millions* of others, was a sucker. He fell for it. He didn't see through the con. He was a patsy.

But he was hardly alone, and this, too, is certain: Vincent *deserves* the greater truth, and *deserves* the vindication that that truth alone can bring him. And so, only when his iniquitous, execrable, vile, quisling murderers are finally exposed, named, prosecuted, and punished, only then can it be said either honestly or truly that he, and the many like him, was not a sucker, but a martyr, and a true one, a martyr to their lies.

Until that happens, all is hopeless, undistinguished, and putrid. Until that happens, all is deceit. Until that happens, all is poison, disease, and death.

3.

The Truth

It shouldn't take long to bring an end to this particular section of our look at the left gatekeepers—although it's clear that another section will be necessary before we visit the iniquitous Nicholas

Lemann, quisling and left gatekeeper, in his Santa's workshop as he puts together the pieces of his own repugnant and vile toys.

Before we go to Lemann, though, let's follow Arianna Huffington another step—this time as she returns to her earlier unwitting truth and (again unknowingly) reveals the enormous relevance of that truth to the life or death of our nation:

> The refusal by the Bush administration...to acknowledge reality is sick—and potentially lethal to the well-being of our country. But it's clear they're not going to get better, because to do so would require they acknowledge reality enough to know they're sick in the first place. And they're not going to do that. They actually believe there's an alternative to the "reality-based world," and that they live in it.

The allusion to Ron Suskind's famous essay, "Faith, Certainty and the Presidency of George W. Bush," in the *New York Times Magazine* of October 17, 2004, is aptly made, and Huffington deserves credit for making it. It's in that essay, readers will remember,[35] that a strong case really *is* at least strongly suggested that the Bushiscti actually should be diagnosed as pathological and megalomaniacal deniers of empirically based reality.

And yet, however strong that case may be, it doesn't change our subject here and now. That's because the great point here and now isn't whether the Bushiscti and Cheneyiscti are fruitcakes or not, but whether they are treasonous or not. The point for us is that, whatever the Bushiscti may or may not be *clinically*, the unalterable fact remains that the left gatekeepers—which now include the Democratic party—in their aid and abetment through covering up the 9/11 crime, are all exactly the same as the *Bushiscti.*

If the perpetrators' side tells lies, so does the abettors' side. If the perpetrators' side "denies reality," so does the abettors' side. If the perpetrators' side ignores "facts," even though "facts are stubborn things," so does the abettors' side.

And the significance of all this? Well, the significance, according, implicitly, to Arianna Huffington, is that both sides are "sick." I tend to agree with her—although she doesn't know that she's admitted her own side is also "sick."[36] And the additional significance of all

---

[35] "The aide said that guys like me were 'in what we call the reality-based community,' which he defined as people who 'believe that solutions emerge from your judicious study of discernible reality.' I nodded and murmured something about enlightenment principles and empiricism. He cut me off. 'That's not the way the world really works anymore,' he continued. 'We're an empire now, and when we act, we create our own reality. And while you're studying that reality—judiciously, as you will—we'll act again, creating other new realities, which you can study too, and that's how things will sort out. We're history's actors...and you, all of you, will be left to just study what we do."

[36] That is, it certainly seems that she doesn't know.

this—and the guilt for it falls every bit as heavily on the left gatekeep-ers as on the Bushiscti—is that the sickness really, truly, actually is *"potentially lethal to the well-being of our country."* [emphasis mine]

As for that poisonous and lethal part, you can bet on it with god's own nickel and be certain of winning—as you're crushed by the sor-row and ruin all around you. The membranous sac of poison that is the hidden crime of 9/11—that sac of toxins has got to be removed from its place deep inside the body politic or it will burst, poison the republic's blood itself, and the entire organism will necessarily and consequently die.[37]

Great haste is essential, because that toxic sac of lies, fraud, puru-lence, hypocrisy, and fascist-style grabbing for hegemony is *already* leaking out its poisons, and the body has *already* lost an arm (habeas corpus), a lower leg (torture), one eye and half its hearing (FISA spy-ing), and the coherence of its central nervous system (arrest without cause, incarceration without limit).

The country is dying. The cause is known, the cure available, the surgeons standing by to aid in the lancing. But nothing good will happen until the gatekeepers give up their despicable feasting on lies and deceit.

Now let's take a look at a few of them at work.

Eric Larsen
December 2, 2006

---

[37] Update: See Linh Dinh, "Collapsing America" (Online Journal, Sept. 13, 2010): http://onlinejournal.com/artman/publish/printer_6313.shtml He writes: "If we don't have the courage and clarity to confront this evil, we won't regain our sanity or move forward. We might as well be dead. We're dying."

6.

OUR ENEMIES, THE LEFT GATEKEEPERS, PT. 2
LET'S WATCH NICHOLAS LEMANN
AND OTHERS OF THE SOCIETY OF GATEKEEPERS
ACTUALLY AT THEIR WORK
DECEMBER 7, 2006

To the Reader:

The more one learned or knew about 9/11, the more inescapably clear it became that in order to write—or report—on that subject in *any* mainstream media outlet, it was absolutely necessary to avoid telling the truth. This, of course, could be done by omission, by distortion, by outright prevarication, or by the sheerest and most absurd uses of chopped and jejune logic imaginable. Papers and magazines eagerly traded their integrity for 9/11 copy that would pass the censors—and in so doing compromised themselves all the way from the very deepest foundations of honest journalism right on up to the roof beams. How writers, editors, commentators could go on living with themselves after becoming prostitutes this completely, I had—and still have—not the least idea. I take that back. I *do* have the least idea. That kind of compromise, complicity, and deceit is a form of moral death. It's true that, as Linh Dinh said, "We're dying." Those writers, editors, and commentators can be able to look at themselves in the mirror for only one conceivable reason, and that's because something inside them has died. Something *moral* in them has died. Only through that death of a moral sensor—a death that in the coming years was to batten ever more greedily on the conscience of America—could such people look at themselves and remain blind to the moral truth of what they had become.

1.

Love Those Gatekeepers: Elliot Spitzer, Leader of The Pack

In 2004, John Perkins came out with a widely read and intended-to-be shocking book, *Confessions of an Economic Hit Man*.[38] More

---

[38] Berrett-Koehler Publishers, http://www.amazon.com/Confessions-Economic-Hit-John-Perkins/dp/0452287081/sr=1-1/qid=1165419366/ref=pd_bbs_sr_1/104-4231058-3189532?ie=UTF8&s=books

41

important than the book, however, was a piece written about it by Catherine Austin Fitts[39] called "Will the Real Economic Hit Men Please Stand Up? Meditations on 9/11 Truth."[40]

Fitts began her piece with a definition *à propos* to our consideration of the writers and media people I'm calling (after Barrie Zwicker, in *Towers of Deception: The Media Cover-up of 9/11)*[41] "left gatekeepers." Perkins' book, Fitts says, is "a limited hangout." Her words:

> A "limited hangout" is a partial confession, a mea culpa, if you will, that leaves the essence of a crime or covert reality hidden. Because it includes some small part of the truth, the limited hangout is irresistibly attractive to dissidents and political critics whose thirst for such truth makes them jump at the dangled scraps. Once the system's watchdogs are busy chewing on the limited hangout, the guilty players can go about their illegal business for a new round of unaccountable, semi-secret mayhem.

While readers "jump at the dangled scraps," the *real* truth is purposely left out:

> The phenomenon that Perkins writes about is well known. But his personal "how to" account of an economic hit pertains to an apparently cold case, far in the financial past. While this story is very instructive for those who have not yet dealt with professional fraudsters or been targeted by economic warfare (whether in the Third World or in the First World nations) it is even more instructive for its omissions—and for its timing as an *apologia* intended, we are led to believe, somehow to assuage guilt for harm done: it relates to events occurring twenty-five or thirty years ago, involving players who are, for the most part, dead or retired from the business of economic warfare and companies that have morphed into later incarnations.

The Perkins book, in other words, is essentially a fraud, its "dangled scraps" of sensationalism being in fact bits of old scenery from a drama played out long ago and now lying somewhere in the dust of an empty theater. Catherine Austin Fitts is certainly one to know about such things, herself having been powerfully victimized—attacked[42]—by the anonymous thugs of government-military-corporate-financial power. So let's read one of her paragraphs where she tells us a bit of what the *mea culpa* writer Perkins doesn't even touch on. She prepares for this paragraph by remarking that "In the process of providing a colorful account of a 1970s whodunit (complete with low

---

[39] http://www.solari.com/

[40] http://www.scoop.co.nz/stories/HL0503/S00090.htm

[41] New Society Publishers, 2006: http://www.amazon.com/Towers-Deception-Media-Cover-up-11/dp/0865715734/sr=1-1/qid=1165590900/ref=pd_bbs_sr_1/1044231058-3189532?ie=UTF8&s=books

[42] See *Crossing the Rubicon*, pp. 55–57.

tech strategies devoid of the dazzling technology toolkit that is now an essential part of the economic hit man's weaponry of economic warfare), Perkins delivers to readers the 'big lie': he reveals the [false] secret that there is no greater conspiracy."

That is, Perkins tells an outdated, tame, and partial tale, all the while positive that his gullible readers will swallow it as the whole and real truth. In short, he lies like a rug, his whole book (like the *9/11 Commission Report* itself) being one big lie of omission:

> Nowhere does Perkins introduce the notion that cartels in a "New World Order" (the phrase coined and promoted by George H. W. Bush) use covert manipulation of the global financial system to centralize and concentrate economic and political power. Assassinations by "jackals" aside, Perkins barely hints that for fifty years the US military-industrial complex has been developing and testing powerful black budget technology, satellite and other invisible weaponry and surveillance technology and insider-trading tools behind the veil of national security secrets. Indeed, it was the need for a means of financing black budget operations and weaponry outside the view and control of Congress and the appropriations process—rather than the mere pursuit of corporate profits—that provided the political air cover for Perkins to do what he did as his covert counterparts marketed drugs in American and Third World communities alike.

Fitts can be seemingly gentle with Perkins when she suggests that, after all, the truth might be more than his readers—we—are as yet ready or able to accept:

> Understanding and facing the economic warfare responsible for slowly poisoning us and our families and wiping out our retirement savings is a complex and very scary undertaking in comparison to Perkins' concerned confessions. Perhaps we prefer to disassociate from our present circumstances, live in a perpetual state of cognitive dissonance, and focus on the study of yesteryear.

But that *we* may not be quite ready for the truth is an insignificance in comparison to the *importance* of that truth. That things are tough is no excuse for hiding from them:

> Complex and scary as it may seem, the growing body of evidence makes a compelling case that officials of the US government, its contractors and the military abetted the 9/11 attacks. With the help and complicity of the US Congress and corporate media, they are engaged in the most profitable war and enforcement profiteering in history. This is a terrifying picture to contemplate.

---

43 Update: Reading these words now, four years later, is even more terrifying. The profiteering and destructive ruin that have been accomplished since Catherine Austin Fitts wrote these words, and that continue to be accomplished, are very nearly beyond the layman's ability to conceive.

The enemy within, that is to say, consists of the very "leaders" who at the least "abetted" 9/11 and at the worst brought it about, the same who are now making out like gangbusters, being war profiteers successful beyond precedent. And lucky us—us New Yorkers, that is—to have just elected a brand new state governor who is one of the most high-profile and guiltiest 9/11 gatekeepers of all:

> Look how tough it has been for New Yorkers, the constituency most adversely affected by the 9/11 tragedy. A recent Zogby poll indicates that 49.3 percent of residents of New York City hold the opinion that officials "knew in advance that attacks were planned on or around September 11, 2001, and that they consciously failed to act." Yet, despite this widespread conviction and the mounting evidence that sustains it, no serious support has developed for the November 2004 citizens' complaint requesting that Elliot Spitzer, the Attorney General of New York, finally open a criminal investigation into the tragedy.

What, then, can be the motives of gatekeepers? Well, in Spitzer's case, an apparent motive for ignoring the people's petition[44] for a New York State investigation into 9/11 was high political ambition—wanting the governorship. And what do you suppose Spitzer plans to *do* with the governorship of New York State to *help* people—when, unexposed, unpunished, and unproscribed, the perpetrators of 9/11, the drainers of the treasury, the profit-makers from war, the economic hit men, the crooked Congress and their myriad corporate and financial henchmen continue going about their business of widening the state of war, channeling profits into their own pockets, and in general pursuing "the strong dollar policy" that was begun under Clinton, that sagged a bit *before* 9/11 but then got a major jolt *from* 9/11 and that, as "it turns out. . .[is] a policy that intentionally destroys the value of the dollar"?

What will Gatekeeper Spitzer do for New York State *then*, at the time not so far in the future when, through the crimes of the big winners and in the *interest* of the big winners, the value of the dollar is destroyed? Will Spitzer be sorry *then* that he didn't take sides with the truth? Not likely.

It's clear to Catherine Austin Fitts what he should have done and why: "Getting to the truth of 9/11," she writes, "offers an opportunity to ask and answer the unanswered questions of who is running our world, and to illuminate how the covert cash flows really work."

But Gatekeeper Spitzer didn't care to illuminate (or change) how "the covert cash flows really work."[45] By extension, that means he

---

[44] A petition signed by yours truly, I might add.

[45] Update: Such Wall Street reforms as he did want or dare to want to bring about—the ending of government support for predatory lending, for example—were sufficiently hateful to the morally-dead high powers that assassination of Spitzer's character was quickly arranged for and he was driven from office just as effectively as if he had been literally assassinated.

must also not have opposed the "Patriot" Act, or, later, the criminal spying on people and the cavalier ignoring of FISA, or, later—*before* his victorious election—the legalization of torture and the tossing out of habeas corpus.

What a governor! What a guy! What a force for truth, good, right, and freedom!

Ah, the gatekeepers, how you gotta love 'em.

Spitzer and the *New York Times*—thick as thieves and faithful to the end, god bless 'em both.

All right, I'll shut up and let Catherine Austin Fitts say a few more words:

> Although fifteen NYC legislators have also called for such an inquiry [that is, a New York State inquiry into 9/11], there has as yet been no effort locally to hold the New York Senate and Congressional delegations accountable for failing to hold the executive branch responsible for its failure to perform, or for its potential complicity. While the New York firemen booing Hillary Clinton off the stage at the 9/11 Concert was a start, the sentiment expressed has not translated into political action or market action. How many New Yorkers have cut off their subscriptions to, ads in or investments in the stock of the *New York Times* when the *Times* helped to facilitate the 9/11 cover-up by failing to ask probative questions or hold officials accountable?

Yes, moral and responsible leadership is grand, especially when it comes from such unimpeachable and truth-seeking sources as the New York State Attorney General's office (soon enough the governor's office) and the editorial offices of the *New York Times*.

And it's especially grand the way the gatekeepers stick with their lies no matter how obvious it becomes that those lies are aiding and abetting the big-guy executive-level honcho-murderers in bringing about ever more swiftly their master plan for an American Police State. That's where you really begin to love Spitzer and really love the *Times*, when you begin to really love the gatekeepers of every type and stripe, high and low, from Amy Goodman and Frank Rich all the way up to Spitzer himself—for valiantly sticking with their lies even as the nation is plunged into a worse-than-Orwellian travesty of a nation, whose Kaiser's motto is pick 'em up, torture 'em up, lock 'em up, murder 'em up, forget 'em up.

Now, a last word not from some thug, cheat, criminal, hypocrite, murderer, or liar, but, instead, from the dignified and intelligent, penetrating, morally powerful, unflinching, courageous, ever-ethical and ever-humane Catherine Austin Fitts:

> The answer to the question *Cui Bono?* ("Who benefits?") from the strong dollar policy suggests that allegations that members of the Bush

Administration fully expected, welcomed and even facilitated 9/11 should be taken seriously. Trillions of dollars have been moved out of the US economy under the umbrella of the strong dollar policy—much of it in what appear to be criminal ways. The 9/11 tragedy conveniently necessitated a sudden, centralized control over government and theretofore private activities in the name of protecting national security interests and addressing the threat of terrorism. 9/11 diverted attention from and shut the door behind that money movement. It ushered in a wave of legislation rushed through Congress that would make it much more difficult for the American people to do anything about it. The events of 9/11 have acted as a "lock-down" on a financial coup d'état at the core of the "strong dollar policy."

2.

Yes, From *The New Yorker*! Half-Truths!! Quarter Truths!!!
Eighth Truths!!!! And Getting Still
Smaller...

Nicholas Lemann's piece in *The New Yorker* for October 16, just like Perkins' entire book, is an example of a "limited hangout." It disgraces not only Lemann, and therefore the Columbia School of Journalism, of which he is the head, but also the entire once-grand tradition—institution, one may say—of *The New Yorker.*

Yet again, we're slapped in the face with a "textbook example," as the half-aware Arianna Huffington put it in *The Progressive Populist,* "of how the relentless denial of reality perverts judgment and rots the soul."

In this way, as the gatekeepers go on living as liars and living *within* their lies, the judgment is perverted and the soul is rotted not only of individual media people, but the judgment is perverted and the souls are rotted of entire media organizations and, worse by far, of once-venerable but now utterly compromised and all-but-strangled print institutions—*The New Yorker, The New York Times, The Atlantic Monthly, The New Republic, The Nation,* even what for a long time remained the best of the hold-outs, *Harper's* magazine.

A reader of *A Nation Gone Blind* and a follower of my web site wrote me the other day about this series of pieces on the left gatekeepers. He said:

> Frankly, I don't see why we couldn't have foreseen homegrown fascism as a reality sooner, given our decades-long love affair with "authoritarian" (a euphemism for "disappearance," jack-boots, torture, election rigging— assuming there are elections at all—state-sponsored terror against your own citizens, rampant militarism, etc., etc., etc.) regimes world-wide. If you lie down with fleas (e.g., the Shah, Marcos, Pinochet, Thieu, Lon Nol, any

number of South Korean, Guatemalan, Honduran, Paraguayan, Bolivian, Argentinean, Indonesian "strong men," not to exclude Franco), logic would seem to dictate that you are (a) a dog or (b) hell-bent on becoming one.

Over the past five years, exactly the same thing has happened to America's mainstream print journalism—and that includes its *literary* print journalism: It has lain down with dogs and, big surprise, been transformed into a craven, mangy cur.

•

Let's see the bare-fanged animal at work. Here's the opening paragraph of Lemann's despicably-titled "Paranoid Style: How conspiracy theories become news."

But *wait* a minute. Let's talk about that title first.

It's a "despicable" title exactly *why*, you ask? And I: It's despicable, first, because of its cheap stooping to the smarmy trigger-phrase "conspiracy theories" (à la Frank Rich with his "conspiracy nuts"); and, second, it's despicable because of the concomitant and simultaneous lie—whether a white one or a black one, *you* can choose—nesting in the glib assumption that nothing about 9/11 truth could possibly be *real* news, since nothing about 9/11 truth can possibly possess either importance or merit.

"Terence, this is stupid stuff," wrote A. E. Housman, and I cry out here in echo. It's true that Lemann, lest he seem *only* to be name-calling, props up his essay on—and takes his title from—Richard Hofstadter and his 1965 book, *Paranoid Style in American Politics* [46] (containing Hofstadter's essay of the same title, which ran in *Harper's* magazine in 1964).

Let's get to Lemann's opening paragraph:

"On September the 11th, enemies of freedom committed an act of war against our country," President Bush declared nine days after the 2001 attacks, during an address to a joint session of Congress which may turn out to be the high-water mark of his Presidency. Not only was September 11th the first major attack on American soil since Pearl Harbor; it was a blow struck to the heart of the country's major centers of finance and government, with total surprise, by a shadowy opponent not susceptible to direct counterattack. It is hard to think of any event in our national life at once so devastating and so puzzling since the assassination of President Kennedy.

If this paragraph had been written *four years ago*, back in 2002, it could well enough have been taken as possessing a shred of honesty,

[46] http://www.amazon.com/Paranoid-Style-American-Politics-Essays/dp/0674654617/sr=1-1/qid=1165605311/ref=pd_bbs_sr_1/104-4231058-3189532?ie=UTF8&s=books

since at that time so very much less was known about 9/11 than is known now. Written today, however, it shows one of two things: It shows either so unbelievably towering a degree of ignorance about an event of such mountainous and obvious importance that in an *honest* world the author would avoid the opening of his mouth on the subject at all lest he look absurd, ignorant, and ridiculous; *or* it shows that it's comprised of a deliberate set of distortions and lies *and* that Lemann is absolutely certain his editors won't expose his ignorance *or* his fraud, but that they'll go along with him in pretending that these humungous lies and slurs aren't really humungous lies and slurs at all.

Does it matter? In things *this* dreadful, do one or two degrees of dreadfulness more or less count for anything? Lemann may just as well be aiming only to please his editors, giving them what they want to hear: That is, doing the equivalent of writing for his fourth-grade teacher "I will be a good boy" five hundred times.

But whether what we're reading is the result of naiveté, the intention to lie, or of pure, slavish ignorance preening itself in order to please its editors, seeing a *professional writer* compose this way— naively, ignorantly, or deceitfully—is at the very, very least *embarrassing*. And then, considering that this writer is dean of the Columbia University School of Journalism, that embarrassment turns quickly enough to plain, simple, outright disgust and despair.

It's an irony of its own that a patent weakness in a piece of writing might be preferable to what turns out to be the real truth of it. Let me explain. By way of making, first, a perfectly standard freshman-English criticism of Lemann's paragraph, let's take a look at the veritable devil's riot of cliché in it—"on American soil," "high-water mark of his Presidency," "total surprise," "blow struck to the heart," "shadowy opponent," "our national life."

Is Lemann *that bad* a writer? Or is he writing this "badly" for a shrewd, conscious reason? I don't know and probably never will know, since I very, very much doubt that the likes of Lemann would ever confess, even if he did know. Still, what could his "shrewd, conscious reason" for writing so abominably conceivably be?

Well, here we go: It could be that Lemann wants to *sound* knowledgeable, wants to *sound* like an expert on 9/11, so that readers— lulled half to sleep by the dull, unflappable, professorial tone he achieves through cliché and false confidence in the "truth" and in himself—*won't pick up on* all his many lies of omission, commission, and artful dodging.

In other words, it could be that he's practicing the art, as we know it from Catherine Austin Fitts, of the limited hangout.

Take a look at Lemann's next sentence:

Bush quickly, and evidently correctly, identified Al Qaeda as the party responsible for the attacks on the United States, but he chose to present the nation with a different, more mysterious enemy: a broad category of terrorists, people scattered all over the world who "hate our freedoms" and want to "disrupt and end a way of life."

Can we pardon a dean of the Journalism School at Columbia University for failing to avoid that tin-eared triplet of "quickly, and evidently correctly"? Can we pardon the copy editors at *The New Yorker* for such an ear-jangle—they, an editorial unit that once, back before the Age of Simplification, consisted of the most impeccably talented and fastidious guardians of the language? Well, I myself forgive neither, and I myself think, further, that both Lemann *and* the copy department at *The New Yorker* have given us yet another hint of the professional decay in writers and writing that is everywhere around us and that is *not* unrelated to the deep crisis the entire nation is now in or to the death that it is slowly dying.[47]

Terence, this is stupid stuff. But there's stupider yet to come. Lemann is dean at Columbia Journalism. Lemann is an author. Lemann is a professional journalist. Lemann is a Harvard graduate, *magna cum laude.* And right now, here, with this particular piece of journalism that we're studying, Lemann is a professional journalist on assignment. And yet one of two things appears inevitably to be the case.

Either this professional journalist and academician, over a span of five years, so great is his evident ignorance of the topic, has read *nothing whatsoever to prepare or equip him for his assignment.*

Either that, or *else*—there being again only these two possibilities—or else, as may have been the case also with Frank Rich—Lemann is simply, shamelessly, and obediently lying through his teeth.

•

The president "quickly, and evidently correctly" pinned the job on Al Qaeda, says Lemann. Does Lemann know that Al Qaeda is a creation of the United States, whose CIA created it as a way of helping push the Russians out of Afghanistan? And does he know that the primary asset fully funded and put to use by the CIA and by the United States in order to bring Al Qaeda ("The Base") into existence was Osama bin Laden? Does he know that now Al Qaeda, an organization nebulous at best, is stirred, strengthened, and brought to focus purposely and primarily by the United States' continual irritating,

---

46 Another note about "evidently correctly" before we leave it. How would the Orwell of "Politics and the English Language" react to this innocuous little pair of words? "*Evidently* correctly"? Something is either correct or not, and Lemann's "evidently" makes of him a fawning dog, lapping up the vomit of the party line while at the same time breaking every rule about verification of the truth before the printing of it.

attacking, offending, and arousing it in ways that are the equivalent of jabbing a hornets' nest with a stick? Does he know (remember his saying that the attacks came "with total surprise") how multitudinous were the warnings given to the United States by other countries and agencies of the looming certainty of the 9/11 attacks? And does he know how systematically, deliberately, and criminally the United States made certain to ignore those warnings? Does he have any idea at all of the extent to which the United States falsely demonizes Al Qaeda and uses this demonization unceasingly and relentlessly as a propaganda device to terrorize and subjugate American citizens by causing them to fear this putative "enemy"?

Does he have any idea that the United States intentionally let Osama bin Laden escape from Tora Bora when America's own generals, or those not inside the loop, were begging for added forces that would enable them to capture him? Does he have any idea why the United States was so firm and focused in its insistence that Osama *not* be captured or killed?

Well, what do *you* think? Please don't pull a Frank Rich on me and say that what you think is that I'm a conspiracy nut. No, *I'm* not a conspiracy nut. I'm a reader. I've been reading about 9/11 since June of 2003—a date with a story attached to it that maybe I'll tell sometime.

Another thing: I'm not a professional journalist. I'm not a dean of the nation's foremost journalism school. I'm not even a graduate of Harvard, let alone a *magna cum laude* one. And, most important of all, I'm not on assignment to write an article for one of the nation's most prestigious magazines purportedly telling the truth about alternative views of 9/11, about those opposed, that is, to the "official" explanation of the attacks.

If Lemann, being all of those things, is so completely uninformed about his assignment as he appears to be—well, then that's an ignominious, pathetic, unprofessional, fraudulent, absurd situation, and he deserves to be publicly scorned and made a model of failure, fraud, intellectual penury, and deceit, and to be removed from his position as dean of the journalism school three days before yesterday.

On the other hand, *do* Lemann and *The New Yorker* know a whole lot more than they're saying or showing? Is it really conceivable that Lemann—and *The New Yorker*—are, as said before, lying through their rotten, despicable, self-serving, cowardly, fascism-bringing teeth?

Or put it this way. We know for an absolute certainty that Lemann and *The New Yorker* have been lying down with fleas. But we still don't know whether they've become mangy curs or—well, whether they're in actuality just simple-minded and non-reading dummies.

December 7, 2006
65th anniversary, Pearl Harbor

7.

OUR ENEMIES, THE LEFT GATEKEEPERS, PT. 3 ON OUR WAY TO CONCLUDE OUR VISIT WITH NICHOLAS LEMANN, LET'S STOP OFF AT JACOB WEISBERG'S PLACE DECEMBER 14, 2006

To the Reader:
I'm often told that my criticisms of the left gatekeepers are unfair, since I'm blaming them for one single failure while ignoring the many *good* things they do, write about, and say. I wish only it were so simple a matter. But it seems to me that such an argument is like claiming that it's unfair to criticize a doctor who treats patients for every manner of ailment but *never says a word to them* when he discovers they have cancer, simply, by remaining silent, letting them die. Or that it's like claiming that it's unfair to criticize a thief since this thief steals only a *single kind* of gem and never any other. Add to it that this particular kind of gem is the *one kind* essential for ending the slaughter of millions and restoring the republic and its constitution—you see the point, I'm sure.

1.

We've Got Plenty of Trouble

Well, well, well—it never rains but it pours, so they say. Readers of *Tristram Shandy* will know about the difficulty that Laurence Sterne had getting Walter Shandy down the stairs of his house, since each step Mr. Shandy took awakened new (or old) memories and considerations that drew him—his mind, that is—farther into the past. And Sterne himself? Well, Sterne had the job of following and describing Walter's mind but also the job of getting him bodily *down the stairs—* with the result, a bit like a paradox of Zeno, that Walter would seemingly never, ever go forward in the narrative (or down the stairs), at least not for so long as Sterne remained true to his artistic-intellectual task, which was, of course, the task of truthfully and fully describing the nature of Walter—and Tristram—Shandy's mental, emotional, *and* physical life.

Now I'm in the same boat as Sterne was—or in a parallel boat, at any rate. In trying to reach Nicholas Lemann, we're distracted by John Perkins, who leads us to Catherine Austin Fitts, and now—as you're about to discover—we find ourselves sailing the black seas of the "mind" of Jacob Weisberg. Will we *ever* get back to where we were going?

2.

Shove On Over, Nicholas Lemann, There's *Company Coming!!!*

If only those whom we're calling left Gatekeepers were *fish*, we'd have been rid of the whole mob of them long ago. How could it be otherwise, since they're so incredibly good at eagerly swallowing hook, line, and sinker whenever that barbed and glittering trio is tossed or dangled their way?

Unless, of course, they're lying about it all. We've got to keep in mind here, as ever, that we may be dealing with lies uttered by quislings rather than with ideas actually believed and burbled out by putatively honest and profoundly ignorant fish. Either way, there's one type of an especially shallow piscine breed among the Gatekeepers, and I had a sighting of that type last fall as it was having an especially dramatic feeding frenzy—that is, if one fish alone can have a feeding frenzy.

In any case, the feeder that time around, swallowing hook, line, and sinker to beat the band—again and again—was none other than Jacob Weisberg, to whom all are grateful for his studious and diligent collecting of Bushisms in *Slate* magazine.[48] But on the other hand a person can hardly be grateful for *Slate*-editor Weisberg's demonstration of what's either myopia in a degree qualifying as clinical blindness, *or* his demonstration of culpability as user of the most fraudulent imaginable of gatekeeper ploys, deceptions, and lies.

Called "Five Years Free: Why Haven't We Been Attacked Again?"[49], the piece was posted at *Slate* magazine last September 6.

You may have guessed—9/6 being so close to 9/11, and 2006 being exactly five years after 2001—that Weisberg's title does indeed refer to the fact of there having been no further 9/11-style attacks in the five years somnolently following one after another after the original 9/11.

In opening, Weisberg says that before 9/11 "We had been living in a fool's paradise," whereas *afterward* everything was going to be

---

[48] http://www.slate.com/id/76886/
[49] http://www.slate.com/id/2149078/

very, very different, because "Now we would have to learn to accommodate the ongoing threat of terrorist violence," comparable to "the Israelis, Spaniards during the era of Basque separation, and Brits in the heyday of the IRA."

Okay. Enormous new fears. Now, here's Weisberg's *second* paragraph:

> As the fifth anniversary of the attacks approaches, perhaps the most surprising result is that American life has not changed very much at all. We worry more about terrorism and have to allow more time to negotiate airport security. But amazingly, al-Qaida hasn't claimed a single additional victim inside the United States. This fact is all the more remarkable when you consider the special challenges America faces in preventing terrorism: thousands of miles of porous border; an open, mobile society; and easy access to firearms.

I ask, unable to believe my own poor eyes and ears, "What can this man be *thinking?*"

At the very least, we've stumbled on another High-Profile-In-The-Media figure who claims he can read but apparently actually can't or at very best doesn't. Or, at the worst, we've stumbled on another High-Profile-In-The-Media quisling, working for the enemy, lying through his teeth and at the same time *apparently* having no trouble either sleeping or getting up in the morning or looking at himself in the mirror.

Is our entire editorial nation, from top to bottom, from Bill Keller at the *New York Times* on down to Jacob Weisberg at *Slate*, made up of professional journalists and editors who either *can't* read or are *non*-readers? Or is our entire editorial nation, from top to bottom, from Bill Keller at the *New York Times* on down to Jacob Weisberg at *Slate* made up of journalists and editors who are, wittingly and willingly, quislings?

At this point, I can do nothing more than leave the question for you to answer.

After all, what surprise can there conceivably be in another 9/11 not having taken place in five years? Since the Bushiscti themselves, along with whoever their many fellow felons were, *perpetrated* 9/11, isn't it self-explanatory? The Bushiscti et alii pulled off their inside job, got away with it, and got what they wanted from it—namely *carte-blanche* war-making powers from "congress," a wide-opening of the purse-strings for said war-making, a magically created ersatz enemy to war *against*, and, hardly least, the best opportunity conceivable to begin their program of the crushing, or, if you wish, the stripping away, of Constitutional liberties. They started with the so-called Patriot Act[50] and now—these famous five years later—have

---

[50] http://en.wikipedia.org/wiki/Insurrection_Act

legalized torture, gotten rid of habeas corpus, gutted the Insurrection Act, and gotten "legislators" to ante up $38 million for spiffing up concentration camps inside the U.S.[51] —an event about which one typical Gatekeeper wrote the following: "Notorious internment camps where Japanese-Americans were kept behind barbed wire during World War II will be preserved as stark reminders of how the United States turned on some of its citizens in a time of fear."[52]

I'm so angry I can hardly breathe. I need to calm myself. I think we should listen for a moment to Shylock:

> Hath
> not a Jew eyes? hath not a Jew hands, organs,
> dimensions, senses, affections, passions? fed with
> the same food, hurt with the same weapons, subject
> to the same diseases, healed by the same means,
> warmed and cooled by the same winter and summer, as
> a Christian is? If you prick us, do we not bleed?
> if you tickle us, do we not laugh? if you poison
> us, do we not die? and if you wrong us, shall we not
> revenge?

.

Hath not a Jew *eyes*? Have *none* of us eyes? I, as the author of a book whose very title is *A Nation Gone Blind*, find myself unable to believe either my own eyes or my own ears.

Weisberg's subject is a perfect Gatekeeper false-subject. Why in the world would even the *Bushiscti* do a rerun of 9/11 if they don't need to? It's expensive, takes many years of planning (Nafeez Mosaddeq Ahmed is the best scholar/writer[53] on this point), and, most of all, they might *get caught* if they tried it a second time.

Would that they'd been caught the first time, as in any *normal* world would have been the case *tout de suite*. Of course, on the other hand, there is also the truth that they *were* caught, *have* been caught, and *have been* exposed time and time again. It's just that that truth is and has been suppressed, distorted, denied, ignored, or outright lied about not only by most of the inhabitants of a nation gone blind, but by *all* the corporate-owned and corporate-controlled mass media—by *all* the Gatekeepers great and small, whether the ignorant ones, the quisling ones, or the ersatz-whatever ones.

---

[51] http://p135.news.scd.yahoo.com/s/ap/20061205/ap_on_go_co/congress_rdp
[52] http://p135.news.scd.yahoo.com/s/ap/20061205/ap_on_go_co/congress_rdp
[53] The War On Truth: 9/11, Disinformation And The Anatomy Of Terrorism (2005, Olive Branch Press):http://www.amazon.com/War-Truth-Disinformation-Anatomy-Terrorism/dp/1566565960/sr=1-1/qid=1166033053/ref=pd_bbs_sr_1/104-4231058-3189532?ie=UTF8&s=books

Still, take heed, Gatekeepers, and listen closely. Take heed, listen closely, and consider exactly, carefully, and well what it really is that you're doing, you—the *New York Times* and *The New Yorker*; you, Jacob Weisberg and *Slate* magazine; you, Nicholas Lemann; you, Amy Goodman; you, Frank Rich; you, National Public Radio; you, *The Nation*; you, Noam Chomsky; you, David Corn; you, the myriad others great and small, inside academia and out—consider carefully what it is you're actually doing in helping to *prevent* the "[restoration] of lawful government" in our poor, betrayed, dying nation.

•

All right. Let's get back to the fakir Jacob Weisberg.

I ask you to decide which it is, perversion of judgment or deadness in the moral soul, that leads Weisberg to write this paragraph (please note its third word):

> But any honest appraisal has to recognize that President Bush has indeed played a role in keeping the United States free from another attack. To say this is not to say that his policy choices have been wise or that they have truly made America safer over the long term, but simply that our avoidance of domestic terrorism over the past five years is not entirely coincidental.

But let it go. Whether caused by rot or by perversion, by ignorance or by treason, these words cannot help but trigger once again that same question, "What can this man be *thinking*?"

The word "toady" doesn't come even close to the word we need as we set about to characterize Weisberg here, to conjecture as to his motives, and as we wonder whether his ear, his perception of irony, of ambiguity, of complexity in thought and expression are at all within the normal range.

Does he have any *idea* what he's saying? Does he have any *idea* of the absurdity of that word "honest" in the context he's putting it in? Does he have any *idea* of the actual truth—that is, that yes, Bush has indeed, along with the Cheneyiscti and the Gatesiscti and molesiscti and the Bilderbergiscti— "played a role in keeping the United States free from another attack."

Those who have followed this far know exactly why all of that is true. If a guy shoots you in the shoulder one afternoon in, let's just say, September of 2001, and if that same guy *doesn't* shoot you in the shoulder again, not even *once*, as five long years roll by—well, then, may I just ask, has that guy "indeed" played a role in keeping you from being shot in the shoulder again?

As the kids everywhere around me say, *"Duh!"*

Talk about *dumb*-sounding journalism. Talk about *embarrassing* journalism. But it's still not as embarrassing and still not as dumb as what's to follow. If you think you can stand it, come on along and see. We'll start with part of Weisberg's very next paragraph:

> To begin with, the Bush administration deserves credit for its role in in-capacitating al-Qaida. U.S. military and intelligence operations have not succeeded in killing or capturing Osama Bin Laden or his deputy Ayman al-Zawahiri. But surreptitious American-led efforts, some of which Bush acknowledged in greater detail in his East Room address, have wrecked al-Qaida as a centralized organization. The war in Afghanistan took away its operating base.

Even I begin to tire after all these words and all this exertion, though the stakes are high, the villains contemptible, the emergency great, and, if we remain patriots and lovers of the truth, we must push on. What is the truth, at this point? The truth at this point is that the Bush administration doesn't deserve credit for *doodly squat*, as the late Kurt Vonnegut might have said.

And certainly it—or they—deserve not one *iota* of credit for "inca-pacitating" Al Qaeda, but, if anything, they deserve credit for pur-posely stirring it up, and (along with Poppy and Clinton as forebears) they deserve credit for creating it in the first place, just as they deserve credit for pulling off the 9/11 attacks themselves and making "Al Qaeda" and Muslims in general take the fall and become the instant-ly-created and unequivocally demonized new enemy, the rapacious devil itself, the insidious disease that preys maliciously on the hale, hearty, firm, heroic flesh of the wholesome West—the wholesome West, I mean, that no longer has habeas corpus, New Orleans, fair taxation, or Posse Comitatus but *does* have lots of internment camps getting fixed up all pretty and nice.

Yes, they deserve credit—for murder, treason, rapine, robbery, treason, betrayal of the Constitution, violation of their oaths of office, abandonment of the people of the United States, abandonment of the poor, as well as for committing of war-crimes of multiple kinds and crimes against humanity of multiple kinds.

Why is Jacob Weisberg so set upon being a bald-faced anti-truth-teller? Why Frank Rich? Why Amy Goodman? Why David Corn? Why Nicholas Lemann? What do they hope to gain? Do they think the Bushiscti will be *nice* to them in return for their craven fidelity, or *good* to them when the rest of the population goes to its ruin, falls into penury, need, and want, or goes to the camps being readied for all those *others* of us who were faithless? Do the gatekeepers actually *trust* in the Bushiscti and in the Cheneyiscti? Do they actually *believe* that, in payment for their quisling-behavior now they'll be paid back later in the coin of favor? Could the gatekeepers conceivably be *that* depraved? Could the gatekeepers conceivably be *that* deceived? Could the gatekeepers conceivably be that *dumb*?

What else could explain it? How can *any*thing explain it?

Except, well, maybe threat of death. Never something to be overlooked in America, the land—once—of Paul Wellstone.

•

Well. As we know from Arianna Huffington, lying makes you sick, makes you rotten, and makes you stupid. Catch this, coming after his limited hangout admission (his "dangling scrap") that said "A second factor [in our five-year reprieve], Bush's domestic assault on potential terrorists, has been a more mixed blessing," Weisberg actually goes on to write *these words*:

> A final factor in our avoidance of terrorism is Bush's poorly judged, dishonestly sold, and incompetently executed war in Iraq. Bush didn't occupy Iraq hoping to draw all the terrorists to one place—to "fight them over there so we don't have to fight them here," as he sometimes puts it. But the "flypaper" effect is genuine. The occupation of Iraq has created a convenient target of opportunity, drawing terrorists who would otherwise be plying their trade somewhere else, including against Americans abroad, or by attempting to sneak into the United States.

Is Weisberg *really* ignorant of the fact that there were no terrorists in the first place beyond those the Clintoniscti and Bushiscti and Bildenbergeriscti and CIA-iscti themselves created for use as "patsies," setting them up to do things like bomb the African embassies, the *USS Cole*, and the WTC the first time around? Ah, I hear roars, shouts, screams of denunciation. And what I say in return to those roars, shouts, and screams is this: Read Nafeez Ahmed Mosaddeq[54] first, and *then* permit yourself to log in on these particular matters. And, as for the war, does Weisberg *really not know* that the only reasons for the Iraq war—ever—were profiteering and the making of opportunistic grabs for global hegemony and oil mastery?

Well, whatever dangling scraps he gives us, Weisberg's own logic is rotten, sick, and stupid (thank you, Arianna Huffington):

> The occupation of Iraq has created a convenient target of opportunity, drawing terrorists who would otherwise be plying their trade somewhere else, including against Americans abroad, or by attempting to sneak into the United States.

[54] The War On Truth: 9/11, Disinformation And The Anatomy Of Terrorism http://www.amazon.com/War-Truth-Disinformation-Anatomy-Terrorism/dp/1566565960/sr=1-1/qid=1166125709/ref=pd_bbs_sr_1/104-4231058-189532?ie=UTF8&s=books

Has anyone of woman born *ever* heard a thing more depraved? More myopic? More amoral? Or more simple-minded, as in its absolutely tone-deaf and out-of-place "plying their trade," as if *real* terrorists were no more significant than, say, hookers or pickpockets? Or that the war, like Weisberg's flypaper, is a pretty neat way of keeping the bad guys out of our own backyards—because, like maggots to carrion, they're drawn instead to the war, preferring the vast opportunities of *that* death- and horror- and ruination-machine to the far slimmer pickings in the hale and pure and wholesome and honest *west*. Ah, war! Ah, what a fine way for keeping the undesirables out of the neighborhood! Hail the Bushiscti for their tactical brilliance!

Well, the fact is that I *do* know something equally or even more depraved. Or certainly *just* as ignorant and uninformed and rudderless and embarrassing and dumb and debased. And here it is, expressed in Weisberg's last two sentences:

> We all know that our immunity over the past five years has also been the result of extraordinary good luck. One of the lessons of Sept. 11 is that such luck can run out on any day.

Permit me to object:

1) We *do not* all know that.

2) The "reprieve" *has not* been the result of luck of *any sort.*

3) And the notion that luck may run out is not *in any way whatsoever* "one of the lessons" of 9/11. And *you* perhaps can tell *me* how any capable or conscientious or experienced writer could use *so* frivolous and *so* juvenile and *so* classroom-y a phrase as "one of the lessons" in so absolutely serious a context as the context of 9/11. *Lessons* are for school kids. Knowledge and understanding are for grownups. But how would Weisberg ever know *that*?

3.

A Note on Sickness, Treason,
Murder, and Guilt

"[The] relentless denial of reality perverts judgment and rots the soul." Thank you again, Arianna Huffington. However much of a Gatekeeper you may be, you've touched on a truth. Let's look into it.

On his web site "Common Wonders," Bob Koehler puts up a piece of his writing each week, and he also emails these pieces to you if you subscribe. I would recommend subscribing.

Yesterday, "Rules of Engagement"[55] appeared in my mailbox, and

---

55 December 14, 2006: http://commonwonders.com./archives/col375.htm

in this piece, Koehler opened by asking, "What illegitimate secrets lie hidden behind the word 'classified'?" He went on:

> "The government is stalling us," Marguerite Hiken of the Military Law Task Force told me. "They're going to be embarrassed and they're scared to death of war crimes charges."

> Could it be that some high-level secrets are that tawdry? Could it be that war is waged—not fought, but set into motion—by, well... cowards, who feel themselves entitled to protection from the consequences of their decisions?

Well, one responds to Koehler, it certainly *could* be that way, couldn't it. We know plenty already about the Chenyisctis' preference for starting wars rather than fighting in them, and plenty, too, about their vindictiveness, viciousness, and lack of compassion—except, of course, for victims of Katrina. Fascists are *often* sadists and cowards.

"For that reason," Koehler goes on,

> I'll be interested to see how the lawsuit that Hiken's organization recently filed against the U.S. Defense Department plays out. The Task Force, which is part of the National Lawyers Guild, has a simple question for the DoD, the answer to which it was unable to get through a Freedom of Information Act request: What were the rules of engagement for soldiers at Fallujah, the Cincinnati-sized city leveled in Operation Phantom Fury two years ago, and in the shooting of Giuliana Sgrena, the Italian journalist who had written about Fallujah, whose car was riddled by bullets at a U.S. checkpoint in Iraq?

> In other words, what acts are off-limits in this war? What casualty-limiting moral restraints are put on soldiers—or maybe I mean not taken away from them—as they are sent into battle? And why is this classified? Why is this a secret?

What the Military Law Task Force wants to know, adds Koehler, "is whether the orders U.S. soldiers were given violated international law. And what the public needs to know is whether those orders turn the stomach."

And they do. Koehler gives us testimony from eye-witnesses: An *ambulance* being directly and repeatedly fired at by U.S. Marines within eye-view distance of the red-cross-marked vehicle; civilians waving white flags as they run, trying to flee the battle area—and being picked off as they go. And this:

> "I watched them roll over wounded people in the street with tanks," said Kassem Mohammed Ahmed, a resident of Fallujah. "This happened so many times."

Ah, crushing people who are still alive by rolling over them with tank treads. How glorious. How typically an action of those who fight for democracy and for freedom, for the rights of the individual and for *tolerance*. How typically the sort of thing done by the "good guys," by the "Yanks," by the liberating Americans and their enlightened allies.

"[The] relentless denial of reality perverts judgment and rots the soul," said Arianna Huffington, not knowing the half of what she was saying.

One wonders what soul we have left that's even capable of rotting.

And, said Webster Tarpley, "Above all, we want 9/11 truth as the essential precondition for restoring lawful government."[56]

It has got to be so. This lying and this covering up of the vile iniquities and malicious crimes that have been committed *in our name* by our criminal "leaders" and that continue to be committed will kill us all in spirit and in body—if it hasn't killed us already—unless what has been done is revealed openly and honestly for precisely what it is and what it has been. It has been, and it continues to be, a great, heinous, on-going string of acts of treason and of crimes against humanity.

Until we see this truth for what it is and until we speak this truth openly, clearly, and honestly—until that happens, the iniquities will continue, they will breed and increase, and we will, with absolute inevitability, be crushed, doomed, and destroyed.

It's up to us.

December 14, 2006

---

[56] "Filibuster Al Qaeda Founder Robert Gates" (Dec. 6, 2006) http://911blogger.com/node/4864

2007

8.

U.S.A.—LAND OF LIARS
JANUARY 22, 2007

To the Reader:
More often than you might expect, I have been criticized for writing these pieces on the grounds that in
them I excoriate others just because they don't "agree
with me." Again, I turn to the analogy of the doctor. If
there is a doctor whose "opinion" is that cases of acute
appendicitis aren't worth operating on, how wrong am
I in excoriating that physician? The unattended patient
will contract peritonitis and die—and this is a matter of
"opinion"? Ignorance—if that be what it is—does not
constitute "opinion." And deliberate repression or misrepresentation of the truth—if that be what it is—does
not constitute "opinion" either, but constitutes lying
or, if the stakes are high enough, criminality. Shouting
"Fire!" in a crowded theater is a crime when there is no
fire. But *refusing* to shout "Fire!" when there is a fire—
well, which is worse? The latter is the crime, or the
crime-equivalent (if genuine ignorance really is what
gives rise to it) that is today destroying our own nation
and bringing about the death and suffering of millions
upon millions abroad. The latter is the crime I excoriate.
I wish it didn't exist. I wish that there were no need for
me so much as to address it.

As a point of information, let me clarify that I no longer
believe explosive charges were the cause of destruction
of the World Trade Center towers (as will be mentioned in the following essay), but that the buildings
underwent a molecular dissociation brought about
by directed energy weaponry. This fact is proven by
Dr. Judy Wood's long and extraordinarily thorough-
research, which began on the day of 9/11 itself. See
http://www.drjudywood.com/

1.

The Unforgivable Guilt of the American Press

I used to be sort of proud of Madison, Wisconsin. This was partly
because I studied there for a while, partly because I got married there,
and partly because I more or less came of age politically there. Part
of the reason for *that* was not just the Goldwater-Johnson campaign

that was going on when I studied there, and not just the beginnings of Vietnam, but also the fact that Madison still held on to a good part of its progressive and populist legacy from the old days of Robert La Follette. That illustrious legacy was reflected not only in the wonderful local paper, *The Madison Capital Times*, but also by the existence, right there in Madison, of nothing less than *The Progressive* magazine, which dated all the way back to 1909, when Robert "Fighting Bob" La Follette himself founded it.

And now? I'm afraid things have changed. The "*Cap Times,*" as we used to call it, fares quite well, I'm happy to say[57]—but *The Progressive* is dead as a doornail. *The Progressive* is a corpse, slain and dead just as surely as Frank Rich has called me and others "conspiracy nuts." Oh, yes, the magazine still *appears* each month; you can still *buy* it and you can still *subscribe* to it. But what's the point? What's the point of reading a dead magazine, a magazine still pretending to be progressive while in actuality it's been sleepily letting things shuffle along, just like Chomsky, Goodman, and all the other Gate-keepers, toward the fascism whose structure is now just about all set up, and toward the nuclear Armageddon that at the present moment looks likely to arrive in six weeks or so.[58] No, skip *The Progressive.* There's nothing there.

•

Strong talk? Yes. Polite? No. I apologize, since, truly, I have no desire to be offensive. But I do have a desire, burning and consuming, for the truth. And, yes, I do find lying despicable. And waiting—as we appear to be right now—for the start of the first nuclear-initiated war in human history, waiting for *that*[59] rash and ungodly act to be undertaken by the insane war criminals who—child's play compared to this—orchestrated 9/11 just because it was useful as a jump-start for their monstrous global grab—well, these aren't matters of a kind to calm a person down. These are not events, expectations, affairs of

---

[57] Update: "(AP) Madison's afternoon newspaper, The Capital Times, will move to an all-Internet edition in a transition that could be the first of its kind in the struggling industry. The 17,000-circulation newspaper announced the changes, which include publishing twice-weekly free print editions, to staff and with a story [sic] on its Web site [http://host.madison.com/ct/opinion/] Thursday. There will be job cuts and a buy-out program, but details and how many staff will be affected were not immediately released. This is the first daily newspaper of any stature or prominence to basically move to all-Internet, said Joe Strupp, senior editor at Editor & Publisher."

[58] "US military strike on Iran seen by April '07; Sea-launched attack to hit oil, N-sites." By Ahmed Al-Jarallah, Editor-in-Chief, the Arab Times 01/14/07 http://www.information-clearinghouse.info/article16169.htm

[59] "Iran: Pieces in Place for Escalation: 'The fuel for a fire is in place,' by Colonel Sam Gardiner" http://www.globalresearch.ca/index.php?context=viewArticle&code=GAR20070116&articleId=4483

a kind to cause a person to polish up on good manners and set aside fear, terror, and anger.[60]

•

So, it's likely enough that I won't get my good manners back until things change for the better, *if* they do. And they never *are* going to get better until such time as the "left" Gatekeepers do some changing of their own, since they're the drop-dead-guilty ones, wittingly or unwittingly, who allowed us to get into such as impasse as this in the first place. Yes, you heard me right. The absence of a free press in America is, in my view, a criminal, and extraordinarily desperate, matter. All of those elements of the press that have blocked 9/11 truth are in fact directly responsible for the unconstitutional policies of the Bushiscti having come to the point of fruition—grimly ironic word in *this* context—that they *have* come to.

In the plain truth of what was done on and before 9/11, there's enough concrete and provable evidence of treason and high criminality to impeach, try, and convict Bush, Cheney, and scores beyond scores of accomplices very nearly over night. That being the case, exactly why and how is it that not only has no such prosecution moved forward, but, instead, why and how is it that the very nation has meanwhile moved *backward* in actually *losing* habeas corpus, *losing* the protections of Posse Comitatus, *losing* the moderating protections of The Insurrection Act, *legalizing* torture, *accepting* extreme rendition, *not* stopping the building of massive concentration camps within our own borders, and now facing the horrible prospect of becoming that ugliest and most ruinous of all things, the first nation in the history of the world to *initiate* war by thermo-nuclear attack. All of this, and *still not*, even at so late a date, have we so much as even seriously moved toward the necessary course of bringing impeachment charges against the administration, *based on 9/11 truth*, charges that would, in a normal world and a fair one, swiftly bring about impeachment, trial, and conviction.

And so the great question: Why and how is it that the transparently evil, criminal, treasonous, treacherous, indescribably dangerous things, actions, and events that have been done by the Bush administration before, on, and since 9/11—why and how is it that these have not over the past six years met with *any* significant challenge or impediment, have not been stalled, slowed, resisted, and, above all, either *exposed* if already done or *prevented* if not yet committed?

---

[60] Update: See Sheila Samples, "Will Americans be Lulled by Blatant lies into waging war on Iran?" (Oct. 20, 2010): http://onlinejournal.com/artman/publish/printer_6474.shtml

The hideous and contemptible answer: Because the free press in America no longer exists. Because the free press in America—just like *The Progressive*—is dead as a doornail: Because the press in America—all of it—has been bought out, bought up, compromised, paid off, threatened and bullied into being the deceitful, mendacious, passive, contemptible, lying, hypocritical, diseased, complicit, criminal, and treasonous "institution" that it now is. And thus it is—in light of every one of these characteristics and abysmal failures—that this "institution" is absolutely and unequivocally guilty of aiding and abetting the criminals who have repeatedly committed treason, murder, and other high crimes, who have not been brought to a reckoning of any kind, and who have—let it be said once more—taken away our republic.

Let's name some of the tentacles of this grotesquerie: ABC. NBC. CBS. PBS. NPR. *The New York Review of Books. The New York Times. The Nation. The New Republic. The New Yorker. The Atlantic Monthly. The Chicago Tribune. The New Republic. The Los Angeles Times. The Washington Post. The* . . . It could grow tiresome to continue, couldn't it. The list, if continued, would become very long indeed. Simpler might be just to go online[61] and take a look, state by state, at every newspaper in America. And then go there again[62] and take a look at a list of every magazine in America. If you find *any magazine or any newspaper* that tells the truth about 9/11 and that, consequently and accordingly, speaks out about the fraud, treason, and criminality of the Bush administration and declares itself, accordingly, in favor of restoring the Republic of the United States of America to a free republic, declares itself also in favor of impeachment proceedings and—accordingly and in consequence—declares itself in favor of turning back the "Doomsday Clock" of the Bulletin of Atomic Scientists from its recent advance to five minutes from midnight—well, if you *do* find such a newspaper or magazine anywhere in America, I beg of you, do me the favor of letting me know about it.[63]

2.

The Unforgivable Guilt of *The Progressive* Magazine

Its roots deep in history, *The Progressive* magazine today has as its editor Matthew Rothschild. On the magazine's website—on September 11, 2006—Rothschild posted a piece called "Enough of the

---

[61] http://www.50states.com/news/

[62] http://en.wikipedia.org/wiki/List_of_United_States_magazines

[63] Update: At the time of this writing, the remarkable Rock Creek Free Press didn't yet exist: http://www.rockcreekfreepress.com/about.html

9/11 Conspiracies, Already."[64] The piece is so typical of its kind, either so uninformed or so *dis*informative, in any case so false, so incomplete and so mendacious that it is a model of the gate-keeping genre as grimly revelatory as the one we saw, just say, by Nicholas LeMann in *The New Yorker* for October 16, 2006.

Rothschild's piece, especially coming as it does from a magazine with so long and illustrious a progressive tradition, is—well, pretty much incredible.

Its opening:

> At almost every progressive gathering where there's a question and answer period, someone or other vehemently raises 9/11 and espouses a grand conspiracy theory.
>
> If you haven't had the pleasure of enduring these rants, please let me share.
>
> Here's what the conspiracists believe:
>
> 9/11 was an inside job.
>
> Members of the Bush Administration ordered it, not Osama bin Laden.
>
> Arab hijackers may not have done the deed.
>
> On top of that, the Twin Towers fell not because of the impact of the airplanes and the ensuing fires but because the Bush Administration got agents to plant explosives at the base of those buildings.
>
> Building 7, another high-rise at the World Trade Center that fell on 9/11, also came down by planted explosives.
>
> The Pentagon was not hit by American Airlines Flight 77 but by a smaller plane or a missile.
>
> And the Pennsylvania plane did not crash as a result of the revolt by the passengers but was brought down by the military.
>
> *"Extraordinary claims require extraordinary evidence."*—Carl Sagan
>
> I'm amazed at how many people give credence to these theories. Everyone's an engineer. People who never even took one college science course can now hold forth at great length on how the buildings at the World Trade Center could not possibly have collapsed in the way they did and why the Pentagon could not have been struck by that American Airlines jet.

---

[64] http://www.progressive.org/mag_wx091106

Alas, the poor *Progressive* magazine. And alas, our poor nation of baby-talkers and baby-thinkers. Is Rothschild—a *professional journalist*—really as ignorant as he appears in this piece, or is he actually just acting, pretending to be greatly more uninformed than he really is in order to disparage his targets and imply *their* greater "dumbness"—that is, to assert the sheer simple-mindedness of anyone who could take the least bit of the 9/11 Truth movement at *all* seriously?

It's the same with Rothschild as it has been with other of the Gatekeeper cases we've looked at: If Rothschild is really this ignorant about the most important public issue in the world today, shouldn't he by rights be fired from his job? On the other hand, if he's just *playing* the role of the uninformed in order to kowtow to his magazine's owners and advertisers by disparaging 9/11 Truth—well, then shouldn't he be charged with the conscious dissemination of known falsehoods, and of doing so for the purpose of covering up the guilt of perpetrators of crimes including murder and treason, thus making *himself* complicit in those same crimes and an abettor of them?

Out of plain old human feeling, I hope that Rothschild really is just that incredibly out of the loop, out of touch, that he's *really* this entirely uninterested in the subject he's writing about, *really* this abysmally ill-informed. It hardly makes him a great editor, but so it goes. Either way, though, in a more rigorous or in an honest world, he'd be outta here day before yesterday. In a world of truth, honesty, and rigor, being *either* uninformed *or* uninterested would disqualify a person from the editorship of a historic and major political magazine. But our world right now is not honest.

Is Matthew Rothschild insecure? Out of his depth? Protectively nervous at the sense of his own guilt? Why is it that Rothschild follows the same pattern of putting smear, innuendo, and "attitude" in the place of reasoning—the same way we saw with Walter Kirn in the depravity he pawned off as a "review" of Cynthia Ozick in *The New York Times Book Review*?

À la Kirn, Rothschild can't just *say* "someone raises 9/11" but instead has to stick in the little stiletto-adverb "vehemently"—just the touch that will imply naiveté, youthfulness, hotheadedness, and un-*coolness* in the 9/11 question-raiser while at the same time implying the author's own superiority to the inexperienced rube.

Ditto with the smarmy addition of the tiny adjective "grand" that does its sarcastic bit to disparage further the already pejorative phrase "conspiracy theory." And, oh, yes, there's one other little authorial brush stroke, but nobody really needs help with that needless use of the pejorative "rants."

However condescending and dirty-trickish it's been so far, we ain't seen nothin' yet. Take another look at the last paragraph from the section I quoted a moment ago:

> I'm amazed at how many people give credence to these theories. Everyone's an engineer. People who never even took one college science course can now hold forth at great length on how the buildings at the World Trade Center could not possibly have collapsed in the way they did and why the Pentagon could not have been struck by that American Airlines jet.

Why the snidely superior tone? Just exactly why is Rothschild "amazed"? Even the complicitous cover-up artist Christopher Hayes in his own hatchet-job in *The Nation* (December 25, 2006: "9/11— The Roots of Paranoia") is more honest, albeit not less condescending, when he replaces Rothschild's "how many people" with something more concrete: "According to a July poll conducted by Scripps News Service," he writes in his own opening sentence, "one-third of Americans think the government either carried out the 9/11 attacks or intentionally allowed them to happen in order to provide a pretext for war in the Middle East."[65]

But let Hayes alone for a minute. Rothschild is too interesting to leave just yet. His declaration of "amazement" at what he considers to be people's gullibility is almost Chaucerian in its fairness and sympathy compared to the sentences that come out with his next two breaths:

> Everyone's an engineer. People who never even took one college science course can now hold forth at great length on how the buildings at the World Trade Center could not possibly have collapsed in the way they did and why the Pentagon could not have been struck by that American Airlines jet.

Again—why the smear and innuendo? Why the blanket generalizations used as put-down? Why the transparently *ad hominem* abandonment of logic, why the attempt to slay the enemy by *tone* and nothing else?

Speak for yourself, Mr. Rothschild. How can a reader *not* say that after reading what Rothschild has written? How can a reader *not* suspect that it's *Rothschild* who "never even took one college science course"? Is there any more likely motive than insecurity that would lead to so condescending, sniping—and false—an assertion? And there again, tagging along after, comes the snootily hyperbolic diction—"hold forth" instead of "talk," and "at great length" to boot, to show superiority and exasperation; and "could not possibly have collapsed" instead of simply "could not have collapsed."

As for science classes, I wonder what Rothschild knows about, say, Kevin Ryan, the scientist at Underwriters' Laboratories who got

---

[65] http://www.thenation.com/doc/20061225/hayes

fired for telling a 9/11 truth participant about the steel that he himself helped test for strength and fire-endurance—I suspect Rothschild hasn't heard about Ryan, but he *can* read about him[66] if he'd like, and can do so again here,[67] or he can read some of Kevin Ryan's *own* criticism of another scientist's work by going here.[68] That other scientist, by the way, is Manuel Garcia, who published *his* piece in *Counter-Punch* magazine, where Alexander Cockburn prides himself, like Rothschild, in being a denouncer of all things related to 9/11 Truth. Manuel Garcia's piece is called "We See Conspiracies that Don't Exist—the Physics of 9/11,"[69] just in case Rothschild would like to read, first, Manuel Garcia, and then, second, Kevin Ryan, in order to do some comparison/contrast thinking and analysis. Wouldn't *that* be an original idea, actually to read the work of two scientific experts whose views are opposed, so that a person could evaluate one against the other? Astonishing to think of, the making of decisions not on the basis of smear, innuendo, and calumniation—but on the basis of solidity of evidence, strength of logic, and empirical observation. What an idea.

It's not likely to work for Rothschild, though—that is, unless his piece of 9/11/2006, which we're now looking at, is in fact *greatly* deceptive and wholly unrepresentative of the editor's overall writing and views about 9/11/2001.

It's no more likely to work, either, for Alexander Cockburn, who positively crows about his own ignorance of the very subject that he calumniates as being based on ignorance. What are we to make of such editors and writers? In the email edition of *CounterPunch* for October 16-31, 2006, Cockburn ran a single-column piece on page one called "On Conspiracies."[70] Here's his opener:

> There are plenty of real conspiracies in America. Why make up fake ones?
> Every few years, property czars and city government in New York conspire to withhold fire company responses, so that enough of a neighborhood burns down for the poor to quit and for profitable gentrification to ensue. That's a conspiracy to commit ethnic cleansing, also murder.

---

[66] "UL Executive Speaks Out on WTC Study" (Nov. 12, 2004): http://www.911truth.org/article.php?story=20041112144051451

[67] "Lab Director Fired for Questioning Official 9/11 Story" (Associated Press): http://www.wanttoknow.info/911kevinrryanfired

[68] http://stj911.org/ryan/garcia.html

[69] http://www.counterpunch.org/physic11282006.html

[70] Online searches provide no longer provide any trace of this piece. But they do very quickly bring up, among other pieces, Alexander Cockburn, "The 9/11 Conspiracy Nuts," Counter-Punch, Sept. 9-10, 2006, a piece certainly comparable to the lost one: http://www.counterpunch.org/cockburn09092006.html, as is also Cockburn's "The 9/11 Conspiracists and the Decline of the American Left," CounterPunch, Nov. 28, 2006: http://www.counterpunch.org/cockburn11282006.html

Thank the deities that Cockburn is just Cockburn and not the Surgeon General or the Commissioner of Health—since, by his extraordinary logic, the existence of *cancer* (that is, criminality against the poor in New York City), a disease greatly dreaded, should result in a total *ignoring* of AIDS (that is, 9/11 truth), since the latter is a disease less well understood by many and almost without doubt feared by a smaller part of the population than is cancer.

Hey, Cockburn! Listen to this! I know you've *got* to agree! You've already made that perfectly clear! Gonorrhea exists, so let's quit monitoring syphilis! The hell with syphilis! And anthrax! how about *anthrax?* The hell with anthrax—after all, the Ebola virus exists, doesn't it? Well, then! no more *anthrax* research!!! Yeah, and starvation exists, so no more research into *obesity. Yeah!!* Heart disease? To the local dump with it! After all, there's *bipolar disorder* to take care of!

Logic to be neither credited nor condoned in English 101 is paraded by the illustrious Alexander Cockburn, with consummate pride, in his own magazine. The slogan atop the front page says that CounterPunch "Tells the Facts and Names the Names." On the basis of Cockburn's piece, it hides the facts and smears the names.

Look how Cockburn's piece ends: "The conspiracy virus is an old strand," he declares, then names some things from the past that people have had "conspiracy theories" about (the lone gunman and JFK, etc.). Then, with 9/11 foremost in the reader's mind, he concludes:

It's all pathetic, but it does save the trouble of reading and thinking.

The insult is obvious—that 9/11 Truth researchers are bigoted, fantasy-driven, half-wit non-readers and non-thinkers. Well, may the guiltless cast the first stone. What has Cockburn read on 9/11? More, do you suppose, or less, than Richard Posner? Has he, do you suppose, even read the fundamental five books recommended and at great effort described by me?[71] Does, he, do you suppose, scan what's offered daily at *Information Clearing House,*[72] or, perhaps, at the indispensible *Online Journal,* [73] or at the equally revelatory *Global Research?* [74]

---

[71] At the time of this writing, the five were 1) Ruppert, Michael C. *Crossing the Rubicon: The Decline of the American Empire at the End of the Age of Oil.* (New Society Publishers, 2004). 2) Griffin, David Ray. *The New Pearl Harbor: Disturbing Questions About the Bush Administration and 9-11.* (Olive Branch Press) 2004). 3) Ahmed, Nafeez Mosaddeq. *The War on Truth: 9/11, Disinformation, and the Anatomy of Terrorism.* (Olive Branch Press, 2005). 4) Chossudovsky, Michel. *America's "War On Terrorism."* (Global Research, 2nd Edition, 2005). 5) Morgan, Rowland, and Ian Henshall. *9/11 Revealed.* (Carroll & Graf, 2005). See the Appendix for more titles.

[72] http://www.informationclearinghouse.info/index.html

[73] http://www.onlinejournal.com/

[74] http://www.globalresearch.ca/index.php?context=home

•

Ah, but why continue? Cockburn, identical in this way to Rothschild and the other Gatekeepers, wears his ignorance on his sleeve.

Remember back when Rothschild told us he was "amazed at how many people give credence to these theories?"? Well, he went on to set us dummies straight by saying that the "Problem is, some of the best engineers in the country have studied these questions and come up with perfectly logical, scientific explanations for what happened."

You don't say. Well, blow me down.

Our progressive leader then cites figures and organizations—a massive name-dropping that does precisely nothing to weaken the 9/11 Truth's position. Take a look, if you can stand it:

> The American Society of Civil Engineers and FEMA conducted an in-depth investigation of the World Trade Center. The team members included the director of the Structural Engineering Institute of the American Society of Civil Engineers, the senior fire investigator for the National Fire Protection Association, professors of fire safety, and leaders of some of the top building design and engineering firms, including Skidmore Owings & Merrill in Chicago, Skilling Ward Magnusson Barkshire in Seattle, and Greenhorne & O'Mara in Maryland.

> It concluded that massive structural damage caused by the crashing of the aircrafts into the buildings, combined with the subsequent fires, "were sufficient to induce the collapse of both structures."

> The National Institute of Standards and Technology did its own forty-three volume study of the Twin Towers. "Some 200 technical experts . . . reviewed tens of thousands of documents, interviewed more than 1,000 people, reviewed 7,000 segments of video footage and 7,000 photographs, analyzed 236 pieces of steel from the wreckage, [and] performed laboratory tests and sophisticated computer simulations," the institute says.

I think "Greenhorne," as in the phrase "Greenhorne & O'Mara," may, however serendipitously, be the word most applicable here. Anyone remember Hurricane Katrina? Remember how reliable, up-and-at-'em, responsive, and trustworthy FEMA was then? FEMA, with a little help from its friends, managed to "lose" an entire major American city. So what, you ask? Well, so I'll trust them all the *more* on their 9/11 and WTC research. Wouldn't *any*one?

It seems that Rothschild would.[75]

---

[75] On the subject of trusting authority because it's assumed to have authority, all readers should study the Qui Tam case brought by Dr. Judy Wood ("on behalf of the UNITED STATES OF AMERICA") against the following list of defendants, the charge against them being science fraud. The case reached the Supreme Court, where it was denied a writ of a certiorari and was thus suppressed. The case arose out of the National Institute of Standards and

Maybe we can help him a little. *Here's* something for him to read, an actually grown-up piece of writing and thinking by Phil Rockstroh from *Online Journal* called "Expanding markets and dying oceans: Eating the planet like a bag of Doritos for Jesus."[76] Ever the consummate thinker and ever the writer extraordinaire, Rockstroh asks this question, its special applicability to Rothschild and Cockburn quite clear:

> How did it come to be that our ability to apprehend reality is in such short supply at a time when the consequences of such dangerous folly will prove so tragic and lasting?

I wonder if Rothschild's own limited "ability to apprehend reality" is what's responsible for his actually suggesting that the *Popular Mechanics* cover story—and subsequent book, *Debunking 9/11 Myths*[77]—is worth the paper it was printed on, which in clear fact it's most demonstrably not?

Terence, this is stupid stuff...
It's time for a letter.

·

January 21, 2007
Matthew Rothschild
Editor, The Progressive
409 East Main Street
Madison, WI 53703

Dear Mr. Rothschild:

When I read for myself the *Popular Mechanics* article that you refer to in "Enough of the 9/11 Conspiracies, Already" (September 11, 2006), I was able to see immediately that the piece was in no way objective or disinterested, but that, instead, it was a job of hack work filled with false assertions, failed logic, important omissions, incorrect

Technology's erroneous and fraudulent report on the causes of the destruction of the World Trade Center buildings. The defendants: Applied Research Associates, Inc. (Ara), Science Applications International Corp.(Saic), Underwriters Laboratories, Inc., Wiss, Janney, Elstner Associates, Inc. (Wje), Rolf Jensen & Associates, Inc.(Rja), Computer Aided Engineering Associates, Inc., Simpson Gumpertz & Heger, Inc. (Sgh), Skidmore, Owings & Merrill, Llp (Som), Gilsanz Murray Steficek Llp (Gms), Hughes Associates, Inc. (Ha), Rosenwasser/Grossman Consulting Engineers, P.C., S. K. Ghosh Associates, Inc. (Ga), Teng & Associates, Inc. (Ta), Ajmal Abbasi, Eduardo Kausel, David Parks, David Sharp, Josef Van Dyck, Kaspar William, Daniele Venezano, Datasource, Inc., Geostaats, Inc., Nustats. See http://www.drjudywood.com/articles/NIST/Qui_Tam_Wood.shtml

76 Dec. 21, 2006: http://onlinejournal.com/artman/publish/article_1554.shtml
77 Debunking 9/11 Myths: Why Conspiracy Theories Can't Stand Up to the Facts, by The Editors of Popular Mechanics, David Dunbar, Brad Reagan, and John McCain (Hearst Communications, 2006): http://www.amazon.com/Debunking-11-Myths-Conspiracy-Theories/dp/158816635X/ref=sr_1_1?s=books&ie=UTF8&qid=1288026341&sr=1-1

words, incorrect wording, and plain, outright deceit. Its purpose obviously was not to clarify but to deceive.

One of the most interesting implausibilities that struck me was suggested by a photograph of the top twenty-five or so floors of the south tower falling *sideways*. On my copy of that picture, I wrote "can't pancake when top 25 floors aren't even exerting a straight downward force." As you, or anyone else, can see very clearly, the top of the tower—whether exactly twenty-five floors' worth, I can't be certain, but a huge amount—is falling at very nearly a forty-five degree angle *to the side*. In the absence of explosive charges,[78] what conceivable force was present to "right" the direction of that huge mass so that it subsequently fell *straight down* and thereby, with its immense weight, began the hypothetical "pancaking" of the entire building beneath? My own understanding of elementary physics is that once the top of the tower had begun falling sideways, the greatest—the only—force that would or could continue to be exerted on it would be the force of *gravity*. In this case, however, since that topmost chunk of the tower never did hit the ground, something other than gravity *must* have been present.

In reading your words, I have gathered that, although you may never have taken a science class in college, you nevertheless, for what may be a psychologically curious reason, do have an inordinate admiration for, if not a near-idolatry of, fancy or long names and titles or strings of names and titles when these are associated with scientific or engineering groups. I wonder whether your sense of awe in cases of this sort might not in fact come about as a result of your own feelings of inadequacy in certain matters, particularly having to do with engineering and science.

If this is the case, then it must have been your awe more than your intellect that guided you in your implicitly favorable evaluation of the *Popular Mechanics* article. In regard to myself, I should let you know that I am recently retired from a career of four decades as a professor of college English. If the *Popular Mechanics* piece that we're talking about had been submitted to me—as, say, a term paper—by an undergraduate in an advanced composition course, or in a technical writing course, or conceivably even in a business writing course, it, because of its many internal failures and weaknesses, would not have received a grade higher than C-minus, more likely not higher than a D-plus.

---

[78] Again let me mention that I no longer believe explosive charges were the cause of destruction, but that the buildings underwent a molecular dissociation brought about by directed energy weaponry as proven by Dr. Judy Wood's long and extraordinarily thorough-going research. The side-ways-tipping top floors of the south tower never did hit the ground but instead were turned into dust long before any material remnants of them would have hit the ground. So-called "pancaking" of the buildings' floors one atop another could not have occurred, further, since they, too, were turned into dust through molecular dissociation. See http://www.drjudywood.com/

So your own judgment of it, and your own holding of it up as a "proof" or "example" of a sort intended to throw 9/11 Truth theorists into shame or disarray—well, your own judgment is therefore itself suspect if not laughable.

You wrote: "Problem is, some of the best engineers in the country have studied these questions and come up with perfectly logical, scientific explanations for what happened." But your own example—in the case of *Popular Mechanics*—refutes the very substance of your implication that the *Popular Mechanics* piece casts doubt on 9/11 Truth. You can't cast doubt on strong and evidence-based arguments with work that's not logically strong, *not* evidence-based, and is written at a D-plus level. Therefore, by corollary, your readers may well have no reason to trust *any* of your lengthy appeals to authority, those strings of name-droppings of the kind I cited earlier.

That fallacy, of appealing to authority as a substitute for the summoning of evidence, is an especially well-known one to professors of freshman English—and a particularly slick and lazy trick it is, guaranteed always to weaken rather than strengthen an argument, as well as to lower rather than raise a grade.

The same is true of your sad little comment that "I made a few calls myself," an assertion followed only by more names and titles in fallacious appeals to authority—the whole then concluding with what may be your most hollow, sweeping, baseless, and extraordinarily broad generalization of all:

> I also contacted engineering professors at MIT and other leading universities in the country, and none of them puts any stock in the 9/11 conspiracy theories. In fact, they view them as a huge waste of time. They are busy trying to figure out how to prevent buildings from falling in the future.

But who were these "professors"? What did they say that indicated they had any knowledge of 9/11 Truth studies? What were their own fields of study? No one in their right mind is going to bow to your false logic in accepting the authority of people merely because they may be among the "engineering professors at MIT and other leading universities in the country."

In a nutshell, only blind faith alone, not intellectual analysis, could lead any intelligent and thinking person to *assume* that at MIT, say, only good guys are at work, never bad ones. Since you presume to know so much about what does and doesn't go on in American universities, I would suggest, as more fundamental background for your highly tendentious writing, that you read (as I have) Jennifer Washburn's *University, Inc.: The Corporate Corruption of American Higher*

Education,[79] perhaps along with Francis A. Boyle's *Biowarfare and Terrorism*,[80] another work that suggests *most* disquietingly some of what actually takes place inside academia.[81] Another of your appeals to authority is to The National Institute of Standards and Technology, or NIST, which, you write, "did its own forty-three volume study of the Twin Towers." You go on in a kind of Paul Bunyan manner of criticism, apparently assuming that if anything is big, it's therefore good:

> "Some 200 technical experts . . . reviewed tens of thousands of documents, interviewed more than 1,000 people, reviewed 7,000 segments of video footage and 7,000 photographs, analyzed 236 pieces of steel from the wreckage, [and] performed laboratory tests and sophisticated computer simulations," the institute says.

"[The] institute says." And well it might, since it has its own reputation to protect. I haven't read the forty-three-volume report, and I doubt that you have, either. But I know someone who has. His name is Mark H. Gaffney, and he has written a scholarly and extremely powerful two-part analysis of it entitled "Dead on Arrival: the NIST Report Part I"[82] and, not surprisingly, "Dead on Arrival: the NIST Report Part II."[83] I'm certain they will be of great interest to you.[84]

It must be growing more clear as we continue that your own credentials—of any kind that might justify the position you take on 9/11 Truth—are themselves increasingly questionable—and that any grade it might be possible for you to receive for your work is rapidly lowering. Your intellectual habit of ignoring the absence of any empirical basis for some of your more flagrant assertions ("How did it come to be that our ability to apprehend reality is in such short supply at a time when the consequences of such dangerous folly will prove so tragic and lasting?") become outright clownish, as in this example of all but unutterably (even though you do utter it) absurd logic:

> Osama bin Laden has already claimed responsibility for the attack several times and boasted of the prowess of the suicide bombers who hijacked those planes. Why not take him at his word?

"Why not take him at his word?" Are you, Matthew Rothschild,

[79] Jennifer Washburn, University, Inc.: *The Corporate Corruption of Higher Education.* New York: Basic Books, 2005. http://www.amazon.com/University-Inc-Corporate-Corruption-Education/dp/0465090516/sr=1-1/qid=1169477219/ref=pd_bbs_1/104-4231058-3189532?ie=UTF8&s=books

[80] Francis A. Boyle, *Biowarfare and Terrorism*, Clarity Press, 2005.

[81] Update: For more on the corruption, dishonesty, and fraud rampant inside academia, I highly recommend Charles Ferguson's 2010 movie, *Inside Story.*

[82] http://thetruthseeker.co.uk/article.asp?id=5697

[83] http://www.thetruthseeker.co.uk/article.asp?id=5695

[84] Also please see footnote number 75, on the lawsuit for science fraud brought by Dr. Judy Wood.

really the editor of *The Progressive?* And, if so, how can you ask of Mayor Rudy Giuliani's foreknowledge that the World Trade Center towers were going to collapse[85] —how can you ask "Is that really evidence?"

"Is that really evidence?" Why, may all the gods in heaven join us in asking whether it be true that you still do keep your job as editor of *The Progressive.*

"Is that really evidence?" And then you ask us to agree that Larry Silverstein can't have had foreknowledge that WTC7 was rigged with explosives for a controlled demolition[86]—even though he said so himself on national television.[87] Worse, you actually ask us to agree that Silverstein had no such knowledge for the most laughable and absurd of all conceivable reasons, namely, that "Silverstein has flat-out denied that."

You not only reveal, Mr. Rothschild, that you must never have read the *Fables* of Aesop, that you must never have read *The Canterbury Tales* of Chaucer, that you must never so much as heard of Uncle Remus or the briar patch; you not only show either your ignorance of *or* your complicity in the crimes of murder and treason committed on 9/11 (by obscuring evidence relating directly to them); but you insist, over and over, upon insulting the intelligence of your readers in ways that are extremely hard to forgive.

Throughout my study and analysis of this piece of your writing, it has become clear to me that all of my professional training to earn a Ph.D., and that all of my ethical responsibilities as I honored and undertook them over forty years as an instructor—all of these, Mr. Rothschild, bring me to the unavoidable conclusion that if your piece had been submitted to me for class credit, I could have done nothing other than give it a grade of F, it being so thoroughly insubstantial in thought, bankrupt in logic, and incompetent in general.

As for your colleague in journalism, Mr. Alexander Cockburn, who wrote the specious, arrogant, unfounded, and, above all, prideful words in regard to 9/11 Truth researchers quoted earlier ("It's all pathetic, but it does save the trouble of reading and thinking"), I know of no grade low enough for him and therefore will award none.

> Yours Sincerely,
> Eric Larsen
> January 22, 2007

---

[85] See David Ray Griffin, *The New Pearl Harbor* (Olive Branch Press, 2004), pp. 181-182. http://www.amazon.com/New-Pearl-Harbor-Disturbing-Administration/dp/1566565529/sr=1-1/qid=1169478593/ref=pd_bbs_1/104-4231058-3189532?ie=UTF8&s=books

[86] Update: In actuality, it was about to undergo molecular dissociation through directed energy weaponry (DEW). Again, see http://www.drjudywood.com/

[87] Watch it here: http://www.prisonplanet.com/011904wtc7.html

9.

AMY GOODMAN: A MIND PROSTITUTED
APRIL 4, 2007

To the Reader:
No one with an innermost secret they don't want exposed should ever put pen to paper if at all possible. Speech is an infinitely better hiding place for the iniquitous inner truth than writing has ever been or ever will be. I knew for some time that Amy Goodman was a major figure among the left gatekeepers (Carolyn Baker even wrote a remarkable essay on the subject: "The Empress Has No Clothes: Amy Goodman's Reality Blackout").[88] But I hadn't known how great a toll—in moral damage and ethical blindness—such gatekeeping may have caused until I'd seen some of the Pacifica commentator's *written* pieces. A few years further on in this book, we will see even more advanced ethical disorientation and moral degradation in other gatekeepers, but back here in 2007 it was already evident that what Linh Dinh recently said—"We're dying"[89]—was already a fast-developing truth.

In its issue for January 1–15, 2007, the *Progressive Populist*[90] filled the top half of its page twenty-two with two columns by Amy Goodman, one called "It's Bigotry That Should be Silenced,"[91] the other "Beyond the Nine-Second Sound Bite." Goodman as a columnist in written form was new to me. In an editor's note, the *Populist* explained that "*Democracy Now!* host Amy Goodman's column... recently started with King Features Syndicate."

Fine. Except for one thing: Both columns were packed stem to stern with hypocrisy and falsehoods.

The forces that have successfully suppressed 9/11 truth for the past five years are turning us into a nation of hypocrites and liars.

---

88 See http://www.fromthewilderness.com/free/ww3/011306_empress_clothes.shtml
89 "Collapsing America," (Sept. 13, 2010, Online Journal): http://onlinejournal.com/art-man/publish/printer_6313.shtml
90 http://www.populist.com/index.html. The article is available now at Information Clearing House: http://www.informationclearinghouse.info/article15840.htm
91 Not available online from Progressive Populist.But the piece can be found at http://www.commondreams.org/views06/1207-33.htm

Amy Goodman, very, very far from alone, is apparently one of these victims. The longer-term psychological, emotional, and political results of living hypocritically and as prevaricators can't yet be known. But let that matter go for now.

In the first of the two pieces reprinted in the *Populist*, "It's Bigotry That Should Be Silenced," Goodman tells the story of Raed Jarrar, "an Iraqi architect and blogger" who was prevented from boarding a plane from New York's JFK to Oakland until he agreed to cover the T-shirt he was wearing with *another*, blank, shirt. His own, you see, had the words "We will not be silent" on it, with the same words, in Arabic, above them.

As Goodman explains, the "two Transportation Security Administration workers and two JetBlue employees" who'd stopped Jarrar "didn't have a translator" and thus "couldn't be sure" that Jarrar wasn't lying about what the Arabic really said. So much for trust. Anyway, Jarrar put on another shirt over his own and they put him on the plane.

End of that story and on to the next. The next is the one about the six imams at the Minneapolis-St. Paul airport on November 20th of 2006 who wanted to fly to Phoenix. It was prayer time and, so as not to draw attention, "the six men decided only three of them would pray. Said [Omar] Shahin, [president of the North American Imams Federation,] 'We picked a quiet area. We did not bother anybody. We did our prayer in a very quiet, lower voice.'"

Trouble is, their fellow passengers were scared of them anyway and, on the plane, went into a mid-western style "racial-profilers'" panic, with the result that, Goodman says, "airport police swarmed [Goodman's word] onto the plane, and the six imams were herded [Goodman's word] out, handcuffed and interrogated for hours." She quotes Shahin as saying that "When I saw the look in the eyes of the other passengers, it became the worst day of my life."

I don't doubt it for a moment.

What I *do* doubt, however, is the integrity or honesty of what's going on—or *not* going on—in the morally confused—or corrupt—mind of Amy Goodman.

After having told her two stories, she feels the need to make application of them to a purpose or point of some kind. So, she traces the origin of the phrase "We will not be silent" back "to the White Rose collective of World War II. A brother and sister named Hans and Sophie Scholl," she explains, "with other students and professors, decided the best way to resist the Nazis was to disseminate information, so that the Germans would never be able to say, 'We did not know.'"

The next, key, paragraph:

The collective distributed a series of pamphlets. On the bottom of one was printed the phrase 'We will not be silent.' The Nazis arrested Hans and Sophie as well as other collective members, tried them, found them guilty and beheaded them. But that motto should be the Hippocratic oath of the media today: 'We will not be silent.'"

At this point, anyone who's done their 9/11 homework will—or will be able to—feel little else than revulsion.

Look closely at what's happening. Amy Goodman knows much of 9/11 truth well[92] and yet won't speak, on air or off, the least hint of what really happened on that day or where the culpability for the crimes lie. Now, how can it be that *this* media person who hides *those* truths can now blithely declare that *this* "motto should be the "Hippocratic oath" of the media today: 'We will not be silent'"?

But that's exactly what Goodman herself is being—silent. As a 9/11 truth denier, Goodman reveals and identifies herself as a hypocrite, a media person who at this particular moment elevates even the Nicholas Lemanns and Frank Riches among us to a rose-scented goodness.

What could be *more* hypocritical? Goodman, by covering up the perpetrators' guilt, aids and abets them, those who planned and executed the greatest crime, the first link in a chain of the most enormous, heinous, ruthless, and treasonous criminal undertakings (excepting Hiroshima and Nagasaki) ever to have been committed by the putative "government" of the United States.

And yet she can write that "'We will not be silent' should be the 'Hippocratic oath of the media today.'" Goodman evokes for her own cover the true but here purely diversionary fact that the Nazis were criminal and evil. Then, exponentially more hypocritical and exponentially more revolting, she compares herself, in her own *false* "truth-telling," to Hans and Sophie Scholl, *true* truth-tellers, not fake, who, thanks to their dedication to the one thing that then mattered most in defense of humanity and freedom, had their heads cut off.

Angels and ministers of grace defend us from hypocrisy of such blind grandiosity, from self-interest of such shamelessness, from exploitation of historical martyrs for so cowardly and self-serving a purpose as disguising one's *own* role as an aider and abettor of the "Nazis" of today. Hans and Sophie Scholl were beheaded. Amy Goodman hides her own role in the cover-up of present-day Nazi atrocities behind the Schells' *genuine* martyrdom and is "punished"—well, by

---

92 See Emanuel Sferios' "Five Years Later: What Have We Accomplished" (available at: http://pilotsfor911truth.org/forum/index.php?showtopic=1191) and also http://video. google.com/videoplay?docid=-4094539209684370800&pr=goog-sl# for a video showing Goodman running from the collapse of WTC 7. What foreknowledge drew her there to "watch"? She denies having been there.

being carefree and prattling on daily in her broadcasts as a "progressive" commentator and investigator.

Goodman's version of the Hippocratic oath as she applies it to journalism—the oath not to be silent—is an oath, then, that she herself breaks even as she speaks of it. Given so perverse and corrupted a situation as she has trapped herself in so far in this column, what will she do next, in an attempt to bring her reader-deluding piece to *some* kind of logical conclusion?

Let's watch and see. And the answer is—she *doesn't* bring it to a conclusion. Like Elmaz Abinader, Sven Birkerts, Robert Olen Butler, Richard Ford, and other of the writers in the first chapter of *A Nation Gone Blind*, she doesn't conclude her essay but, instead, simply ends it—and she does so, like the other writers mentioned, by abandoning the essay, jumping ship, and changing the subject—reaching out, in effect, for any old sort of life raft that may happen to be floating by.

Like the writers in *A Nation Gone Blind*, Goodman appears to be blind to her real subject; like them, it seems that she's *unable to see it*, although in her case, admittedly, we don't know for sure whether she's blind to it because she *must* not see it or because she *can* not see it.

Now, Goodman does seem to think—or to *want* to think, or to want *us* to think—that her real subject is "racial profiling." Accordingly, she provides us with these few phrases just before going off into her opportunistic background talk about the Nazis:

> Racial profiling does not make us safer. It simply alienates and marginalizes whole populations. Whether it is African Americans driving while black, or Muslims trying to fly home.

Now, if the essay *were* coherent, and if the writer *did* have an interest in penetrating into her subject past the level of cliché and the obvious—what would she do? Think for a moment of a medical researcher. Suppose this researcher had identified a disease and observed it to be harmful, much as Goodman has here identified "racial profiling" and has observed it to be harmful. What two courses of action might the medical researcher—and, by analogy, Goodman—take?

The medical researcher might, for example, set out to research exactly what the mechanism is by which the disease produces harmful results, the purpose being that with an increased understanding of the precise nature of the disease's progress in an organism, it might become possible to ameliorate, protect against—or even prevent—the harm it does.

On the other hand, the medical researcher might move in a different direction. He or she might choose to study not *how* the disease is harmful to an organism but, instead, choose to study the cause or etiology *of* the disease. Once the origin of the disease is understood, it may become possible to avoid or eliminate it altogether.

Makes sense to me. But does Goodman take a route like either of these? Let's take the first one first—and the answer is no, Goodman doesn't take it. Instead, after merely asserting that "racial profiling" is harmful (it "marginalizes whole populations" and it "does not make us safer"),[93] she drops the subject and takes us "Back to the T-shirt story." From there, she disappears further backward into time with her two paragraphs about the Nazis beheading those who distributed pamphlets with "We will not be silent" on them.

So much for any analysis or insight that might, say, actually help reduce the harmfulness of "racial profiling."

But there's still hope, am I right? It's still possible—isn't it?—that Goodman will take the other and even richer direction and will explore where it is exactly that this harmful "disease" of "racial profiling" originates *from*? Taking *this* direction could be absolutely packed with potential for significance and good: If a murder has been committed, the mere feature writer might study the harmful effect of the murder on others—grief in the family, and so forth—but it's the true reporter who will dig into the roots of the crime, ever in the hopes, of course, of exposing the murderer.

But it's quite obvious by now that that is a direction Goodman is forbidden to go in, whether because she has accepted hush money[94] and is thus sworn to secrecy—has prostituted herself, in other words—*or* because she's a committed non-reader and non-seer who in actuality knows nothing whatsoever about 9/11: Not a reasonable probability in a nationally known "left" journalist or in someone with Goodman's experience.

Either way, skip the deeper story she does. Let me be more forceful: Either way, she skips the one, single, absolutely most significant, unspeakably important, treasonous, poison-spreading, republic-destroying, Constitution-shredding, concentration camp-causing, habeas corpus-denying, torture-permitting, totalitarian future-creating story that's smelling to heaven right there in front of her nose just as it's smelling to heaven right there in front of the nose of every American who isn't either blinded by deepest ignorance or in so powerful a state of denial as to be no longer able to eat, stand up, or breathe.

That's the story Goodman skips. *That's* the story she averts her gaze from. *That's* the story she ignores, and *that's* the story she

---

93 Goodmann's assertion, accompanied by no evidence, reasoning, detail, or exploration, is boilerplate, not thought.

94 See Barrie Zwicker, http://www.amazon.com/Towers-Deception-Media-Cover-dp/up-11/0865715734/sr=1-1/qid=1167929084/ref=pd_bbs_sr_1/104-4231058-3189532?ie=UTF8&s=books Towers of Deception, p. 223. You'll find there a full-page flow-chart under the title "THE GATEKEEPERS: Foundations Fund Phony 'Left' Media." Zwicker provides a quote from http://www.TomPaine.com Executive Director John Moyers that explains the power of foundation-derived "hush money": "If they don't like what we're doing, we don't get funded next year." Look closely on p. 233, and you'll find Amy Goodman's name.

replaces with—diversionary pablum. Incoherent diversionary pablum, at that.

Uh, uh, uh—we mustn't say a *word* about Cheney at the controls on the morning of 9/11, not a word about the long-planned war games taking place on 9/11 as a means of keeping military interceptors away from the "hijacked" airliners, not a *word* about the fact that at least seven of the supposed 9/11 hijackers are still alive,[95] not a *word* about the fact that all three huge buildings, defying the laws of physics, came down at near-free-fall speed,[96] and not a *word* about the fraud, lies, distortions, and omissions in the NIST report on the WTC Collapse,"[97] and *certainly* not a word about Larry Silverstein knowing ahead of time that WTC 7 had been *made ready* for collapse whenever that destructive event might be desired,[98] and *just* as certainly not a word about boy scout Rudy Giuliani knowing ahead of time that WTC 1 and WTC 2 were going to collapse,[99] and not a word, either, about the hilarious and revealing fact that BBC-TV announced live that WTC 7 had collapsed—but announced it twenty minutes before the building actually did go away. The media Brits who were in on the whole thing had read their part of the script too fast.[100]

Well. It must take a lot to keep a journalist silent on every detail of a story as big as that one. But, whatever it does take to do it, it's been done to a T-shirt on Amy Goodman. Instead of looking into the fraud of 9/11, or into the false blaming of the "attacks" on "Islamo-terrorists," instead of acknowledging the resultant, planned, deliberately-created national Islamo-phobia that has led inevitably and predictably—precisely in accordance with the playbook—to the virulent, irrational, near-universal "racial profiling" of Muslims across the gracious plains and mountains of the entire United States—well, Goodman has remained content to rest on a couple of easy, empty, and tired platitudes: "Racial profiling does not make us safer. It simply alienates and marginalizes whole populations."

Duh.

No, we can't expect Amy Goodman to look into the true etiology of a vile disease. We understand how it's preferable to speak only in clichés—"racial profiling" and "marginalizes whole populations."

---

[95] See http://www.whatreallyhappened.com/hijackers.html

[96] For scientific study of this aspect, and many others, of the destruction of World Trade Center, see again Dr. Judy Wood's immeasurably important web site: http://www.drjudywood.com/

[97] Again, see "Dead On Arrival: The NIST 9/11 Report on the WTC Collapse, Part 1" by Mark H. Gaffney: http://thetruthseeker.co.uk/article.asp?id=5697 as well as the second half of this same work: http://www.thetruthseeker.co.uk/article.asp?id=5695

[98] See the video here of him saying so: http://video.google.com/videoplay?docid=-775053 2340306101329

[99] http://www.whatreallyhappened.com/wtc_giuliani.html

[100] Watch it here: http://www.ericlarsen.net/foodforthought8.0.2007.html

That's much better than getting at the actual truth of *how* and *why*. Here's a way of understanding, by analogy, what's really going on with fake progressives like Amy Goodman and others. Imagine if it had been Amy Goodman instead of Jonas Salk who was dedicated to studying the scourge of polio. If it had been Amy Goodman, she'd never have done anything more than prattle on about how polio is harmful, about how it "does not make us safer." But she'd do nothing *about it*. She wouldn't delve into the cause of the disease. The result? We'd *still have polio*.

How progressive.

In our own world of "real reality," however, in our actual, malicious, criminal, and unamusing world, we're faced with the task of doing what Amy Goodman doesn't and won't do—that is, *look at and expose* the truth that if properly understood could save our republic, restore the Bill of Rights, resurrect habeas corpus, bring our nation into compliance again with the Geneva Conventions, rejoin it to the World Court, eliminate torture as state policy, and bring a cessation to the building of domestic concentration camps.

A tall order, I'll grant. But Amy Goodman is up to the task. She aspires high, aims high, and hits high. Take a look, for example, at the truth she gives us that may and will and can allow us to keep our republic, freedoms, and—very possibly—our lives:

She speaks again of media people, of those whose "Hippocratic oath" should be "We will not be silent." And, after that, she arrives at her grand, climactic pronouncement:

> Our job is to provide a forum for people to speak for themselves, to describe their own experiences. This breaks down stereotypes and bigotry, things that fuel racial profiling, which ultimately endangers us all.

To which I, for one, can say only that I have seldom read such a perfectly dinky little parade of falsehood and cliché, such a prime-quality anti-climax, such a freshman English-worthy example of disunity, evasion, cliché and non sequitur in a piece of writing by an adult human being—especially an eminent, nationally known, progressive journalist.

If *this* is what "progressive" means in America, surely we all are doomed to life under fascism.

To read such as Amy Goodman wrote, to be cheated so, to be manipulated by such puerile banality as this from a person of widely-recognized "progressive" influence, to see revealed through the writing itself what the vapid, jejune, essentially un-serious quality of the mind and thinking behind it really is—this is an experience incompatible with any hope that such leadership or guidance as Amy

Goodman—or Pacifica Radio and its ilk—provide can *conceivably* be tonic to anyone's dying hope for the survival of the United States of America as a free republic.

The entirety of the closing paragraph, in essence, is a pack of church-basement lies, poisonous ones, words wholly and perfectly acceptable to the enemies of the republic though spoken by a putative ally of those faithful to it. The exercise is diseased, ruinous, treacherous, and contemptible. From Amy Goodman and her like, one learns not only that the "progressive left" no longer exists in the United States, but that it has taken the form of a serpent, complete with its own late-model forked tongue.

The great question, very nearly the only question remaining to a patriot, is the question of where to turn *now* to find representation of the truth and to assemble power on its behalf.

Eric Larsen
April 4, 2007

10.

POISONED NATION, POISONED TRUTH: A READING AND A QUIZ APRIL 12, 2007

To the Reader:
When I was in high school, one of the things I most disliked was being told by a teacher, usually in English class, to "read between the lines." It was no good. I found nothing there but white space. If the teacher had said what he or she had really meant, the task would have at least been understandable although probably—given the tiny amount of reading I'd done—no easier. What the teachers meant was that we should read for connotation, or sometimes for symbolism, difficult things to sense or see until much more reading—and experience—is under one's belt. In college came reading for logic, continuity, clarity, and completeness. Bit by bit, a person got better at reading. But over the past six decades, as the "age of simplification" has grown from infancy to full pseudo-adulthood and the republic has regressed into a disease-plagued near-infancy, Americans have become less and less and less good at reading. "Poisoned Nation, Poisoned Truth" talks about it.

On Monday, April 2, 2007, *The New York Times* led off with "New Generation of Qaeda Chiefs Is Seen on Rise." First subhead: "Consolidation of Power." Second subhead:
"Surprise and Dismay at Perception That Group Is Rebounding." Byline: Mark Mazzetti.[101]
So? Well, so this: Reading that lead news item makes one realize that the continued suppression of true information and the continued issuance of *dis*information have become so commonplace by this point in the planned fascist takeover of the U.S. that even the nation's foremost newspaper can cook up an opener-of-the-week lead article that's a slumgullion of disputed truths, half truths, falsehoods, and

[101] http://www.nytimes.com/2007/04/02/world/middleeast/02qaeda.r=1&_1&sq=New%20Generation%20of%20Qaeda%20Chiefs%20Is%20Seen%20on%20Rise&st=cse

plain lies—knowing that the whole wretched thing will pass unchallenged, will hardly be noticed, will cause no resistance, opposition, or demand for corrections.

Now, I'll bet my underpants and a two dollar bill with a cherry on top that of all the phrases in that last paragraph, there's *one* that's more likely than any others to cause a good number of readers to quit reading in disgust and skip on out here to—well, god knows where.

So, you who are still here, take a minute and choose a phrase. My own bet (same as yours, I'm sure) is on "by this point in the planned fascist takeover of the U.S."

I might be wrong and hope I am. But suppose people *were* to quit reading at that point. If they did, it would mean we'd stumbled on yet another "truth test," akin to the famous one when the BBC generously provided proof that all of 9/11 was a fraud. That was the occasion when the BBC news staff, on air, prematurely read a certain piece of their "script" of the dread day's events. That is, they read the script correctly—announcing that WTC 7 had collapsed—but they did it *twenty minutes too early*, while WTC7 was still standing, firm and tall and *very* visible in the background over the commentator's shoulder. You can take this particular BBC "9/11 truth test" yourself, if you like, and watch for yourself the poor Brits caught with their pants at their ankles and, thus encumbered, running like mad to *try* to cover up their blunder. They attempt heroically to fill up the empty air time until—please! please!—the cursed thing actually does collapse the way the script said it was supposed to.[102]

In my own experience, the most interesting thing about the BBC "9/11 truth test" was that when I wrote about it, my doing so had the effect of turning readers *away* and causing them to demand I drop them immediately from my email list. That was the opposite of what I'd *wanted* to happen, which was that after seeing for themselves this indisputable example of set-up, treason, and fraud, they would become more rather than less inclined to look further into 9/11 truth and the near-countless ways the standard Bush administration version of what actually happened on that day were fraudulent and absurd.

But what does it mean if people see this kind of "truth test" and then just turn away and say "count me out"? It means the same thing as it would if people were to read the phrase "by this point in the planned fascist takeover in the U.S." and then just turn away and also say "count me out."

In other words, it would mean that such people actually prefer lies and falsehood over truth. We've looked at this syndrome before,

---

[102] Actually, the BBC couldn't quite make it through the whole twenty minutes, and so—hilarious to watch—they "dissolved" their on-site reporter, Jane Standley, saying they'd "lost" her. You can watch the whole thing here: http://www.youtube.com/watch?v=ltP2t9nq9fI

in "Our Enemies, the Left Gatekeepers, Pt. 1," where I quoted the Arianna Huffington piece called "Living in Denial":

> Let's face it: the Bush administration is sick. The fall of Ted Haggard is just the latest manifestation of the central disease of President Bush and his cohorts: the pathological refusal to accept reality, and the delusion that reality can be changed by rhetoric.

Powerful words, "pathological refusal to accept reality," and also hypocritical ones, since Huffington, who prides herself on blindness to 9/11 truth, suffers from the same pathology she accuses others of suffering from. Whether she knows it or not really makes no difference, but she remains a hypocrite by demanding that others change *their* ways and stop denying truth, while she derides, eschews, or is blind to the need for any such change in her own opinionated self.[103]

Now, not everyone is a columnist, journalist, editor, analyst, or public figure. Most people, in fact (unlike, say, Arianna Huffington, Frank Rich, Matthew Rothschild, Nicholas Lemann, Christopher Hayes,[104] or Alexander Cockburn—just for a few examples that pop into mind) don't write for their livings, don't make public arguments, don't advocate things in print, don't preach at all. But it's still entirely possible that they might take one of the "9/11 tests"—that is, take a look at the indisputable truth—and *still* turn their backs and say, "Oh, no. Count me out."

What's the difference? Well, those non-public and non-publishing people can't so easily be declared hypocrites, since they preach nothing. These are plain, regular people with no claims toward convincing anyone else of *any*thing. So hypocrites, arguably, they're not. And yet, if they're people who, when shown the truth, turn their backs and say "Count me out"—then they're *still* people with "a pathological refusal to accept reality."

There may well be *some* sort of reasoning involved. Some people may refuse to believe the truth out of a craven selfishness that makes them not want to be bothered, while others may be un*able* to believe it, whether out of fear ("that's too frightening to think about") or even the power of habit ("our leaders have never been that evil before, and therefore they can't be that evil now").

But whatever the case—fear, refusal, selfishness, or habit—these are people who *choose* to remain blind to a truth that they've in fact themselves actually seen some part or evidence of, large or small.

---

[103] Update: Evidence of Huffington's own pathology was offered by her March 9, 2010, excision from *The Huffington Post* of a 9/11 truth piece written by Jesse Ventura. See the censorship here: http://www.huffingtonpost.com/jesse-ventura/for-some-the-search-for-w_b_491504.html
[104] See his essay in The Nation for December 26, 2006, "9/11: The Roots of Paranoia." http://www.thenation.com/article/911-roots-of-paranoia

These are blinded Americans. The question of whether they've been blinded by themselves or by other agencies or forces is of no consideration or consequence for our purposes here. The deed, either way, is done. The significance here is that these people, *being* blinded, are every bit as much supporters, friends, and allies of the fascists, neocons, and the corporatocracy as are all those many hypocrites and media-insiders themselves whom we've been talking about, from Huffington or Rich on high to the likes of Rothschild or Jacob Weisberg down low. All of *them*, whether by speaking against 9/11 truth or whether "only" by remaining silent—the silence of a doctor who knows of a disease's cure but says nothing—these, all of them, function as friends of fascism and enemies of the republic.

In times like such as we're living through now, a time of war against the citizenry, even the common person's saying "count me out" is a form of desertion, a form of aid to the enemy, and therefore traitorous. And certainly more so is the *purposeful and professional* distorting or covering up of known truths that could disempower or even defeat the enemies of the people and the destroyers of the Constitution—the kind of distorting and covering up that we find daily, all the time, for example, in *The New York Times*.

•

So let's go back to April 2 and the lead article in the *Times*. In fact, I'll quote bits of the piece and then ask quiz questions. See if you can make your own response before you look at the answers.

First paragraph:

"As Al Qaeda rebuilds in Pakistan's tribal areas, a new generation of leaders has emerged under Osama bin Laden to cement control over the network's operations, according to American intelligence and counter-terrorism officials."

Q: Which two groups of words or phrases cast greatest doubt on the truth of this sentence's content?

A: First, "according to American intelligence and counter-terrorism officials," since they're unidentified. Second, "under Osama bin Laden." Osama bin Laden has been dead for years.[105]

Second paragraph:

"The new leaders rose from within the organization after the death or capture of the operatives that built Al Qaeda before the Sept. 11, 2001, attacks,

---

[105] See "Osama bin Laden: A dead nemesis perpetuated by the US government" at What Really Happened: http://whatreallyhappened.com/WRHARTICLES/osama_dead.php. Also see this video, "Benazir Bhutto: Bin Laden was Murdered," at http://www.youtube.com/watch?v=UnychOXj9Tg.

leading to surprise and dismay within United States intelligence agencies about the group's ability to rebound from an American-led offensive."

Q: What infamous geographical location is alluded to, however faintly, by the phrase "after the *death or capture* of the operatives that built Al Qaeda"?

A: Correct: Guantanamo Bay, Cuba. Equal credit for Bagram or Abu Ghraib.

Q: "What historical fact is being ignored, not so much as alluded to, in the phrase 'the operatives that built Al Qaeda'"?

A: Correct: The fact that the U.S. itself, or, more accurately, the CIA, was the first "operative" to create Al Qaeda and give money to Osama bin Laden for the purpose of creating and expanding "The Base." The intent, as all know (or should know), was to create a force to resist and ideally end the Russian occupation of Afghanistan. Only after Russia's pullout did the question arise of what to "do" with Al Qaeda, the "monster" self-created by the CIA.[106]

Q: Considering the answer to the preceding question, what is the most ominous two-word phrase in "the operatives that built Al Qaeda before the Sept. 11, 2001, attacks"?

A: The phrase "the operatives."

Q: Considering the answer to the preceding question, what is the true meaning of the phrase "the operatives"? That is, who *were* "the operatives"?

A: The "operatives" were the U.S. and the CIA. We have met the operatives and they are us.

Q: Considering the answer to the preceding question, explain the irony in the phrase "*before the Sept. 11, 2001, attacks*" as it appears in the longer phrase, "the operatives that built Al Qaeda before the Sept. 11, 2001, attacks."

A: The irony is that the U.S. and CIA "operatives" who "built" Al Qaeda *had* to have done so "before the Sept. 11, 2001, attacks," since otherwise Al Qaeda couldn't have been blamed for them. Remember the classic rule from Strunk and White: Omit needless words.[107]

Two more passages from the *Times* piece before we end. Fourth paragraph:

"American, European and Pakistani authorities have for months been piecing together a picture of the new leadership, based in part on

---

[106] See Webster Tarpley at http://www.911blogger.com/node/4864 to the effect, in reference to Robert Gates, that "Most damning of all is the fact that Gates was one of the founders of al Qaeda, the CIA's Arab Legion which was assembled to attack the Soviets in Afghanistan. Gates is thus part of the infrastructure that produced the patsies of 9/11..."

[107] To help keep yourself from writing the way the *Times* does, read the famous "little book," *The Elements of Style*: http://www.amazon.com/Elements-Style-Fourth-William-Strunk/dp/020530902X

evidence-gathering during terrorism investigations in the past two years. Particularly important have been interrogations of suspects and material evidence connected to a plot British and American investigators said they averted last summer to destroy multiple commercial airlines after take-off from London."

Q: Considering the answer to the question just above this quote, what single, two-syllable word beginning with the letter "t" comes immediately to mind when one reads this phrase: "Particularly important have been interrogations of suspects"?

A: Correct: "torture."

Q: For a well-informed reader, what is the most notable thing about the fact that the *Times* article refers to "a plot British and American investigators said they averted last summer [i.e., summer 2006] to destroy multiple commercial airlines after takeoff from London"?

A: Exactly. What's notable is that, pokerfaced, the *Times* refers to a plot that never happened, and that, though it may have passed through a mind or two, was never in any credible or realistic way achievable. See "Liquid Bomb Pakistan Link Is False Flag Smoking Gun,"[108] with its subhead, "Veracity of liquid explosives method also put under... doubt." Or maybe "What Does A Terrorist Preparing To Bomb 10 Airliners Do Beforehand? Buys Cakes."[109] And next time you have to leave your cosmetics at home, you might, first, enjoy looking at this article, "Liquid Bomb Plot a 'Fiction.'"[110]

Q: One word appears in the fourth paragraph that *may* conceivably suggest that the *Times*—or Mark Mazzetti—*knew* at the time of writing that the "liquid bomb" plot was a fraud relentlessly hyperbolized by Bush/Blair/CIA *et alii* as real, authentic, and highly dangerous.

A: Correct. The word "said"

Our final passage, the eighth paragraph of the Mazzetti piece:

"The evidence officials said was accumulating about Mr. Masri and a handful of other Qaeda figures has led to a reassessment within the American intelligence community about the strength of the group's core in Pakistan's tribal areas, and its role in some of the most significant terrorism plots of the past two years, attacks in London in July 2005 that killed 56."

Q: I'm sure you're growing tired from all this work, so let's have just one last question. We'll leave all the slippery, suspicious, code-and-cover-up words alone—"evidence" "officials," "said," "accumulating," "reassessment," "American intelligence community"—and

---

[108] http://www.prisonplanet.com/articles/august2006/130806liquidbomb.htm
[109] http://www.prisonplanet.com/articles/august2006/160806buyscakes.htm
[110] http://www.911blogger.com/node/2984

ask this one thing: In light of your answer to the question about a "plot that never happened," what is most notable to a well-informed reader (not counting "the airline plot," already discussed) about the deadpan phrase "some of the most significant terrorism plots of the past two years, including the airline plot and the suicide attacks in London in July 2005 that killed 56"?

A: Right again: The London attacks of 7/7/05 were another "false flag op" perpetrated to raise the sagging terror-level among the populations of the U.S. and Great Britain. No point in re-creating the argument here yet again, but those sufficiently interested—interested, that is, in just how much we're being lied to, by whom, and why—can read "July 7th as Machiavellian State Terror?"[111], a scholarly article by Professor David MacGregor of King's University College at the University of Western Ontario. Those interested—and how, I ask, can anyone not be interested? Unless, of course, they've cast their lot with the enemy—can also take a look at this paragraph[112] from Webster G. Tarpley's indispensable book, *9/11 Synthetic Terror: Made in USA*. Finally, everyone can also take a look at this trim and helpful "9/11 'Fact Sheet,'"[113] first brought to my attention by Carolyn Baker—to whom my thanks—and available to all.

Eric Larsen
April 12, 2007

---

[111] http://julyseventh.co.uk/july-7-article-david-macgregor-july-7th-as-machiavellian-state-terror.html

[112] http://www.ericlarsen.net/foodforthought9.3.2.2007.html

[113] http://911proof.com/FactSheet.html

11.

THE PERNICIOUS HYPOCRISY OF FRANK RICH
OF *THE NEW YORK TIMES*
PART I
OCTOBER 11, 2007

To the Reader:
The title of this piece speaks for itself, and I will add
nothing to it here. The point needs to be made clearly,
however, that my turning to individual figures among
the gatekeepers in order to analyze their writing—
Nicholas Lemann, Amy Goodman, Jacob Weisberg,
Frank Rich, and so on—is not, can not, and must not be
taken as a choice having any impulse of the *ad hominem*
as its basis. The truth is that I don't set out to analyze
or criticize *anyone*. All I do is read pieces that come my
way or that appear in places I tend to follow. And then
all I do is study and analyze what I've read—if, indeed, it
raises questions or demonstrates qualities, for better or
for worse, deserving of analysis. It's absolutely true that
characteristics in the writing may and most likely *will*
lead back to the writer of them, and I myself see no way
that this pattern could be otherwise. The Comte de Buf-
fon famously wrote "Le style, c'est l'homme même,"
and he was quite right. I cautioned in the headnote to
chapter 9 that the last thing anyone with a secret should
do is take up pen and ink. Nothing is a more unforgiving
revealer than writing. If any aspect of this note seems
disingenuous to the reader, so be it. Admittedly, some
things I do indeed find unforgiveable. Being a human
being, however, is not one of them. Things that human
beings may *do*, however, or things that they may be
caused to do—these may be another matter altogether,
and I don't see how it can be otherwise than that the
responsibility for them must lie with the *doer* of them.

1.

Just imagine this for a moment. Just imagine that you could actually set aside the *fear* of the criminal leadership of the United States
that any normal thinking citizen *should* be feeling right now. Imagine
that you could set both your fear and anger aside because somehow
you could be *certain* that the Bush-Cheney junta *will not* perpetrate,

between now and November 2009,[114] some godawful variant of 9/11 that will allow them to declare a national emergency and lock all of us down in their perfectly prepared-for police state—this new false event being contrived so that they could the more easily, unhindered by *us*, go about their adolescent games of bombing much of the Middle East into oblivion in order to "save" it for Halliburton and the oil men.

I can't do it, can't put aside the fear. The terrorists—*our* terrorists—have done their work too long and too well. I've been terrorized and remain so, scared to death of every move in Cheney's reptilian little brain and every psycho-triggered tic in The Boy's behavior that might incline the pair of them the more readily to "Cut the Big One," as the clear-sighted and strong-hearted Sheila Samples put it not long ago.[115]

Therefore I'll just have to *pretend* that I'm not terrified, at least for right now. How else can I possibly concentrate on writing an essay that's not only political but also literary?

It's not an easy thing, paying attention to the arts when terror seizes you—but if it isn't done, then the degradation everywhere will occur all the faster and the ruin in the end will be only and all the greater. That's another thing I fear in the U.S., the exponentially increasing *rate* of degradation in a nation where the arts, already, are hardly any longer even breathing.

Even though terror and foreboding are omnipresent and witheringly powerful, that's still no excuse for anyone in the arts to squeeze their eyes shut, cower down, and give up. Many will remember the famous Yeats poem, "Lapis Lazuli," written in another year of great dread, 1938. *Some* people argue, says Yeats, that the arts are of no conceivable use or importance at a time when the realities of destruction and war loom:

> I have heard that hysterical women say
> They are sick of the palette and fiddle-bow.
> Of poets that are always gay,
> For everybody knows or else should know
> That if nothing drastic is done
> Aeroplane and Zeppelin will come out.
> Pitch like King Billy[116] bomb-balls in
> Until the town lie beaten flat.

True? Maybe, or partly. But this is only the *start* of the poem, and as it goes on, Yeats produces a powerful and eloquent NAY, declaring that the arts remain just as important (how important? *absolutely* important) in time of threat and dread as at any other, and that even

---

[114] That is, between Oct. 11, 2007 and the election to follow on Nov. 3, 2009.
[115] http://www.smirkingchimp.com/thread/4188
[116] This particular "King Billy" is the Protestant William III (of Orange), who defeated Catholic James II in the 1690 Battle of Boyne.

if the whole world were about to end, even "should the last scene be there, / The great stage curtain about to drop," even *then* those who "perform their tragic" roles,

> If worthy their prominent part in the play,
> Do not break up their lines to weep.

"If worthy their prominent part. . . " I have been interested for my entire adult life in knowing and hoping to emulate what it is that makes a person "worthy" in the sense Yeats means here—and elsewhere too. But the question of worthiness aside, it's obvious—isn't it?—that if you've got a heart as dedicated and passionate as Yeats', then you're going to *see to it* that the arts be *made* to stick around no matter what. And, I might add, you're going to do all you can to make them stick around *without* their degenerating into the shallow, the cheap, the meretricious, or the political. Instead, you're going to see to it that they stick around the way they're *supposed* to stick around and the way they *must*: Big and grand and bold and high and essential to the heart, the self, the mind—and to the people, the nation, the kingdom of humankind.

Ah, yes, grand thoughts. *My* heart be with the old poets,[117] that's *my* view, as it's been since I was a student. And that's the reason why, even though the Bushiscti may be about to spark the blinding, world-white-flash any second now ("The great stage curtain [be] about to drop"), even though they may be about to fill "this excellent canopy, the air"[118] with cancerous malignancy and the dust of nuclear death—all for the sake of their snake-skin wallets and their phallo-centric boyish greed-lust—well, that's the reason why, in spite of my terror at what the boy-bastards might do next, I'm nevertheless going to embark on a big and grand and bold and high *literary* essay. And it's going to take on a *big* subject.

Namely? Well, in general, the subject will be those hundreds of thousands of men and women throughout the media who out-Faustus Faustus[119] in their having made a pact with Mephostophilis himself,

---

117 "My ghost be with the old philosophers!" (Christopher Marlowe, *The Tragical History of Dr. Faustus*, I,iii, 59.)

118 I have of late—but wherefore I know not—lost all my mirth, forgone all custom of exercises; and indeed it goes so heavily with my disposition that this goodly frame, the earth, seems to me a sterile promontory, this most excellent canopy, the air, look you, this brave o'erhanging firmament, this majestical roof fretted with golden fire, why, it appears no other thing to me than a foul and pestilent congregation of vapours. What a piece of work is a man! how noble in reason! how infinite in faculty! in form and moving how express and admirable! in action how like an angel! in apprehension how like a god! the beauty of the world! the paragon of animals! And yet, to me, what is this quintessence of dust? man delights not me: no, nor woman neither, though by your smiling you seem to say so. (*Hamlet*, II, ii, 291-296; Hamlet to Rosencrantz and Guildenstern)

119 O, it offends me to the / soul to hear a robustious periwig-pated fellow tear / a passion to tatters, to very rags, to split the ears of the / groundlings, who for the most part are capable of / nothing but inexplicable dumbshows and noise: I would / have such a fellow whipped for o'erdoing Termagant; / it out-herods Herod: pray you, avoid it. (*Hamlet* III, ii, 1-16. Hamlet to the Players)

although for what end I have no clear idea, other than to destroy the republic and bring ruinous harm to the globe and perhaps an end to us all. Whatever their reason, these legions of men and women putatively serving the nation's people have agreed—against ethics, against morality, against decency, against *good*—on a full-time basis to lie, deceive, occlude, obfuscate, distort, twist, ignore, to do anything, in short, so long as it's *not* tell or speak or reveal to regular American people the *least iota* of simple plain truth about the secret, hidden, rogue, or "overworld" government that's now malevolently *and* maliciously determining life-and-death matters for us all on the local, the regional, the national, and the international level. (See Peter Dale Scott's *The Road to 9/11*[120] for the most recent of the several important scholarly analyses of this awful truth.)

But back to those in the media. Liars on so massive a scale as we see among media people today—such enormous numbers of hypocrites and fraudsters all busy at one concerted task—may be a thing unprecedented in human history (outside, I quickly add, of organized religion). On top of the enormity in numbers, those among them who are actually *on* air or *in* print (not to mention their *own* writers and packagers and producers) are so practiced and so devoted in employing their deceit that these wretches very, very often are able to deceive so skillfully and so subtly that they *actually cause their audiences to experience both gratitude and an increasing fidelity* to them: To those very liars who are lying to them, misleading them, and above all blinding them to the truth of 9/11 and therefore to the truth of the malicious, dangerous, traitorous government that now has us under its control.

Shhh. Some quiet and respect, please, say these sanctimonious peddlers of deceit. We're talking here about "poverty," or "gender issues," or "women's rights," or "electoral reform," etc., etc.—but, however reverently such "progressive" media people bow their heads to these "good" and "humane" and "democratic" and "fairness-centered" topics or "issues," all of this "coverage"—in light of the *huge* true and present danger—is nothing more than fluff, chaff in the wind, just like those diversionary aluminum strips that used to be tossed into the high atmosphere to confuse radar by functioning as false targets and thus diverting airborne enemy predators. It's snake oil. It's hokum. Every bit of such coverage is used divert attention from the one enormous lie of omission, the one lie of over-arching importance. The truth is that none of those peripheral subjects matters a hoot in comparison with the enormously more pressing truth that, thanks

---

[120] The University of California Press (2007) http://www.amazon.com/Road-11-Wealth-Empire-America/dp/0520237730/ref=pd_bbs_sr_1/105-4791811-3350040?ie=UTF8&s=books&qid=1191764020&sr=1-1

to the policies of our present junta-"leadership," we're about to lose the entire republic itself and *all* our freedoms while this malignant and malicious "government"—one that can be halted only and solely by the exposure of 9/11 truth—embarks upon its further plans not only for implementing the domestic prison-state but for achieving the even greater prison-state of permanent global war.

In a situation such as we're now in—*all* of us—to lie about 9/11 truth, by commission *or* by omission—seems to me treachery against the republic, against the Constitution, against the people, against the human race.

To speak of such things is to speak of enormities. But it is also to speak the simplest truth. We are in a state of emergency such as our own republic has never before been in, and we are being lied to about it, massively and absolutely, by the entirety of that very element of socio-political society that at one time in history was the *indispensable* freedom-preserving element—namely, the "Fourth Estate," now become, in Paul Craig Roberts' words, "propaganda ministry for the government's wars and police state."

The Fourth Estate is now our most vile enemy; it is more vile, by merit of being *willingly* in lying servitude to it, even than the traitorous and putrescent government it perversely enables and nourishes, a government whose aim is to impoverish and imprison us all.

2.

The phenomenon of a lying media, then, is my general subject. My specific subject, on the other hand, is a single and very powerful person at work within that media, namely, the outstandingly sophisticated master of mendacity who deceives for *The New York Times* op-ed page on Sundays, Frank Rich. I have chosen to discuss Rich because of the several of his pieces I've read that bear directly on 9/11. He is, further, an extremely visible writer. It can hardly be denied that his eminence and high profile, along with the very large numbers of readers he reaches, serve to create in certain of them a greater than average revulsion at his effectiveness as a betrayer and misleader of the people. That he *so willingly* works to help keep in power the malignant and pernicious "leaders" who in turn seem aimed to destroy us—such apparent zeal elevates him both in the interest he holds for a reader and in the repugnance he creates. That he does his work with so apparently *perfect* an absence of the agenbite

---

121 "Conservatism isn't what it used to be,"(Information Clearing House, Sept. 17, 2007) http://www.informationclearinghouse.info/article18409.htm

of inwit makes him, in short, simultaneously fascinating and abominable, as does the fact additionally that he does his treacherous work while, with masterly success, leading his not-very-skillful readers to believe that he's actually telling them the truth only most soulfully, serving only most devotedly their best interests.

Before we get to specifics in Rich's writing, though, I think I should clarify two points that I consider axiomatic and that will help show why I consider the matter at hand—our lying media—to be a matter so extremely, in fact absolutely, important.

After reviewing six years' worth of study by numerous scholars and writers over a period of four years (I didn't begin studying and reading about 9/11 until June 2003), I take it as a proper, just, and correct view, a view properly to be shared by any intelligent, reading, thinking, and seriously observant person, that the events of 9/11 were, in Carolyn Baker's words, "premeditated mass murder by the United States government."[122]

Exactly what elements of "government" executed the crimes is still inexactly known. Almost certainly, it was in large part a "shadow" or "rogue" element, as Webster G. Tarpley calls it in his brilliant 2005 *Synthetic Terror: Made in U.S.A.*,[123] or an "overworld" element, as Peter Dale Scott calls it in his new and extremely revealing study, already mentioned, *The Road to 9/11*.[124]

But, though it may not yet be known precisely what domestic United States elements (along with with what non-domestic allies) perpetrated the 9/11 crimes, some such elements did do it. And now, with that said, I come to the second point that I consider axiomatic and that, again, should help show the importance of the subject of the lying media. This point has two parts or steps to it, and the first has to do with what the purpose of the 9/11 murders and destruction was. It's now irrefutable that a good part of the purpose was to scare and intimidate the American people so badly that they would permit their "leaders" to use any methods they wished in order to "protect" the republic and its people from the enemy that "attacked" them on 9/11. That this "enemy" was fictional and the attack self-created and self-inflicted didn't then matter. Americans were scared enough to believe that the enemy was real, and our criminal leaders immediately scared them further by making use of the frightening

---

122 Carolyn Baker, "The Empress Has No Clothes: Amy Goodman's Reality Blackout" at http://www.fromthewilderness.com/free/ww3/011306_empress_clothes.shtml

123 *9/11 Synthetic Terror: Made in USA* (2005), http://www.amazon.com/11-Synthetic-Terror-Made-Fourth/dp/0930852370

124 The University of California Press (2007) http://www.amazon.com/Road-11-Wealth-Empire-America/dp/0520237730/ref=pd_bbs_sr_1/105-4791811-3350040?ie=UTF8&s=books&qid=1191764020&sr=1-1

name "Terrorism." Thus the "War on Terrorism" was born out of falsehood and lies and went forward amid falsehood and lies. The "war" included the dual plan of stripping Americans of their civil and Constitutional liberties at home, and without hindrance waging unjust and illegal war abroad.

•

The first step in the point I take as axiomatic, then, is that 9/11, a fraud through and through, was the visible starting point of—*and* the faked excuse for—a concerted program of reactionism, theft, treason, crime, and global militarism both illegal and unchecked.

The second part of the point I take as axiomatic is very simple and I think also indisputable. The Bush junta is responsible now for a six-year-long string of crimes. That it has proven itself unstoppable for that long is a grim gift for which we can give thanks in very great part to a corrupt, bought-off, complicit congress that has either *approved* every single one of those crimes or at the very least has failed to hold the junta *accountable* for a single one of them—including the one very, very, very important crime, the one that made all the subsequent crimes possible, namely, of course, 9/11 itself.

This is why I said before and say again that only the exposure of the truth about 9/11, followed by appropriate measures holding accountable those responsible for the crimes of 9/11 or for enabling those crimes (Cheney, Rumsfeld, and Air Force general Richard Myers, for three) or abetting them (Giuliani, Rice, Powell, for three more)—only such measures can slow the pace of destruction and allow even the *consideration* of ways to reclaim and save the republic.

One of the significant things about this point—that 9/11 truth alone can slow the junta, make it accountable for its crimes, or end its diabolic work—is that *six years is long enough to prove that no established branch of government or of law inside the United States is going to expose this truth or begin prosecutions because of it.* Therefore? Therefore, the job must be done—and can be done only—by the nation's people.

The central facts of the case in the heinous and witheringly cold-blooded 9/11 crimes, in spite of certain remaining unknowns, are evident, transparent, and *eminently* provable. Any thinking, reading, intelligent, and observant person can discover this inexpressibly important fact simply by taking the time and mustering the interest to familiarize him- or herself with even *some* of the essential scholarly work that has been done on the history, evidence, facts, and truth of 9/11.[125]

---

[125] A partial yet helpful list of works on 9/11 can be found in the Appendix to this book.

The situation is this: A third of the population of the U.S. doubts the "official" story about 9/11 and either suspects or is convinced that 9/11 was an "inside job."[126] A person might wish it were two-thirds instead of one-third, but this number is still momentous and significant.

Let's hypothesize for a moment how we might reasonably classify the American population into the *smallest* number of groups possible without there being overlap among them. This is a good and useful exercise in thinking and logic of the kind once included during fall semesters in English 101 classrooms all over the land, yet now as likely as not to go untouched. I will propose, given our present interest here, that all Americans can be distinguished as belonging to one of *three* groups, groups that will be distinct from one another and yet that will leave no one out. Hence:

1) Thinking and observant Americans.
2) Blind Americans, those for whom the media determine most if not in fact all reality
3) Bought, guilty, complicit Americans, those who continue to deny and suppress 9/11 truth while at the same time *knowing* that truth.

Anyone who went through a good English 101 course knows that these groups *need* not be and very likely *will* not be equal or anywhere near equal in the number of their members. A great discrepancy in numbers is very clear here. The likelihood is that Group 2 will be the largest, since the polls telling us that one-third of Americans embrace or lean toward 9/11 truth[127] suggest also that *two*-thirds don't. It follows that that two thirds must be the less-informed, less-observant, and less-inquisitive two thirds. I'll call them "blind."

And where does this leave us? Two thirds of Americans—roughly—are blind. One third of Americans—roughly—is thinking, observant, and inquisitive. This means that only the leftovers fill up Group 3, making it clearly, patently, and obviously the smallest group of the three. And yet, though the smallest, it is also—as things stand now—far and away the most powerful.

It's the most powerful, and it's also the group that could be renamed the group of liars, the group of deceivers, the group of falsifiers and repressors, the group of quislings, the group of those who

---

[126] "Third of Americans suspect 9-11 government conspiracy" (Scripps News, Aug. 1, 2006): http://www.scrippsnews.com/911poll

[127] "Was 9/11 an 'inside job'?" (*Seattle Press-Intelligencer*, Aug. 3, 2006): http://www.seattlepi.com/national/279827_conspiracy02ww.html

are *complicit* in the crimes of 9/11 by merit of hiding the truth of the crimes, the group of those who are treasonous by merit of *covering up* the known crimes of treason, and, finally, those who could be renamed the group of *explicit enemies* against the entirety of Group one, while simultaneously being *implicit* enemies of all of Group two (even though those in Group two don't *know* this, since they don't understand that those in Group 3 are liars but, if they believe anything, believe them to be truth-tellers).

And exactly who is in the contemptible Group 3? Well, Amy Goodman is in it, Frank Rich is in it, Nancy Pelosi is in it, Harry Reid is in it, John Conyers is in it, all the media people I mentioned before as choosing to be liars are in it, Adolph Giuliani is in it, Elliot Spitzer is in it, and Larry Silverstein is in it[128]—and so on.

Members of the Bush administration, members of the Houses of Congress, many members of state and local governments, and the huge numbers of people who work in the mainstream media—these are the members of Group 3. What do you suppose their actual numbers come to? How many of them do you suppose there really *are*? Well, there are one hundred in the Senate and 433 in the House for a total of 533. What shall we say for the number of people constituting the Bush administration, including cabinet members, close advisors, ambassadors, and so on? How about five hundred, for a running total now of 1,033. And how many work in the mainstream media, print, video, and radio—*including* NPR, Pacifica, and the like? Let's estimate that those working *in* or influentially *near* the editorial side of the media come to something like 25,000, including everybody from the tiniest little radio stations in the tiniest little towns, every reporter in every paper, every advisor in every station, every announcer, every editor, every columnist. If we're at all close, we've got a total now for the membership of Group 3 that comes to 26,033.

Now we've got to add every corporate owner of the media, the membership of every corporate board that *controls* the media, and every head of and influential staff in pertinent agencies from, say, the FCC on through the Motion Picture Association of America.

Let's say there are a thousand people—a well-dressed yet sleazily reptilian in-group of business slicks and their like-minded "friends" who make up among themselves the membership of all the most important corporate boards in America. That means we're up to 27,033. Let's triple—no, let's quadruple—the total just to be sure we've got everyone, including high elements of the military and of the numerous intelligence agencies. Quadrupling gives us a grand total of 108,132.

---

128 See "Insurers Agree to Pay Billions at Ground Zero," http://911blogger.com/node/8886

Now. Those hundred-thousand people—*they're* our enemies. *They're* the obvious enemies of Group 1 and, as I suggested, the enemies also of Group 2, even though Group 2 doesn't know it.

What do you think? Let's say there are 300,000,000 people in the U.S.[129] We know already that 100,000,000 of them are in Group 1 and either know, suspect, or lean toward 9/11 Truth. Even leaving Group 2 out of the argument for the moment, that suggests that 100,000,000 people are being held hostage by 108,132!

I, for one, hate being ruled by gangs. I, for one, hate being ruled by thuggery. I, for one, hate being ruled by deceit, deception, cover-up, lies, thievery, criminality, treason, and fraud. I, for one, hate the "left gatekeepers," some of whom you can see cited by Barrie Zwicker in his book, *Towers of Deception: The Media Cover-Up of 9/11*.[130]

I, for one, heartily agree with Zwicker when he writes in *Towers of Deception* (pp. 238–239) that

> Revealing the fraud of 9/11 in my opinion is the single most important task faced by civilization today. That it was dared is the... Achilles heel of the Fourth Reich. If enough people could be awakened to the enormity of the crime, and who its perpetrators are, they become a politically-relevant

---

129 See "2000 United States Census," http://en.wikipedia.org/wiki/United_States_Census,_2000

130 "A surprisingly large number of Left media outlets—most of them, in fact—have adopted the same stance on 9/11 as Chomsky's: refuse to investigate 9/11, and discourage or ridicule those who do. Most wind up using the familiar "wacky conspiracy theorists" putdown to describe others on the Left who want to discuss the evidence of an inside job on 9/11. The almost total uniformity within Left media in sync with the White House and Right media is more than puzzling. In other cases, the Left media pursue questions of malfeasance on the part of the power elites, including some conspiracies such as Iran-Contra.

"Individuals and media outlets that have exhibited this stay-away-from-9/11 stance, entirely or in large part, for more than four years now include David Corn and *The Nation*; Amy Goodman of Democracy Now!; Chip Berlet, senior analyst at Political Research Associates in Somerville, Massachusetts; David Barsamian of Alternative Radio; Michael Albert of *Z Magazine*; Alexander Cockburn; Norman Solomon; *The Progressive*; *Mother Jones*; Alternet.org; Global Exchange; PBS; South End Press; Public Research Associates; FAIR/ Extra!; *Counterspin*; *Columbia Journalism Review*; Deep Dish TV; Working Assets; Molly Ivins; *Ms Magazine*; Inter Press Service; MoveOn.org; Greg-Palast: David Zupan; Northwest Media Project....

"Of course, different people can independently or through dialogue arrive at the same or similar conclusions. But it is a startling anomaly for so many organs and leaders of the conscious Left to be seemingly unconscious regarding 9/11. More than a few on the Left share the opinion of progressive film maker Roy Harvey that "the greatest single obstacle to the spread of 9/11 Truth is the Left media." To my mind, the relationship of Chomsky and the Left Gatekeepers on 9/11 is analogous to the relationship of the White House and the 9/11 Commission. Both relationships are so tight as to invite close scrutiny. Elementary pattern recognition reveals a common agenda among these otherwise well-informed, intelligent, investigative critics of corporate greed, the power elite and US hegemony. The agenda, completely atypical of their approach generally, is to vigorously reject investigation into 9/11. This is prima facie. One example, that of perhaps Chomsky's best known protégé and amplifier, David Barsamian, is typical of 9/11 blindness on the Left." "The Left Gatekeepers," from *Towers of Deception* (New Society Publishers, 2006), pp. 218–219

constituency. Then *the possibility of a cleansing transformation would emerge.* [my emphasis] Every worthwhile initiative you can name, be it environmental, social, political or economic, would benefit from politically-relevant exposure of the Great Deception.

And with Paul Craig Roberts when he wrote a month or two ago that

Unless Congress immediately impeaches Bush and Cheney, a year from now the US could be a dictatorial police state at war with Iran.[131]

I *don't* heartily agree with Nancy Pelosi, Harry Reid, the tragically disappointing John Conyer, with Hillary Clinton or Barrack Obama or John Edwards, or with Adolph Giuliani, Elliott Spitzer, Larry Silverstein, or—one who ranks in his own variety of eminence among this company, with Frank Rich of the *New York Times.*

In 1960, in the spring semester of my freshman year, I began learning about writing, though most of the time not even *knowing* I was learning. Much later, somewhere in the 1980s, in a faculty seminar at the Graduate Center of the City University of New York, the seminar leader happened to ask me—seminar members were from all different CUNY colleges and all different disciplines, and I was there as a literary member—how I would define writing. He knew that I wrote both fiction and non-fiction, and I knew that any *good* definition of good writing would necessarily be equally applicable to both (and, I would say now, also to poetry). What I found myself telling him, not knowing before that moment that I'd already formulated the definition, possibly over the span of a couple of decades, was this:

Writing is telling the truth in a way that itself is also true.

It's a literary definition, but I told you that this was going to be a literary essay—and, besides, *all* writing should be literary writing.

Now, as we draw closer to the subject of Frank Rich himself, I would invite readers to consider what things I learned when, on Sunday, September 17, 2006—a bit over a year ago—I opened up the *Times* and found this passage in Rich's op ed piece, "The Longer the War, the Larger the Lies."[132]

You'd think that after having been caught concocting the scenario that took the nation to war in Iraq, the White House would mind the facts now. But

---

[131] "Impeach Bush And Cheney Now," Jul. 15, 2007 http://www.vdare.com/roberts/070715_impeach.htm

[132] "The Longer the War, the Larger the Lies," the New York Times, Sept. 17, 2007: http://query.nytimes.com/gst/fullpage.html?res=9902EFDB1331F934A2575AC0A9609C8B63&scp=1&sq=the%20longer%20the%20war%20the%20larger%20the%20lies&st=cse

this administration understands our culture all too well. This is a country where a cable news network (MSNBC) offers in-depth journalism about one of its anchors (Tucker Carlson) losing a prime-time dance contest and where conspiracy nuts have created a cottage industry of books and DVD's by arguing that hijacked jets did not cause 9/11 and that the 9/11 commission was a cover-up. (The fictionalized "Path to 9/11," supposedly based on the commission's report, only advanced the nuts' case.) If you're a White House stuck in a quagmire in an election year, what's the percentage in starting to tell the truth now? It's better to game the system.

Just for information's sake, I mention that the next paragraph of Rich's piece begins with this sentence, providing an excellent early example—there will be many more, in Part 2 of this essay—of Rich naming and doing the exact thing (lying) that he's simultaneously accusing others of doing: "The untruths," says he, "are flying so fast that untangling them can be a full-time job."

They sure are and it sure can. What I argued a year ago when I earlier wrote about this piece is worth going back to—and I'll do that in Part 2. For now, let's just take care of that question—of what a person *learns* from reading this one paragraph plus one more sentence of Frank Rich.

Another question as a way into the first one: Is Rich a *writer*, by our definition?

And it's impossible—isn't it?—for the answer to be anything other than "No." Is Rich telling the truth in a way that itself is also true?

No, you can't be a writer by that standard and at the same time use smear and innuendo; assert half-truths as though they were whole truths; and—at the end—twist things so as to allow yourself acquittal for doing the very thing you're condemning others for doing.

Let's pin this down. The smear and innuendo lie in the cheap and slummy phrases "conspiracy nuts," "cottage industry," and "the nuts' case." Now, just consider this fact: By September 2006, I know with absolute certainty that, at the very least, *these* books on 9/11 had been published, were in print, and were available for anyone to read (as I had); and I know also that any single one of them would reveal to a serious and open-minded reader that research into 9/11 truth is hardly the domain solely of "nut cases" but is predominantly the domain of serious, principled, dedicated, broadly experienced researchers, scholars, commentators, and historians:

> Ahmed, Nafeez Mosaddeq. *The War on Freedom: How and Why American was Attacked September 11, 2001.* (2002)[133]

---

[133] *The War on Freedom: How and Why American was Attacked September 11, 2001* (Tree of Life Publications, 2002) http://www.amazon.com/War-Freedom-America-Attacked-September/dp/0930852400/sr=1-1/qid=1167587018/ref=pd_bbs_sr_1/104-4231058-3189532?ie=UTF8&s=books

Ahmed, Nafeez Mosaddeq. *The War On Truth: 9/11, Disinformation And The Anatomy Of Terrorism.* (2005)[134]

Chossudovsky, Michel. *America's "War on Terrorism."* (2002)[135]

Griffin, David Ray. The 9/11 *Commission Report: Omissions and Distortions.* (2005)[136]

Griffin, David Ray. *The New Pearl Harbor: Disturbing Questions About the Bush Administration and 9/11.* (2004)[137]

Hicks, Sander. *The Big Wedding: 9/11, The Whistle-Blowers, and the Cover-Up.* (2005)[138]

Morgan, Rowland, and Ian Henshall. *9/11 Revealed: The Unanswered Questions* (2005)[139]

Ruppert, Michael C. *Crossing the Rubicon: The Decline of the American Empire at the End of the Age of Oil.* (2004)[140]

Tarpley, Webster Griffin. *9/11 Synthetic Terror: Made in USA.*[141]

If Rich is writing in late 2006 and is still taking cheap shots at the 9/11 truth movement with smears and half truths—if he's still doing that sort thing *in late* 2006, what does a person learn about him?

[134] *The War on Truth: 9/11, Disinformation and the Anatomy of Terrorism* (Olive Branch Press, 2005) http://www.amazon.com/War-Truth-Disinformation-Anatomy-Terrorism/dp/1566565960/sr=1-1/qid=1166125709/ref=pd_bbs_sr_1/104-4231058-189532?ie=UTF8&s=books

[135] Global Research (2005) http://www.amazon.com/Americas-War-Terrorism-Michel-Chossudovsky/dp/0973714719/sr=1-1/qid=1167594566/ref=pd_bbs_sr_1/104-4231058-3189532?ie=UTF8&s=books

[136] The Olive Branch Press (2005) http://www.amazon.com/11-Commission-Report-Omissions-Distortions/dp/1566565847/ref=sr_1_1/105-4791811-3350040?ie=UTF8&s=books&qid=1192117097&sr=1-1

[137] The Olive Branch Press (2004) http://www.amazon.com/New-Pearl-Harbor-Disturbing-Administration/dp/1566565529/sr=1-1/qid=1167586758/ref=pd_bbs_1/104-4231058-3189532?ie=UTF8&s=books

[138] Vox Pop (2005) http://www.amazon.com/Big-Wedding-Whistle-Blowers-Cover-up/dp/097527631X/ref=pd_bbs_sr_1/104-4231058-3189532?ie=UTF8&s=books&qid=1181360078&sr=1-1

[139] Carroll & Graf, New York (2005) http://www.amazon.com/9-11-Revealed-Unanswered-Questions/dp/0786716134/sr=1-1/qid=1167600574/ref=pd_bbs_sr_1/104-4231058-3189532?ie=UTF8&s=books

[140] New Society Publishers (2004) http://www.amazon.com/Crossing-Rubicon-Decline-American-Empire/dp/0865715408/sr=1-1/qid=1167586584/ref=pd_bbs_sr_1/104-4231058-3189532?ie=UTF8&s=books

[141] The Progressive Press (2005), http://www.amazon.com/11-Synthetic-Terror-Made-Fourth/dp/0930852370

Well, a person learns that he's 1) either a far greater dissembler even than he seems, since he's claiming not to know things he really does know; or that 2) he's a dismal competitor if not a mediocrity as a reporter, since he's failed totally to make contact with any or to make use of any of the most visible and essential research materials relevant to his subject; or you learn that he's 3) neither a writer of principle nor a man of principle, since he's willing to slur, smear, defame, lie, and present truth as falsehood (after all, the 9/11 commission really *was* a cover-up, in a league up there with soviet-style show trials)[142]—all because his owners *tell him* that's what he's got to do if he wants to keep his job.

What was that definition of writing—something about telling the truth in a way that itself is also true, I believe?

And here what do we have *instead* of someone fitting that definition? The actuality looks extremely grim. We're dealing with the one subject—9/11 truth—that's more than just arguably the most important matter that exists in political and cultural affairs today. Whether the free republic will become a police state within the next ten months depends on it; whether the cultural, artistic, and literary life of the nation will continue its decline into the empty and ephemeral rather than strengthening once again depends on it; whether genuine care and husbanding of the planet itself will ever actually occur depends on it; the lives of millions, and the safety from fear, disease, penury, suffering, and starvation of millions upon millions more in countries at home and abroad depend on it; and the historic grounding, the dignity, the preserving of any meager part of what may still be left of human and common good in the United States, depends on it. All of these things and more depend on the exposure of the high crimes of 9/11 and the holding accountable of those responsible for them.[143]

It seems to me that 9/11 truth is one of the most, no, is *the* most important matter in the world today. And what do we have in Frank Rich when he looks at it? Well, a year ago we had 1) a dishonest, contemptuous, smearing journalist who either *really was* totally ignorant of the truth of his subject, or 2) a person who was dissembling about something he *did* know while claiming *not* to know it, or 3) a person who was the true and *complete* lackey, performing *anything*

---

[142] See David Ray Griffin, *The 9/11 Commission Report: Omissions and Distortions* (Olive Branch Press, 2005) http://www.amazon.com/11-Commission-Report-Omissions-Distortions/dp/1566565847/ref=sr_1_1/105-4791811-3350040?ie=UTF8&s=books&qid=11 92117097&sr=1-1

[143] Update: "An American Police State was inevitable once Americans let 'their' government get away with 9/11." Paul Craig Roberts, "It Is Official: The US Is a Police State," September 25, 2010 http://www.lewrockwell.com/roberts/roberts283.html

whatsoever that his paying client, in this case the *New York Times*, asked him to do, and doing *nothing whatsoever* that that client would *not* pay for, however globally pressing, serious, or of absolute importance that other thing might be.

This is not a matter of telling the truth in a way that is also itself true.

Instead, this is—well, being struck speechless, let me leave the burden of work to you. I suggest that you choose one, none, some, or all of the following:

- *This is fraud;*

- *This is hypocrisy;*

- *This is treachery;*

- *This is the aiding and abetting of monstrous criminality;*

- *This is frivolity, depravity, a poisonous non-seriousness;*

- *This is total indifference to the welfare of the nation and its people;*

- *This is total indifference to the welfare of the world and its people;*

- *This is conscious enmity toward the nation and its people;*

- *This is a vivid example of the moral penury, the absence of conscience, and the wholesale depravity, fraud, and deceit, of the mainstream media today and of those working within it.*

•

And so we pause. Part Two is next.

Eric Larsen
October 11, 2007

12.

THE PERNICIOUS HYPOCRISY OF FRANK RICH
OF *THE NEW YORK TIMES*
PART II
OCTOBER 11, 2007

1.

After I began writing pieces attacking what Barrie Zwicker calls the "left gatekeepers," I started seeing a pattern that I was unable to attribute to anything other than some kind of self-destructive and yet also self-imposed blindness to certain vitally important aspects of plain reality—the plain reality, specifically, of 9/11 and the events surrounding it.

How and why would a person *choose* to become part of a conspiracy to deny, hide, and suppress the truth of what actually happened that day, along with the truth of *why* it happened? Why would anyone, especially a left-leaning person, actually opt to join a conspiracy that would and could function only in the service of the neoconservative criminals and traitors, those visible and those retiring in deep shadow, who over the past six years have gone forward steadily about their business of destroying the republic *and* its Constitution and of establishing by force a hegemonic control over not only the Middle East but the world?

Barry Zwicker, in the previous section of this essay, provided a generous sampling of just who some of these people are who have made the choice to cover up for the traitors.

On the subject of that list, Zwicker writes that "The almost total uniformity within Left media in sync with the White House and

Right media [on the subject of 9/11] is more than puzzling"—and the reason it's "puzzling" is because the left media, on *other* issues, "pursue questions of malfeasance on the part of the power elites" and continue doing the job that's traditionally—and importantly—the job of a free liberal press.

And so *why* the closed ranks and the great unity of silence on the lone and single subject of 9/11 truth? People can reasonably differ in opinion and view, Zwicker grants, then adds: "But it is a startling anomaly for so many organs and leaders of the conscious Left to be seemingly unconscious regarding 9/11."

What can a person conclude? What does it *mean*, this 9/11 gatekeeper-blindness "on the Left," this refusal to open up the one thing that's now of the greatest importance imaginable?

If and as the nation goes fascist; if and as the Iraq war proves to have no end—no end ever having been *intended*; if and as Iran goes under U.S. attack and the Middle East falls into chaos; if and as things such as these take place *only because* impeachment was made impossible, impeachment having been made impossible *only because* of the stonewalling from the left that buried 9/11 truth and covered up *the one weapon that the people really have and could use against the junta*—*then*, when all of *that* has happened, whose fault will it be?

Whose fault? Well, whose fault is it *so far* that the junta hasn't been braked? And *why* is it their fault? Why has the "left" media behaved in a way *so patently against the nation's best interest and even against the likelihood of its survival?*

2.

I began growing aware of the full intensity of this self-imposed blindness among left-leaners and pseudo-progressives when I started writing about Amy Goodman. I hadn't sensed it as strongly before then, not even when I wrote "Our Enemies, the Left Gatekeepers, Pt. 1," or "U.S.A.—Land of Liars," about Matthew Rothschild and Alexander Cockburn, or pieces about Nicholas Lemann or Jacob Weisberg or Arianna Huffington.

I wrote angry and bitter pieces about these figures and yet nobody responded. Silence reigned. But when I took on Amy *Goodman* as a gatekeeper, angry letters arrived from incensed readers demanding *immediately* to be dropped from my mailing list.

A typical one went like this:

While I am [a signer] ... of the 9/11 truth statement and I routinely publish articles exploring 9/11 truth, your attack on Amy Goodman and the statements you make in this email about liberals and progressives in general are toxic and destructive, and clearly desperate.

I still believe that the 9/11 commission was a coverup and [I?] even commissioned polling that showed that the majority of Democrats and over 40% of the public believe that the investigation was inadequate. But you are misguided. Please remove me from your mailing list. NOW!! And don't respond to this email either. I will label as spam any further email I receive from you.

The piece that elicited that email was something called "The Traitors in Our House," which I had turned over to two guest writers—although the piece before that one ("Does the CIA Own Amy Goodman?")[144] may have offended the writer equally.

Most interesting to me, however, was what exactly it really was that made the writer so angry. She or he referred not just to the articles about Amy Goodman but also to the May 2007 email that I'd sent out to my recipients' list as an introduction to "The Traitors In Our House." Here's that email:

Dear Readers of *A Nation Gone Blind*, Other Recipients, Writers, Thinkers, Patriots, and Friends:

I can do no more than trust and hope that everyone really does understand the reason for this series of pieces about Amy Goodman, or pieces largely about her. The reason isn't to be unfair to Amy Goodman. The reason is to analyze her work and then, if necessary and appropriate, to condemn certain aspects of her performance as a journalist. I've chosen to focus on Goodman (although in truth she's hardly alone on the little stage of this web site) partly because she's so clearly associated with the left-leaning and "progressive," partly because she's so well known, partly because she's so well trusted, partly because she's so well loved (by many), partly because she's recently turned to *writing* instead of remaining with just radio and TV—and partly because she is so quintessentially typical of numerous other erstwhile progressive or left-leaning American journalists and commentators who—known or unbeknownst to themselves—have metamorphosed since 9/11 into the greatest and most dangerous liars in the entire land outside of politicians themselves or figures in the true mass media, like, say, executives for Fox News or corporate purveyors of pop music.

Harsh to say, perhaps, but it's the result of close examination, and I believe it's true. Frank Rich, Nicholas Lemann, Matthew Rothschild, Arianna Huffington, Jacob Weisberg, et al—the list is long, demoralizing, and suggestive of a grave and extreme danger—a danger given sinister but truthful implication by Paul Craig Roberts in his recent words, "Normally, this

---

144 A title, again, that owes its origin to Carolyn Baker.

is called dictatorship." (See "The State or the People," April 2007.)[145]

In fact, Amy Goodman, Frank Rich, and the others like them are aiders and abettors in the bringing about of dictatorship to the United States. This is so because they are all liars by omission—that is, by refusing to acknowledge, credit, stand behind, or publish the truth about 9/11, they effectually both aid and permit the continuation of the guilty and as yet unaccountable Bush administration's attack not only on the Iraqi and Afghan people but also on the American people, in the last case through gutting of the Constitution and clear and evident preparing for the imposition of martial law and a police state.
[Material about my guest authors has here been deleted.]
As for the actual situation: You may not agree, but it looks to me absolutely clear that the criminals are on the loose; are in fact holding the reins of government; are as yet beyond the reach of law or accountability; and can be reined in and made accountable only through the just and proper prosecution of those—that is, themselves—who are responsible for the extraordinary crimes of 9/11.

Eric Larsen

Now, I wonder how many readers would agree that what I say here about Amy Goodman and "liberals and progressives in general" is really "toxic and destructive," let alone "desperate." Granting that it was evidently toxic indeed to the angry letter-writer, why was it so? Before getting at the answer to that question, though, let me give another example of the denial that seems to me rampant.

This is something more recent, just a week or two ago. I'd seen an essay attacking the Bush junta for its illegal war policies and calling for impeachment of Bush and Cheney. Since I admired it well enough and shared its views, I wrote the author:

10/1/2007
Hello, X. X.,

I saw your [unnamed] piece and think it's inestimably strong and good and thorough and powerful. Thank you for it. I only, only wish that more would come your way and bring about the necessary impeachment you urge. Why is there such mad resistance?

I'm working in similar veins, though usually from a more "literary" approach, but trying to expose hypocrisy in the press and media, doing it in my own small ways. Also have a book out, *A Nation Gone Blind: America in an Age of Simplification and Deceit*. I'm afraid the co-opted media have been instructed or have learned to ignore books of its kind, since notice of it has been nil.

---

[145] http://www.lewrockwell.com/roberts/roberts205.html

But may I put you on my list of people to alert when new pieces go up on my site? Here's the most recent—today—letter I've sent out. Just let me know if you want off. And may your work prosper and harvest peace and good. The times are bad.

Yours,
Eric Larsen

To my own small horror, here is what I got back:

10/07/07
Mr. Larsen,
Please forgive me for being so tardy in answering your kind email of Oct. 1 —and now here is another.

I appreciate and applaud your stance on these interlocking issues, and urge you to continue daylighting the one about which you are far better informed than I am: the facts of 9/11.

Let me implore you, however, to cease the attacks on those who fail to match your passion: the Amy Goodmans of the world and, as you know, there are a lot of doubters on the left. (Cf. Alexander Cockburn.) Internecine invective serves no one but the True Believers, those who, tragically, have fallen under the spell of the Bush intrigue.

We are all fighting the same war: the hideous presidency we endure. There are many battlefields, and none is demonstrably the only true and correct one. Yes, arguments can be made to rebut that statement, but those who make them seem to me more interested in being RIGHT than in a successful ending of the nightmare.

Please do not send me any more criticisms of people I see as effective antagonists to the Bush regime.

Am I alone in the world in thinking that the arguments in this letter and in the one preceding it are the sheerest—well, let me warble out "malarkey" in order to prevent myself from soiling the page with a truly vile or at the very least scatological term? What are these letters and others like them *saying*? I might ask the second writer—I in fact *did* ask, in a follow-up letter, one that resulted in stony silence—how he can conceivably see left-progressives like Goodman or Weisberg—or like "Frank Rich, Nicholas Lemann, Matthew Rothschild, Arianna Huffington, Jacob Weisberg, et al"—as being "effective antagonists to the Bush regime"? In what way is *any* of them being "effective"? In what way is *any* of them altering, ending, or ameliorating the course of the inhuman and wasteful wars in Iraq or Afghanistan? in helping diminish the threat of even wider wars through attack, perhaps nuclear, on Iran? in—above all—opposing a cowardly, complicit, and petrified congress in order actually to help bring about the impeachment of the Bush-Cheney junta, a Constitutional action[146] without which we're doomed, at the very best, to a repetition of Bush-Cheney "policy," including increasing domestic lockdown, for at least another eight years no matter *which* "party" may sit in the White House or hold majority control of congress?[147]

The "left-progressive" media is talking about such things, I'll immediately agree, but so help me god I can find no way under the stars, sun, or the heavens themselves that they could rightly be declared as "effective" in opposition to the junta or its ruinous, rapacious, and murderous policies. Well, maybe they are "effective antagonists," as the writer said. But only "antagonists," I would add, in the sense of flies on a cow's hide in summer—an irritation to be brushed away with a sweep of the tail.

Two points:

I. First, what is it that *really* makes left-leaners or putative left-leaners get *so* mad and *so* incensed and *so* righteous when I attack figures like Goodman? I'll tell you. It's that figures like Amy Goodman or even, say, Keith Olbermann, do *some* good things. Maybe they even do a *lot* of good things. And therefore, in this our Age of Simplification, wherein feeling has so largely replaced thinking, it's *forbidden* to attack them on the grounds that they do—or may be doing—one *extremely* bad thing. Anyone who attacks them for that one bad thing is a monster and thereby despicable, treacherous, and unfaithful to the tribe of the left-leaning.

By this logic, it seems to me, a man could do good things for forty years—no, he could do good things for *fifty* years—and then murder his perfectly innocent and nice mother-in-law by garroting her with piano wire. Since he'd done so many *good* things for fifty years, *many* more *good* things than the one *bad* thing he did, he ought to be exonerated entirely, pardoned for the murder, and go unpunished, remaining free to roam the neighborhood. After all, he's a good guy.

Yeah, right.

2. And, second, what *is* the *one* bad thing that Amy Goodman and her left-leaning media colleagues are doing? Answer: They're ignoring, denying, suppressing, minimizing, or covering up the truth of 9/11.

---

[146] See Article II of the United States Constitution: http://topics.law.cornell.edu/constitution/articleii

[147] Update: I am genuinely, even grievously, sorrowful and regretful to have been right in this forecast. Clear to all by now is that Obama is merely George W. Bush with brains and a great voice—but with not a whit more room to maneuver under the lockstep tyranny imposed upon him by his own Bankster and Bushiscti masters.

Pardon me for a moment, but I think I hear distant roars and incensed shouts of disapproval coming from wherever it is that the tribe of putative left-leaning reporters, commentators, broadcasters, columnists, analysts, writers, and audience members are gathered. In fact, I believe that they're *outraged*. They're shrieking and yelling at me to the effect that I *can't say what I just said*, and the reason I can't is that it's *up to each person* what they choose or don't choose to cover or investigate or write about or analyze. It's their *right* to write about what they want to write about. It's only a matter of *opinion* if I think they should cover one subject or another, and one person's opinion is equal to *another* person's opinion, and *that's that.*

Okay, say I. Listen up. It's *all right* to be a news reporter, writer, investigator, or correspondent in 1944, based, perhaps, in London. It's *all right* to investigate and report on what kinds of art Hitler did or didn't allow or approve. It's *all right* to investigate, to follow up on rumors about, and to report on Hitler's quite kinky sexual habits and tastes. It's *all right* to look as closely as possible at his uses of and attitudes toward summary execution by rifle fire for whatever *he* may see as cowardice in the field of battle. It's *all right* to report on his obvious military error in wildly over-extending Germany's military forces by sending them into Russia with the idea of seizing the oil fields east of Stalingrad and beyond the Volga.[148]

And it's okay, too, if you don't *feel* like it, or if in your *opinion* it isn't important—it's okay, too, not to follow up on the increasing numbers of rumors and bits of not-yet-validated information that come your way about the existence of death camps in the eastern regions of Germany, in Poland, and in Austria, camps where it's rumored that millions upon millions of people are being held in slavery, worked almost to death, and *then* gassed and incinerated. And it's *okay*, too, because it's your *opinion* as to whether a lead is worth pursuing or not, and you have a *right* to your opinion, it's all *right* if you decide not to take a reportorial or investigative lick at the awful rumors—let's say it's now the summer of 1944—that hundreds and hundreds of thousands of people are being seized from their homes, put on trains, and taken straight to mass execution sites where they are shot en masse and then dumped into and incinerated by the thousands at a time in gargantuan and newly-designed furnaces.

It's okay if you just don't feel like investigating or reporting on *that* story. It's okay, in fact, if you *sit* on it, *deny* it, *suppress* it.

Ditto 9/11. It's *okay* if you *skip* that one. After all, when you're a professional left-leaning journalist, it's your *opinion* that matters

---

[148] See the extraordinary book by Anthony Beevor, *Stalingrad: The Fateful Siege*, 1942–1943. (Penguin, 1998).

most, not enormous amounts of *evidence*, say, that a society-changing, war-causing, republic-crushing, humanity-destroying, international policy-altering atrocity has taken place.

3.

And so we come at last to possibly the greatest and most visible 9/11-denying figure in the entire tribe of putatively progressive and left-leaning media workers—Frank Rich, of the *New York Times.*

I'm becoming nearly consumed by the feeling of regret that I ever wrote *A Nation Gone Blind.* If I'd known how *monstrously true* the arguments in it were, I wonder if I still would have proceeded with it, or would have dared to. And if I'd known that what the book said—that Americans can't any longer see reality for themselves—was going to be true also in regard to 9/11 truth and thus true also in regard to the ongoing, treasonous, murderous, and rapacious successes one after another of the Bush-Cheney junta: Could I then have gone on writing the damn thing?

I don't know. But I do know that Frank Rich—who may indeed be fully able to see reality for himself—seems to me the greatest and most successful dissembler and con-artist out of all of the tainted 9/11 suppressors in all of the tribes of all the putatively progressive and left-leaning journalists in all of the land.

What do people *think* when they think about Frank Rich? How do people read when they *read* Frank Rich? How can they read Frank Rich without, much too often, being *just revolted?*

Well, I suppose one reason they can do it is that they have poor memories, or at least memories that aren't incessantly on high alert to 9/11 subjects, references, or smears. You see, one of *my* problems with Frank Rich is that I can't forget the genuinely awful piece he wrote back in 2006, a piece I referred to in Part One of this essay and said I'd return to again here. The date was September 17 and the piece was "The Longer the War, the Larger the Lies,"[149] a title that prestidigitator Rich proves, before the eyes of his own easily-tricked readers, to be true not only of his own putative targets but also of *himself.*

I won't cite Rich's third paragraph here again, since I did so in Part 1 of this essay, and any who may not have read it can return there to do so. I will, however, cite again the highly ironic sentence that Rich places after his article's third paragraph:

---

[149] See it at: http://query.nytimes.com/gst/fullpage.html?res=9902EFDB1331F934A2575
AC0A9609C8B63&scp=1&sq=the%20longer%20the%20war%20the%20larger%20the%20
lies&st=cse

"The untruths," says Rich, "are flying so fast that untangling them can be a full-time job."

The gratuitous condescension *toward* and the facile smears *of* the 9/11 truth movement in Rich's third paragraph—and the ignoring of the often towering scholarship that in fact drives[150] the truth movement—obviously and clearly mark Rich as a leading member of the great tribe of deceivers. The arrogance is akin to the arrogance of the Bill O'Reilly-esque right-wingers in that it's as though Rich is *daring* us to take his slummy, cheap, worn and putrid bait—"conspiracy nuts," "cottage industry," "the nuts' case"—and swallow it whole.

The truth is that Rich, like Amy Goodman, could simply have gone on forever covering up 9/11 truth simply by never mentioning it and by not talking about it. But that wouldn't be good enough. There wouldn't be any sport in that. Instead, Rich does a "look-Ma-no-hands" job of powerfully signaling his disdain and contempt *for* 9/11 truth with a dog-that's-just-peed air of pride.

And thus we found ourselves alerted to the position of Rich and of the *Times*. Any reader of "The Longer the War, the Larger the Lies" who happened also to be a follower of the extensive writing and scholarship on 9/11 truth, knew immediately that Frank Rich, having *so* publicly and *so* smugly declared himself such, was an enemy—of the truth, of the republic, and of the people *of* that republic.

Something else he did—by writing the ambiguity that "The untruths are flying so fast that untangling them can be a full-time job"— intentionally or not I don't know, had the same effect of his waving a flag, visible to many, invisible to many more, that revealed *himself* to be not a frequent flier but a frequent liar.

Very frequent, I might add. Anyone who follows Rich's ever-snide and ever-entertaining work in the *Times* knows that even when he's just plain telling the truth about one thing or another, he's superbly cocky and condescending—in a way that seems to say to readers, "here's my arm around your shoulder; come on in as a privileged friend and join me in my salon, in this wonderful dinner-party of superiority-and-scorn."

No one I know does it better than Frank Rich. And *that's* when he's telling the truth. But when he sits down at the keyboard to play "The Hypocrisy Rag," he becomes positively a weasel: Deplorable, conscienceless, destructive.

And, there's no question but that I must add, *successful*. The best in the business.

---

[150] Or should drive it. See again the penetrating, accurate, crushing, and invaluable piece by Emanuel Sferios, "Five Years Later: What Have We Accomplished? An Assessment of the 9/11 Truth Movement" (Sept. 11, 2006), available at: http://pilotsfor911truth.org/forum/index.php?showtopic=1191

•

For an example of Rich as truth-teller, a look at his scorn-filled piece on Clarence Thomas, "Nobody Knows the Lynchings He's Seen,"[151] will suffice perfectly—as will his most recent piece, of this October 21, on the shameful and endemic corruption in the Iraq war (including the absolutely wrenching 2005 death of Col. Ted Westhusing),[152] "Suicide Is Not Painless."[153]

In the much differently-toned Clarence Thomas piece, however, a person could almost think, "Poor Clarence Thomas, exposed to such barbs and slings, such silver-tongued scorn"—but the fact is that Thomas is getting the *truth*, whatever the dish it's delivered in, and deservedly so, as I suspect most readers would agree.

But for the *other* Frank Rich, the one I can't help but call the weasel Frank Rich, let's hop back, say, to an example from May 6, 2007, called "Is Condi Hiding the Smoking Gun?"[154] The subject is the question of who bears responsibility for the Iraq War. Herewith, our first example of the weasel at work:

> The only White House figure to take any responsibility for the fiasco is the former Bush-Cheney pollster Matthew Dowd,[155] who in March expressed remorse for furthering a war he now deems a mistake. For his belated act of conscience, he was promptly patronized as an incipient basket case by an administration flack, who attributed Mr. Dowd's defection to "personal turmoil." If that is what this vicious gang would do to a pollster, imagine what would befall Colin Powell if he spoke out. Nonetheless, Mr. Powell should summon the guts to do so. Until there is accountability for the major architects and perpetrators of the Iraq war, the quagmire will deepen. A tragedy of this scale demands a full accounting, not to mention a catharsis.

Rich once again proves his bona fides as a faithful member of the Amy Goodman-esque "left-leaning progressive" tribe. He does this through phrases like "this vicious gang" for the Bush administration and "the fiasco" for the Iraq war. Meanwhile, "administration flack" offers an allusion to the conventional red herring in the mainstream

---

[151] *The New York Times*, October 7, 2007: http://www.nytimes.com/2007/10/07/opinion/07rich.html?_r=2

[152] See http://www.johntreed.com/Westhusing.html

[153] *The New York Times*, October 21, 2007: http://www.nytimes.com/2007/10/21/opinion/21rich.html?_r=1&ref=opinion

[154] *The New York Times*, May 6, 2007: http://select.nytimes.com/2007/05/06/opinion/06rich.html?pagewanted=print

[155] *The New York Times*, April 1, 2007: http://www.nytimes.com/2007/04/01/washington/01adviser.html

media that "incompetence" is really what's the trouble with "this vicious gang." If you're troubled by the question of how "incompetence" can be the catalyst that creates a "vicious" gang, it's better not to worry about it. When Rich is in weasel-mode, it doesn't pay to concern yourself with this kind of contradiction, since its real purpose is to keep you distracted from the fact that what you're getting isn't the real truth. Are these guys Abbott and Costello bunglers, or are they vicious criminals? You're not going to find the answer in Rich's weasel-mode, though you could *easily* find it in, say, this unusual interview[156] with the peerless, dedicated, and indefatigably patriotic Francis A. Boyle, or in this powerful essay by a simple, actual, everyday American[157] who, unlike Rich, speaks plain English instead of "CorpoMedia," the language that's spoken by those in all the mainstream media—that is, in the corpo-tribes—a language that leaks its way into Frank Rich's columns only too often, where it serves him well by allowing him to *seem* to be telling the truth while *not* telling the truth.

Example:

> Until there is accountability for the major architects and perpetrators of the Iraq war, the quagmire will deepen. A tragedy of this scale demands a full accounting, not to mention a catharsis.

This is grand language, but more is left out of it than is put in. If a person asks just *how* "accountability" for a "tragedy of this scale" will be brought about, he or she comes up empty. Who *are* "the major architects and perpetrators" of the war whose accountability alone can keep the "quagmire" from "deepening"? The grandeur continues with "tragedy," "demands," "full accounting," and "catharsis," a word (Rich *is* the best in the business) neatly echoing "tragedy."

But back to getting *answers*. When Rich is in weasel-mode, the question isn't only *what* the columnist is thinking, but it's also *where* he is thinking. For example, looking "for the major architects and perpetrators of the Iraq war," he turns to—*well*, to Condi Rice, whose appearance "on three Sunday shows. . . raised more questions than they answered." Poor Condi. As *she* takes the heat—sort of—I'm interested in asking the question of where Frank Rich *isn't* looking for the "major architects and perpetrators." If he's serious, after all, he has to look where he's *not* looking and where he *will not* look— and that's at 9/11.

---

156 *The Alex Jones Program,* Oct. 17, 2007: http://www.ericlarsen.net/FOOD%20FOR%20 THOUGHT%2013.2.3.2007.pdf

157 Rand Clifford, "Mud, Fog, and Blackwater," in *Countercurrents,* Oct. 11, 2007: http:// www.countercurrents.org/clifford111007.htm

Or even before 9/11. It's interesting to take a look at this video,[158] where Ron Suskind and Secretary of the Treasury Paul O'Neill show clearly that the Iraq project was under way at least *eight months before* 9/11. So why won't Frank Rich look *there?* Why won't he look back in 2000, or even *before* 2000?[159]

Who might Rich turn up as the "major architects and perpetrators" if he were to look back *there?* Or if he were to look *at* 9/11, and not just look *at* it but look at the *truth* of it? That, however, *will not* happen. One is reminded—yes—of Amy Goodman, who, in Carolyn Baker's words, "will not, absolutely will *not*, deal with 9/11."[160] It looks to me as though a parallel statement can convincingly be made about Frank Rich.

And so the question becomes this: Is Rich *really* looking for the "major architects and perpetrators"? Does he really think that "A tragedy of this scale demands a full accounting"? Does he really want, and is he really pushing to bring about, a "catharsis"?

Or—making good use of weasel-mode—is he just saying so? Is he just making it look that way for certain reasons of his own, like, say, protecting his image as a "liberal"?

Big questions, true, and maybe even seemingly nasty ones, and yet, to my own way of thinking, extraordinarily important ones. In any case, let's hypothesize that what we're seeing here is not true and authentic writing, but weasel-writing. That is, let's hypothesize that we're reading a passage where one liar by omission and master of cover-up and suppression uses a stern and righteous voice to castigate another liar and suppressor of the very same kind.

Let's do that and see what happens.

Thus Ms. Rice was dispatched to three Sunday shows last weekend to bat away Mr. Tenet's book before "60 Minutes" broadcast its interview with

---

[158] The video was so revealing that if you go now to its URL—http://www.youtube.com/index?ytsession=rpFS-gtiPXvlTygazqv6ddw3ulPSu4upgjZv8WQpNEWtC6WS3jnu-JZ5iFzuppOBkMpgZiG7eleq1azwGzjn5UkcxAIYo7ClnxKxsvZvsWpdjMPGBGzXUm-kvcRkDoJioHVeWihjo8d1mqY2JFIDrHiYslbXBiqV9_gVbn5ChtYNR9w7SErL7Kzt-FyLn-BQaZ9A9RJ7nsH_mOb4DAdT3_TZa9-fl_TFUM-Wcp43Nhb-DjFAVZn0tVmbvHeix78Vn XbB_4A0D9Ev4QcCiXt7WlTmnbNkSXjEb8weC7GVp1BGLQzQRBtG_5la5DSj4wqDtH 0XSCst6yhpE32OhxnGzY8moNcaye6Qlpn2NIocsZ67vmz6w3cOetew — you will find the message that "This video has been removed due to terms of use violation."

[159] Rich might, for example, have looked at the web site of the Project for the New American Century— http://www.newamericancentury.org/ At the time he was writing, in 2007, he could still have found there what has since been removed, the famous position paper entitled "Rebuilding America's Defenses." It's in that paper that the equally famous sentence appeared, declaring that "the process of transformation [of the U.S. to a degree of military preparedness suitable for its new aims], even if it brings revolutionary change, is likely to be a long one, absent some catastrophic and catalyzing event—like a new Pearl Harbor." Read about it here: http://en.wikipedia.org/wiki/Project_for_the_New_American_Century#Rebuilding_America.27s_Defenses.

[160] Baker's words are still available at http://www.fromthewilderness.com/free/ww3/011306_empress_clothes.shtml

him that night.[161] But in each appearance her statements raised more questions than they answered. She was persistently at odds with the record, not just the record as spun by Mr. Tenet but also the public record. She must be held to a higher standard—a k a the truth—before she too jumps ship.

The rolling timbre and cadence are astonishing—"higher standard," "the truth"—as the hypocrisy of one dissembler castigating another for the identical sin rises to high melodrama, righteous dissembler number one raising still higher his voice of the good, the right, and the true as he comes nearer the moment when his spear-tip will pierce the very heart of Condi, dissembler number two:

> Ms. Rice's latest canard wasn't an improvisation; it was a scripted set-up for the president's outrageous statement three days later. "The decision we face in Iraq," Mr. Bush said Wednesday, "is not whether we ought to take sides in a civil war, it's whether we stay in the fight against the same international terrorist network that attacked us on 9/11." Such statements about the present in Iraq are no less deceptive—and no less damaging to our national interest—than the lies about uranium and Qaeda-9/11 connections told in 2002-3. This country needs facts, not fiction, to make its decisions about the endgame of the war, just as it needed (but didn't get) facts when we went to war in the first place. To settle for less is to make the same tragic error twice.

So 9/11, mentioned in passing, remains buried under drifts of corpo-media lies, distortions, smears, omissions—while Adjutant to the Liar-in-Chief, in the very act of making up his own fictions, dares to say that "This country needs facts, not fiction," and that "To settle for less is to make the same tragic error twice."

The hypocrisy shines as bright as the gleaming armor of Satan preening in Heaven.

4.

And on it goes. To secure himself a place in the hearts of his "liberal" audience, Rich gives every impression of outrage at the "vicious" Bush-Cheney administration and its dread policies—and at the same time he hides and denies and suppresses and smears the one true and certain thing that could in actuality be brought forth—into impeachment and into court—in order to dismantle, disassemble, and replace the junta he claims so much to despise. The gorge rises again and again for any careful reader of Frank Rich. Take "Don't Laugh at Michael

---

[161] Watch the interview here: http://www.cbsnews.com/stories/2007/04/25/60minutes/main2728375.shtml

Chertoff," from July 15, 2007,[162] and ask yourself what other person besides Bush these words are *most* perfectly applicable to:

This president is never one to let facts get in the way of a political agenda.

Or look at a *combination* of Richian methods, places where the master puts the lie of omission *together* with its equally putrid twin, the lie of *com*mission. A quick trip back to August 12, 2007, and "Shuffling Off to Crawford, 2007 Edition"[163] will give us a look. The subject? This time it's the junta's shameless way of spinning false or pitiable or shocking things—the Jessica Lynch fraud-circus, the Pat Tillman murder, the Daniel Pearl beheading—in order to exploit them for publicity or propaganda benefiting the junta itself.

A good subject. In fact, a great subject—a subject with a *very, very* great deal of power and potential leverage in it for doing real damage to a treasonous and criminal administration that has already killed more than a million people[164] outright in *this* Iraq war, stands to kill many millions more if only through having used and continuing to use depleted uranium in munitions, and, domestically, has lost one entire American city, has cut down whole swaths of previously guaranteed Constitutional rights, from the right to habeas corpus to the right to be free from torture to the right "of the people to be secure in their persons, houses, papers, and effects, against unreasonable searches and seizures."[165]

And more. And potentially worse.[166]

So what exactly will the master do with the subject? First, as usual, he'll condemn the junta as shameless and vile, thereby snuggling up good and tight with his ostensibly left-leaning readership:

But nothing is out of bounds for a government that puts the darkest arts of politics and public relations above even the exigencies of war.

And then? Well, and then he'll behave in precisely the same way as the "vicious gang" he claims to be attacking. That is, he'll lie by

---

[162] http://select.nytimes.com/2007/07/15/opinion/15rich.html?_r=1&n=Top/Reference/Times%20Topics/People/C/Chertoff,%20Michael&oref=slogin
[163] "Shuffling Off to Crawford, 2007 Edition" (Aug. 12, 007) http://select.nytimes.com/2007/08/12/opinion/12rich.html
[164] As reported at the time of writing in the heading of *Information Clearing House*: http://www.informationclearinghouse.info/index.html
[165] Update: For the current state of Fourth Amendment protections, see "F.B.I. Searches Antiwar Activists' Homes" in the *New York Times* of September 25, 2010: http://www.nytimes.com/2010/09/25/us/politics/25search.html?scp=1&sq=F.B.I.%20Searches%20Antiwar%20Activists'%20Homes&st=cse Also see Paul Craig Roberts' response to the "searches" in his "It Is Official: The US is a Police State" http://www.lewrockwell.com/roberts/roberts283.html
[166] See Peter Dale Scott, "Homeland Security Contracts for Vast New Detention Camps" (Feb. 8, 2006) http://news.pacificnews.org/news/view_article.html?article_id=eed74d9d44c30493706fe03f4c9b3a77

commission and he'll do so for the same purpose that 9/11 itself was created—for the purpose of *frightening* people:

> Now that the administration is winding down and the Qaeda threat is at its scariest since 2001, one might hope that such [publicity and propaganda] stunts would cease. Indeed, two of the White House's most accomplished artificial-reality Imagineers both left their jobs last month...

The lie of *commission* is the part about "the Qaeda threat," whereby Rich casually drops a piece of the very propaganda he claims so strenuously to oppose. The lies of *omission* are the leaving out of the actual and simple truth that "the Qaeda," to use Rich's two-language coinage, itself a creation of the United States,[167] is *not* "at its scariest since 2001," *nor* was al Qaeda, as Rich yet again implies, either the propellant or the executor of 9/11.

What does it matter? Propounding these lies, both kinds, is the *purpose* of the column, just as the purpose of it is, as shown before, to imitate the enemy's practices while simultaneously condemning the enemy's practices. And so, here again, after approving of the departure of one of the junta's propaganda agents, Rich writes:

> But while Mr. Feaver and his doomed effort to substitute propaganda for action may now be gone, the White House's public relations strategies for the war, far from waning, are again gathering steam, to America's peril.

Chalk up another point for the Bushiscti, who also want us scared and want us to stay scared. Now, exactly why the *Weasel* should want us to remain in this same condition, terrorized and in "peril," is a question that will lead us to the very darkest recesses of Weaseldom and to a consideration of what the *fuel* is that actually makes Weaseldom continue on its road of double agency, faultless hypocrisy, and impeccably skilled prevarication—so that, in the end, the weasel-writer writes for and serves not we the *people* but *them* the Bushiscti, however deluded and misled on this point Weasel's poor audience of would-be liberals who can't *read* very well may be.

The Bushisctis' war policies do put us in peril, though less certain is that we're equally endangered by the Bushisctis' "public relations strategies for the war." Either way, if anyone can come up with a convincing—repeat, convincing—argument that the Weasel is any less interested in scaring *his* audience than the Bushiscti are in scaring *theirs*, I hope that person will let me know about it. To wit, the

---

167 Again, see Peter Dale Scott, *The Road to 9/11: Wealth, Empire, and the Future of America* (The University of California Press, 2007) http://www.amazon.com/Road-11-Wealth-Empire-America/dp/0520237730/ref=pd_bbs_sr_1/105-4791811-3350040?ie=UTF8&s=books&qid=1191764020&sr=1-1

closing lines of "Shuffling Off to Crawford," replete with frightening lie upon frightening lie, as in "remains determined to strike in America" or "The enemy that did attack us six years ago" or "is likely to persist in its nasty habit," all sweetened with one perfect spoonful of hypocrisy-honey in the slam at "White House fictions," as if we ourselves, here, weren't reading virtually a *festival* of fictions:

> And so the president, firm in his resolve against "Al Qaeda in Iraq," heads toward another August break in Crawford while Al Qaeda in Pakistan and Afghanistan remains determined to strike in America. No one can doubt Mr. Bush's triumph in the P.R. war: There are more American troops than ever mired in Iraq, sent there by a fresh round of White House fictions. And the real war? The enemy that did attack us six years ago, sad to say, is likely to persist in its nasty habit of operating in the reality-based world that our president disdains.

•

A steady diet of scare-mongering and deceit, then, all under the perfected disguise of a pious anti-Bushiscti stance presumed to be in keeping with what his left-leaning "base" expects and wants. *Presumed* to be in keeping. Hypocrisy on this level and hypocrisy sustained *at* this level, however genius-driven, can be the work only of the truly prostituted and/or, in this case, the truly corrupted. If the *New York Times* suddenly weren't interested above all other things on earth in keeping the truth of 9/11 a buried secret so as to permit the Bushiscti to continue its projects, would Rich then, too, suddenly be similarly uninterested? Would his professionalism as a lackey allow him— quick as a snap of the fingers—to turn so readily *away* from servicing the Bushiscti-*Times* and the *Times*-Bushiscti and *toward* serving, say, the Constitution of the United States?

We may never know. For now, certainly, The Weasel-and-Disguise-Artist par excellence is just what the *Times*-doctor ordered, as, week after week, the pandering to the White House *and* the pandering-by-deceit to the "base" goes on while that not-very-good-at-reading base lap it all up as kittens would milk. Take September 16, 2007, for example, and Rich's riffs on the General Petraeus dust-up ("Will the Democrats Betray Us?")[168]

How does it go? Well, again, first come the lies in service of terror—in the service, that is, of causing *our* terror, produced by *our* terrorizers: "On the sixth anniversary of the day that did not change everything, General Petraeus couldn't say we are safer because he knows we are not."

---

[168] Sept. 16, 2007: http://www.truth-out.org/article/frank-rich-will-democrats-betray-us

The day that "did *not* change everything"? Let it go. More important is the bit about General Petraeus not saying we're safer "because he knows we are not." *Does* he know we're not? Says *who*? The truth is that the general, as Rich himself knows full well because he just *quoted* it, said something quite different. What Petraeus actually said was, as quoted by Rich and as cited in the *Washington Post*, "Sir, I don't know, actually,"[169] hardly the same thing as "we are not." But then again, Rich's purpose, like the *Times*'s, is to scare us and to *keep* us scared, to make us ignorant and to *keep* us ignorant.

And then, after the scare tactic hors d'oeuvres come the varied main dishes of falsehoods and hypocrisies. Of the varying proposals regarding time-plans for and levels of troop withdrawal, Rich pulls a swifty by saying that

> Every one of these plans is academic anyway as long as Mr. Bush has a veto pen.

And how might that veto pen be taken away from the Fascistic Boy? Well, a bit of truth-telling about 9/11 and the administration's deep complicity in it would go quite a distance toward effecting that pen-snatch. But truth-telling isn't on Rich's agenda any more than it's on his own string-pullers' agenda. And his string-pullers' agenda *is* the Weasel's agenda, delivered in sanctimonious hypocrisy-gravy ladled over more dishes of falsehoods and dissemblings. The next masterpiece of Richian phrases:

> The security of America is more important—dare one say it?—than trying to outpander one another in Iowa and New Hampshire.

And if the security of America really *is* important—at *all* important—what do you say we do something *about* it? But no, no, no—*that's* not our purpose. Our purpose is to keep the neocon fascist movement *going*, in obedience to the *Times*'s corpo-owners, while at the same time keeping that particular and absolutely shameful—treasonable—truth hidden from the paper's "base." Let those with delicate stomachs not read this, our last, citation of the sheerest hypocrisy from the Weasel's Petraeus piece:

> Our national security can't be held hostage indefinitely to a president's narcissistic need to compound his errors rather than admit them.

•

---

169 See "Officials Cite Long-Term Need for U.S. in Iraq," the New York Times, Sept. 12, 2007: http://www.nytimes.com/2007/09/12/washington/12policy.html

The worst is still to come, I'm afraid, and it's deserving of lengthier treatment than it's going to get here. I tire and weaken under the assault of so *much* deceit, hypocrisy, duplicity, *complicity*, and treachery. Rich goes for the jackpot with the recent (October 14, 2007) column titled "The 'Good Germans' Among Us."[170]

It's about torture, about the war in Iraq, about the lies that made the war in Iraq possible, and about "our" guilt in not having—like the good Germans who failed similarly—opposed the Bush-Cheney administration in its war-mongering.

The opening sentence:

> "Bush lies" doesn't cut it anymore. It's time to confront the darker reality that we are lying to ourselves.

You might *hope* that that's *really* a confession and that it's therefore going to lead to some real, actual truth. But you'll hope in vain. Once again, Rich hides behind every trick in his satanic playbook of deceits and dodges.

The fear, terror, anxiety are again dished out in big heaps as Rich notes that

> [as] Andrew Sullivan, once a Bush cheerleader, observed last weekend in The Sunday Times of London, America's "enhanced interrogation" techniques have a grotesque provenance: "Verschärfte Vernehmung, enhanced or intensified interrogation, was the exact term innovated by the Gestapo to describe what became known as the 'third degree.' It left no marks. It included hypothermia, stress positions and long-time sleep deprivation."

There's terror for you. We've *become* the Fourth Reich, and certain old schoolroom words have nothing in them but a searing, grotesque sense of loss—*"My country, 'tis of thee, sweet land of liberty, of thee I sing."*

Yes, but what *I* want to know—and *do* know, in good part—is how our country degenerated into its disgusting, repellant, criminal state. And how it can be raised up again *out* of that state.

Am I going to find out such things from Frank Rich? No. What's going to happen is this: 1) he's going to scare me; 2) he's going to blame me; 3) he's going to ignore the *one truth* that could uninstall the neocons—or that *could have* uninstalled them; 4) he's going to red herring us by dwelling on a *secondary* subject—the war—in order to hide the *primary* and potentially war-*ending* subject of 9/11, the root and origin (in logistical terms) of all the cancers that have followed;

---

170 "The 'Good Germans' Among Us" (Oct. 14, 2007):http://query.nytimes.com/gst/fullpage. html?res=940DE7DF163EF937A25753C1A9619C8B63

5) he's going to pile one piety onto another, one hypocrisy onto another, until the reader—that reader who *can read*—is sickened unto death; and 6) then, that damage all done, the status quo once again assured, and the utterly fraudulent mask of Rich as an anti-Bush left-leaner and "liberal" once more glued firmly in place, he will 7) take his repulsive, sanctimonious, and hypocritical leave.

Do you want to watch some of this little drama of awful ugliness? Well, here's a bit of purest comedy:

> Call me cynical, but when Laura Bush spoke up last week[171] about the human rights atrocities in Burma, it seemed less an act of selfless humanitarianism than another administration maneuver to change the subject from its own abuses.

Hilarious! After all, who on planet Earth would *ever* think of calling Frank Rich cynical? The very thought is an impossibility! If this really were theater—well, obviously it *is* theater, every bit of it, but it if were performed *in* a theater—the audience at this point would be out of their seats and rolling in the you-know-what.

That's where *I* am, but as I laugh and roll, I'm also sobbing bitter tears, not to mention gasping in despair, shame, and revulsion.

The shame, the shame, the shame. Shame at Bush, at Cheney, at Abu Ghraib, shame at *being* an American, shame at *being* a nation of torturers, mass murderers, liars, criminals, and hypocrites.

Shame at being unable to *use the truth* against the enemies and traitors now ruling us. And anger at the lying media that, so far, have made *using* that truth to restore both freedom and republic *an impossibility*. So massive is their lying, so unified, so base, and so groveling is their submission to the corpo-fascist ownership and "leader"-ship, that truth has all but drained out of the nation like the blood out of Caesar's body, so that only lies remain, lies like the maggots inside the corpse, lies that will hatch out into the swarms of more and greater lies, bringing more death, more loss, more despair, more putrescence, more evil, breeding on through the generations.

"We asked few questions" in the run-up to the Iraq war intones the Weasel, and I say to him, "*We*? Speak for *yourself*, Weasel, don't speak for *me*."

"It was always the White House's plan to coax us into a blissful ignorance about the war," intones the Weasel, and I ask of him, "And exactly *who* 'always had a plan to coax us into a blissful ignorance' about 9/11—*eh*, Weasel?"

---

171 See "Laura Bush: Burma has 'days' to act," *USA Today*, Oct. 9, 2007: "First lady Laura Bush said Tuesday that her husband's administration is prepared to slap additional sanctions on Burma's military government if it does not start moving toward democracy 'within the next couple of days.'" http://www.usatoday.com/news/washington/2007-10-09-laura-bush_N.htm

"Our humanity has been compromised by those who use Gestapo tactics in our war," intones the Weasel, and I ask of him, "Oh, so our humanity has been *compromised*, has it, by our becoming a torture-state, a Gestapo-state? Well my, my, that's certainly tragic and appalling. But isn't there something we could *do* about this dehumanization of our state, Weasel? Isn't there some means toward a *remedy*, Weasel? *Weasel?* Couldn't we all agree to tell not just the truth but also *the whole truth?* What do you say to *that*, Weasel? *Weasel?*"

Into the silence the Weasel, himself the best German of all, intones, "It's up to us to wake up our somnambulant Congress to challenge administration policy every day. Let the war's last supporters filibuster all night if they want to. There is nothing left to lose except whatever remains of our country's good name." And I say to the Weasel, "Oh, it's up to *us*, you say?" And who, exactly, is this *us*, Weasel? Are *you* part of this *us*? And so what exactly are *we* going to do, Weasel? Do you think *we're* going to try telling the *truth?*

"Are *you* going to wake up our somnambulant Congress to challenge administration policy every day,' Weasel? I haven't *seen* you doing that. I haven't *heard* you doing that. I haven't *read* you doing that. *Are* you going to do that, Weasel? Or are you just going to go on as usual, dissembling, prevaricating, *dodging?*

"And let's go a little bit further. Is the truth really that the Congress is *'somnambulant'?* Is that the *right word? Why* has no one in Congress opposed the junta, *why* have they passed one piece of legislation after another *giving away* to the junta ever wider powers of tyranny and oppression, ever easier means of committing the most brutal crimes against humanity? *Why* have they done this, capitulated so whole-heartedly? *Why* have they done nothing to *prevent* this? Is it *really* because they're *sleep-walking*, Weasel?

"No, it's not because they're 'somnambulant,' *is* it. I *know* that you know that that's not it, and you also know that I know, don't you? It's not because they're somnambulant, but it's because they've been craven for so long, they've been *bought* for so long—like *you*, Weasel—that at first they were powerless to oppose their *corpo-owners*, and then, after the stupendous crime and fraud of 9/11, they quickly became too terrified to speak the truth, say the truth, or vote for the truth for fear that the same thing would happen to them—in one terrible variant or another—that had already happened to the three thousand. They were, in a word, terrorized, and so they voted for Patriot Act I and Patriot Act II, foolish, blind, insane votes all in the grip of a fear that had been created by a *fictional* attack that was blamed on a *fictional* enemy so that a very real albeit grotesquely criminal war could then be started *against* that fictional enemy. And then—*don't* you think this is the way it went, Weasel? *Weasel?* Pay *attention*, Weasel!—then the 'somnambulant' Congress found even further that it too had been caught, trapped, and enclosed, *imprisoned* all the further by the very pieces of legislation that it itself, in stupidity, terror, and blindness, had passed—and so now they're *not* sleep-walking, Weasel, but they're exactly where they've been put not only by the likes of themselves but by the likes of *you*, who have refused again and again to speak, say, or write the truth about *who* is accountable for *what* and *who* is guilty of *what*, so that now the same laws that brought about the torture and fake trial and conviction to life imprisonment of an absolutely and incontrovertibly innocent *American citizen*[172] can be used to bring about the torture and fake trial and conviction to life imprisonment, or worse, of anyone in the entire nation that the junta chooses to so punish, *including* members of Congress[173] if they—just perhaps—happen to vote against the junta or stand in the way of the junta, or expose the ugly, withering, truth about the junta, so that they keep their mouths shut, terrified, hoping against hope that time will pass and something different will come about, something that will save them from being murdered on the one hand or that will absolve them of their blood-guilt on the other, a blood-guilt like *yours*, Weasel, for failing to have told the truth when it still *could* have been told, for failing to tell the truth instead of joining the craven members of the house and the senate and choosing, as they chose to serve the junta, to serve your criminal corpo-masters who in turn serve the junta, with the result that you, like Congress and like your corpo-masters, are drenched in blood-guilt for betrayal of the republic, for betrayal of its people, and for the betrayal of and the murder and the suffering of millions across the world, these being the fruits of your having agreed to lie, to live in lying, and to live by lying.

"These crimes are grave crimes, Weasel, these crimes are enormous crimes, and many others are guilty of them as *you* are guilty of them, your colleagues in conspiracy and cover-up and crime like Jacob Weisberg and Amy Goodman and David Corn and Nicholas Lemann and Christopher Hayes and Alexander Cockburn and Norman Solomon and Matthew Rothschild and Greg Palast and the hundreds and hundreds and hundreds more who edit them and who pay them and who praise them just as there are those at the *New York Times* who edit you and who pay you and who praise you for the skillful dissembling that you provide.

---

172 See Mike Whitney, "Jose Padilla and the Death of Liberty," *Information Clearing House*, Sept. 10, 2005: http://www.informationclearinghouse.info/article10223.htm

173 See Sheila Samples, "Ah, Democracy, We Hardly Knew Ye…" in *Political Cortex*, August 23, 2007: http://www.politicalcortex.com/story/2007/8/22/20124/1820

"Do you think that all these people have become weasels like you and have remained weasels like you—because they're *somnambulant?* No, even you would never accuse your own colleagues of being *sleep-walkers.* If you *did* call them sleep-walkers, the logic would turn straight back on *you* and prove *you* to be the same thing, a 9/11 sleep-walker. No, there's something else, isn't there. Way back in the beginning, when you, too, were still frightened and scared, or maybe even *before* then, you were *told* to lie about 9/11, told either directly or by obvious hints, told by your *corpo-masters.* And then after time passed and after some of the decayed and rotten fruits of an unexposed 9/11 began splatting down onto our heads and onto the ground all around us, *other* reasons for keeping mum began appearing. Read this, by Sheila Samples, and please think very, very hard as you do it:

> And Bush grows bolder with each victory. He's determined to have no restraints placed upon him in any area. Immediately upon ramming through the USA Patriot Act just six weeks after 9/11, the administration went on a spree of sweeping up and detaining thousands of citizens without charges and no access to counsel. This act was, and continues to be, the greatest threat to American liberties in our history. It is buoyed by Bush's Military Commissions Act of 2006, or "no consequences torture bill," giving himself the empirical right to torture anyone he views as a "terror suspect."

> Perhaps this act is one reason Democrats remain so subservient. Right up front, in Section 948a(2), Bush has the empirical right to decide who is a "lawful enemy combatant." If you are a "member of the regular forces of a State party engaged in hostilities against the United States," or even a "member of a volunteer corps or organized resistance movement and you wear a fixed distinctive sign recognizable at a distance,"[174] Bush has the power to decide you are not only hostile but an enemy combatant.[175]

"Or how about when Sheila Samples says this, showing that when she wants to, she can get a perfect ten in any style contest:

> Is it any wonder that legislators on both sides of the aisle recoil and beat a fast retreat when they look up and see Bush, caught up in the wild influences of his own idiotic imagination, running at them with a lighted firecracker in each hand? Is anyone surprised that Bush so easily got them to agree to his Protect America Act of 2007, which allows the continued secret collection of Americans' phone calls and e-mails with no oversight. . . no checks. . . no balances?

---

[174] Like maybe, just say, a peace emblem, or an anti-war button? EL

[175] Sheila Samples, "Ah, Democracy, We Hardly Knew Ye. . ." in Political Cortex, August 23, 2007: http://www.politicalcortex.com/story/2007/8/22/20124/1820

"And so *there's* what it comes to. Pelosi is *afraid.* Pelosi is *terror-ized. That's* why she took impeachment off the table, don't you sup-pose? *That* was the quid pro quo—do or die, very simple. Scholars will find out someday, but what does even the *suggestion* say about how things have developed because you and your colleagues kept on lying about 9/11, keeping the people's one power punch under cover, protecting the fascisti, making sure the road was clear for them so they could mess up the Constitution and pass the vile bills they've passed—tell me, how many of *your* colleagues in crime and secrecy and deceit are *afraid?* I know that *I'm* afraid, thanks to the work in treachery that you and the many, many likes of you have done. You and the others in the conspiracy of silence and secrecy and cover-up and distortion and disinformation, *you're* the ones who have enabled and propelled the junta so that by now it may be altogether too late to stop them from the still further and ever more mad and heinous crimes they plan.

"Too late because of people like *you*, Weasel. Are *you* afraid? Are you *also* afraid, Weasel? *Weasel?* Are you there? Pay *attention*, Weasel."

•

There's more. There's worse. About this particular weasel, about *all* the corpo-weasels, and worst of all about the republic itself—the blood it's hemorrhaging, has already hemorrhaged, and with that blood its strength, bringing it already near the point of death, all thanks to the traitors in our house.

There's more. There's worse. But the night is long, the hour late, and we must rest. And perhaps even pray, as if *that* would do any good, given what we're up against.

Eric Larsen
October 22, 2007

2008

13.

THE PREMEDITATED MURDER OF THE UNITED STATES OF AMERICA MARCH 30, 2008

To the Reader:
Here is another title that speaks for itself, and in the gloomiest of terms. The nation is under siege by murderers, is already near-dead from hemorrhaging its life-blood, as I suggested last time. Where to turn for help? Not the media. Not academia. Certainly not government. Not even the "elections." *Where*, then? There's only one thing to turn to. Let's find it.

1.

The Unseen, the Unsaid, the Unknown

What if there were *literary* evidence to show just how and why it is that our nation is dying, is being made to die and is being *allowed* to die, before our very eyes—with nobody doing a thing to stop it?

Well, there is such evidence—literary—and I'll get to it later. First, though, I'd better take up the objections certain to arise from my saying that nobody is doing a single thing to stop the all-but-completed murder of our nation.

We *are* doing things! I hear someone shout. We *do* know what's going on! adds another. And a third: Everybody *knows* Bush and Cheney and Rice are traitors, murderers, and war criminals!

Yes, yes, and yes, I know, I know. But I also know that nothing is *happening* and that—a fact even more grim—nothing is *likely* to happen that will keep our country from being destroyed forever, or from being destroyed, at least, to the point where restoration will necessitate bloodshed, suffering, and ruin not seen inside the U.S. since the Civil War.

Just what is it that's supposed to be happening right now, in this last week of March 2008, that could in any way have the least effect in causing the nation to do anything other than continue lying down as it awaits the completion of its murder?

Several million voices cry thunderously, *The election! The election! The election!*

But that is *not* a good answer. In fact, it's not an answer at all. Those several million voices are the voices of people deeply deceived, people kept purposely in a state of horrifying ignorance by the corporate media, people living merely on hope (to put it nicely) or people (to put it more accurately) living not only by habit but living also in the most acute state of blindness *to* and denial *of* the actualities of the social and political world they're living in that may ever have existed—at least on so large a scale—in the history of the world.

Just to name some of the most pressing subjects and issues *not* being mentioned, let alone talked about, in the presidential campaign or by the presidential candidates is to understand immediately a number of things of very great importance. It is to understand quickly, for example, 1) that all of the candidates are major, world-class, championship liars, their lying being done *primarily* by omission; that 2) all of the candidates are intent upon keeping the world's most pressing and vital truths *out of* the thoughts and minds of the American population for the reason that 3) the candidates are in the service *not* of that population but in the service, instead, of the *enemies* of that population; 4) that none of the candidates is *free* to raise for discussion any of these matters that are of greatest importance to the population, but, instead, must function and behave as what they really are, namely, 5) bonded slaves to their corporate owners, forbidden to speak in the interest of the people while allowed to speak only in the short-term and monetary interest of the owners; and, finally, it is to understand that 6) if any of the candidates *were* to break rank and speak out on— let alone act upon—truths of the greatest interest to the people rather than to their corpo-government owners, the penalty would be assassination. Such a candidate, that is to say, would either be assassinated by being sidelined in the way that Elliot Spitzer was recently and summarily sidelined and politically destroyed, or he or she would be assassinated in the more literal way in which Senator Paul Wellstone was assassinated for refusing, in 2002, to support the Iraq war.[176]

That said, what are the issues that, lest the result be death literal or symbolic, must either be kept by the candidates always and only on the outmost perimeter of the public consciousness or, even better, removed from that oozy swamp altogether?

---

[176] Before denying that Paul Wellstone could conceivably have been assassinated, please read James H. Fetzer and Four Arrows, *American Assassination: The Strange Death of Senator Paul Wellstone* (Vox Pop, 2004)

Well, there's the boist'rous ruin[177] of the criminally-driven and now collapsing economy, for one thing. In a column called "Taming the Beast"[178] (and subheaded "Who's willing to take on Wall Street?"), Paul Krugman just the other day remarked with great simplicity and directness that "We're now in the midst of an epic financial crisis, which ought to be at the center of the election debate. But it isn't."

Okay, so truth about economic collapse has to stay out of the picture. Don't talk about *that* and you can hope to wake up healthy the next morning (after all, keeping his mouth shut about it is exactly what Eliot Spitzer did *not* do when—on Valentine's day, no less, a nice touch—he attacked government failure to move against "predatory lending" in his famous *Washington Post* piece.)[179] And why not talk about that? Well, Patrice Greanville and Jason Miller, in "Hope, Change, and Pissing in the Wind,"[180] put it simply enough for anyone when they write that, whatever may be claimed or said or intoned by candidates like Obama, who seem to bring "hope," the truth is that "we are still stuck with a bourgeois democracy. Which means that despite all the rhetoric and mythologies about equality, freedom, meritocracy, opportunity, and a host of other lies that placate the masses and maintain the social order, the United States is a nation of the rich, by the rich and for the rich."

You can't dis the plutocrats, even when they're criminals. Correction: You can't tell the truth about the plutocrats, *especially* when they're criminals.

Americans, then—all the way through the laborious presidential campaigns that (because of their obvious usefulness as diversion from matters that *matter*) stretch out across ever more and more pages of the calendar leading up to that parched desert of the non-elections[181] themselves; and *then* on through the vast wasteland of a new "administration"—Americans *must* be kept blind every minute of every day of every month of every year to the fundamental truth that

---

177 "The single and peculiar life is bound, / With all the strength and armor of the mind, / To keep itself from noyance; but much more / That spirit upon whose weal depends and rests / The lives of many. The cess of majesty / Dies not alone; but like a gulf doth draw / What's near it with it; or 'tis a massy wheel, / Fix'd on the summit of the highest mount, / To whose huge spokes ten thousand lesser things / Are mortised and adjoined; which, when it falls, / Each small annexment, petty consequence, / Attends the boist'rous ruin. Never alone / Did the king sigh, but with a general groan." *Hamlet*, III, iii, 16–23.

178 *The New York Times*, March 24, 2008: http://www.nytimes.com/2008/03/24/opinion/24krugman.html?_r=2&scp=1&sq=Taming+the+Beast&st=nyt&oref=slogin

179 A piece now—how curious—disappeared from the internet.

180 In *Dandelion Salad*, March 20, 2008: http://dandelionsalad.wordpress.com/2008/03/20/hope-change-and-pissing-in-the-wind-by-patrice-greanville-jason-miller/

181 "Ohio seizes voting machines in criminal investigation," March 18, 2008: http://arstechnica.com/tech-policy/news/2008/03/ohio-seizes-voting-machines-in-criminal-investigation.ars

their country is run and ruled by criminal plutocrats whose greatest and most despised and feared natural enemy is—yes, a conscious, informed, knowledgeable, *thinking* population.

2.

The Untrue
(A Note on History)

And, asks a reader somewhere, "So what? What's the big deal? The populace has always been kept dumber than their leaders."

This sort of response makes me think of cancer, since its logic is parallel to the logic in this sentence: "There's always been cancer, so what's the big deal? Let's quit the whole business of cancer research."

Let's even suppose that it may be true, that the populace *have* always been kept dumber than their leaders. Two points immediately arise: 1) That fact doesn't make it a good thing any more than cancer is a good thing; and 2) it's also quite possible that the people's being kept dumber *now* is a worse or more dangerous matter than it was in the past.

It's perfectly easy to argue that Americans have been sold a bill of goods over and over again. Howard Zinn, for example, is one of those fond of the notion that the *first* such hoodwinking took place at the founding itself. It is "a fact long true about this country," he writes, "that, as Richard Hofstadter said: '[The U.S.] was . . .[ellipsis in original] a middle-class society governed for the most part by its upper classes.'"

The founders, that is to say, were property-owning men of wealth, power, and privilege, and they set things up from the get-go in such a way so as to *protect* wealth, power, and privilege. Furthermore, the founders were, in Zinn's telling, most vile and sneaky about it indeed:

> Those upper classes, to rule, needed to make concessions to the middle class, without damage to their own wealth or power, at the expense of slaves, Indians, and poor whites. This bought loyalty. And to bind that loyalty with something more powerful even than material advantage, the ruling group found, in the 1760s and 1770s, a wonderfully useful device. That device was the language of liberty and equality, which could unite just enough whites to fight a Revolution against England, without ending either slavery or inequality.[182]

---

[182] *A People's History of the United States* (Harper Collins, 1980), pp. 57–58.

Zinn's is an example of thinking that qualifies perfectly as coming straight from The Age of Simplification. For thinkers of this sort, it's both routine and perfectly okay to lay moral blame on figures *from* the historical past for the crime of holding attitudes that were part and parcel *of* that historical past. Jefferson and the other founders are thus morally blamed *retroactively* for having held attitudes and for having acted in accordance with attitudes *of their day* in regard to race, gender, wealth, property, and Eurocentrism.

Now, two problems immediately arise. Both have to do both with logic and, quite curiously, with a kind of righteousness that comes very near to malice. I'm going to number them.

Problem One:

The first problem is this: To place *retroactive moral blame* the way Zinn does is the equivalent, logically, of placing *retroactive moral blame* on those living in the mid-eighteenth century for not having prevented people from dying of cholera or pneumonia.

Few would disagree, I'm sure, that those deaths by cholera or pneumonia were and remain today deeply lamentable and powerfully undesirable. But what moral blame can conceivably—what *moral blame* can logically—be placed on the denizens of the revolutionary era, medically less knowledgeable than ours, *for* those deaths?

Since it's universally agreed that no moral blame can be placed in the cholera and pneumonia case, what chopping of logic *permits* it to be placed in the case of attitudes that to us are admittedly backward and pernicious ones toward property, race, and gender, even though *at the time* of Jefferson and the founders they were customary?

Imputing moral blame *retroactively* is a demonstration of one of the most pernicious abuses of historical thinking—pernicious because it assumes a superiority in the person living *later* in history over the person living *earlier*. This fallacious view of history both arises from blindness and in turn causes more blindness, just as it also both arises from and causes *pride*, which is itself another form of blindness.

Here's a test. Who among us *now* is able to identify or perceive customs followed routinely by us in our own present day that at some point in the future will be looked back upon as retrograde, unbelievable, barbaric, and pernicious?

And a question. What *kind* of person do you expect would be *more* perceptive, insightful, or prescient in identifying habits or attitudes that we ourselves now follow by custom but that in future may be seen as backward and pernicious? Which would it more likely be, a person who considers him or herself *superior* to those in the past, or a person who doesn't?

Obviously, the superior-feeling person will be the less likely of the two kinds, not the more likely, to be perspicacious, insightful, self-analytical, and impartially studious of his or her *own* attitudes, behavior, or unquestioned and unexamined assumptions. A sense of superiority, like pride, is a closer of the eyes.

After all, if you look closely at what it is that Zinn's eyes are closed to in this case, the result makes for a significant discovery. As we've seen, Zinn ascribes only contemptible—not a more realistic mixture of, say, contemptible and laudable—motives to the founders. And as a result, superciliously, he writes that the fathers of the nation "found, in the 1760s and 1770s, a wonderfully useful device." They "*found*" it? And what they found was a "*device*"? In trying to set up his case that the fathers were operating *solely* out of their own propertied self interest and out of no other, Zinn trivializes the entire historical sweep of Enlightenment science, philosophy, and thought into the simple-minded notion of a "device" that was maybe lying around under a corner table in some Boston or Philadelphia pub, a "device" that one of the founders happened to notice, bent down to pick up, looked at curiously, and remarked, "*Voilà!* Here's *just* the device that'll do the trick for our fake and duplicitous revolution!"

It's ludicrous, of course, a childish if not infantile trivialization of the entire and profound sweep of philosophic, literary, and political history that in fact brought into existence the very *concepts* of inalienable individual rights and of the justification for popular revolution against the institution of monarchy. True enough, those rights weren't at the time seen as extending to women, blacks, native Americans, and non-property holders, and thus, an awful truth, were *not* extended in such a way that to us now would mean "extended justly."

For moralizing simplifiers like Zinn, however, the limitation is alchemized into something other than an awful truth that exists as part of a complex and organically evolving history. Instead, it's made into an absolute, or, you could say, an *absolute value*. As soon as this has been done, history is no longer organic and evolving but something quite different.

Any *absolute*, after all, is and must be, by definition, *inert*. Given this fact, how would a person describe the concept of history as it exists in the mind of someone like Zinn? Well, you might think of a very long steel beam, wholly rigid, that's grasped firmly by the historian in such a manner that it extends both deeply back into the past and far forward into the future. The steel beam, obviously, represents the *absolute value* that is to be—how else to say it?—*served* by history, much as such a steel beam might be *served* by electricity through acting as a conductor for it. History, from this point on, must be partial instead of whole, since there's only one conductor, or conduit, and it must be inert instead of organic. This metaphor, however destructive you may find it, demonstrates the way that historical thinking, in our present age, which I call the Age of Simplification, steps away from being real, organic thought or thinking and becomes, instead, a form of zealotry. The thinker no longer arrives *at* conclusions based on the observation of *all* available relevant evidence—the method of thinking known as empiricism—but instead submits the past to his or her domination by a prior fixed idea, and, accordingly, cuts away or ignores all evidence *except* evidence that supports or seems to support the prior idea.

From whatever good intentions it first arose, this highly restrictive formation of "thought," being, as it is, now all but pandemic among the nation's "left-progressive" intellectuals, *certainly* those in academia, has done and continues to do enormous damage intellectually *and* politically. As the birth-parent of "identity politics," "multi-culturalism," the rage for "diversity" and other well-intended but truly pernicious ills, it has had so thorough a fragmenting influence, *and* so thorough an emasculating one upon the left, that there's no longer any political left left in the land. Moral *feeling* (how *awful* and *repugnant* and *unjust* those founding fathers were!) has replaced intellectual *thinking*, with the result that America's progressive left is now almost totally void of ideas—and therefore, the greater disaster, almost totally void also of *power*. You can read issue after issue of the *Progressive* magazine,[183] you can read issue after issue of the *Progressive Populist*,[184] you can read issue after issue of *The Nation*[185]—and still come away empty-handed, without *any* new sense or awareness of plan, policy, project, initiative, idea, or program that could or can or would or will re-*u*nite, strengthen, or re-*i*gnite the doddering, fragmented, insipid, touchy-feely, ever-righteous "progressive left."[186] You will come away, that is, with no sense of having been among the strong, but with the wholly dispiriting sense of having spent much more time than you could ever have wanted to among the kind and well-intentioned—well, *mainly* the well-intentioned, and of course also among the invariably "anti-war"—but also among the shallow, the toothless, the wan, the repetitive, the not-terribly-bright, and,

183 http://www.progressive.org/
184 http://www.populist.com/current.html
185 http://www.thenation.com/
186 Update: See Emma Kate Symons' "The Decline of the Left" in *The Wall Street Journal* of Sept. 23, 2010. The piece is a review of Raffaele Simone's 2008 book, "Il Mostro Mite: Perché l'Occidente non va a sinistra," or "The Sweet Monster: Why the West is not moving to the left," as Symons explains. She adds that "Today it is making a huge splash in France after its publication there last week. It features Silvio Berlusconi on the cover under the title 'Le Monstre doux: L'Occident vire-t-il a droite?' ('The Sweet Monster: Is the West veering to the right?')." http://online.wsj.com/article/SB10001 42405274870412920457550603211561668.html?mod=WSJ_article_related

above all—this being, among all their many varieties, the one hallmark shared by all—among *the moralistic*. But *thinkers*? No. Certainly not. No. You won't find yourself having been among *thinkers*.

Problem Two:

Some way back, I said that *two* problems arose as soon as people began thinking (that is, began "thinking") in moral absolutes, and also when they began (as they couldn't help but do, being absolutists already) applying those moral absolutes *retroactively* in historical studies. I think we've covered the first problem well enough—that "thinking" of this kind is an inevitable creator of tremendous intellectual, cultural, and political destructiveness, fragmentation, simplification, *and* impotence.

The second problem is no less destructive than the first, though it's a good deal more simple. The problem is this: Absolutism in thinking, and absolutism in *historical* thinking, isn't ruinous only in the ways we've already seen, but it's also ruinous *to debate*. Why? Because *it isn't possible* to debate with an absolutist.

Here's where we get some idea of the origins of political correctness—where it came from—and how it took hold. "Political correctness," after all, is nothing other than absolutism practiced on very, very narrow grounds. And *because* it's absolutist—or you could say, because it's *belief*—it pays the least possible *serious* attention to empiricism in any manifestation or from any direction.

As a result, because political correctness is the same as zealotry, people like me get into trouble and make large numbers of enemies. For an example of how this happens, since we've already looked at the founding fathers as treated in the Zinnian mode, let's turn to Shakespeare and consider *him* as treated in—well, let's pick the feminist mode.

Most people at some point have probably heard the charge made that Shakespeare is a misogynist and, even more likely, that *Hamlet* is a misogynistic play. To my own way of thinking, the charges are baseless and not worth going into. But what if I *were* to go about trying to refute them? Well, I could take one of two approaches, or both. And the result, either way, would *not* be a successful refutation on my part. Instead, the result would be only that I *myself* would be charged with being a misogynist.

Why? Let's look and see. In the first of my two available approaches, I could read the play yet again, combing it for evidence of misogyny. Finding none, I would declare the play free of misogyny. My accuser, however, might counter with any of several observations about women in the play—that Gertrude is treated like a sex object, that she is made to appear slow and unintelligent, that *Ophelia* is treated like *and* spoken of as a sex object, and, worse, that she is abused despicably by a cruel and wholly unfeeling Hamlet. *Her* madness and wholly pointless death come about as a result of *his* monstrous cruelty. *He*, on the other hand, in his *privileged male* role and with his *privileged male* status, is permitted to go on and, through his *male* brilliance (or through his dumb luck, given him by the playwright *because* he's male), to become the heroic savior of the kingdom.

Refutation? If this accuser in regard to Shakespeare is like Howard Zinn in regard to the founders, he or she will be "seeing" only *part* of Shakespeare, and will be seeing also only *part* or one aspect of *Hamlet*, just as Zinn "saw" only one side of the actually much more complex founders. Therefore? Therefore the "evidence" of misogyny "found" by the accuser will be the *only* evidence he or she is open to. As a consequence, any counter-arguments I might summon up will fall on deaf ears. I would be dealing, as in the case of Zinn, with an absolutist rather than an empiricist, a person who therefore feels free, like Zinn, to impose moral blame *retroactively* into history in disregard for *historical* custom or attitude. This person will be holding a steel beam just as Zinn did, though this beam, running from ancient past to indefinite future, will have stamped on it "Misogyny," whereas Zinn's had stamped on it "Power, Capital, Property." Against the obduracy of my accuser's a-historicism—or his or her *partial* or *inorganic* historicism—no attempted explanation on my part of, say, the literary, theatrical, or stage conventions of the Elizabethan period, or of contemporary ideas about the Great Chain of Being, or about Shakespeare's perceived relation between macrocosm and microcosm—would avail.

No, what would happen instead is that my accuser would become increasingly baffled as to what conceivable reason or motive I might have that would drive me to *defend* a misogynist—unless—et *voilà*! but of course!—unless I myself were one of the very same as he and was trying only to cover up my guilt by protesting too much.

3.

The Horror

And so we come back, unhappily, to our original question—who and where *are* they, these vitally and desperately needed people, the ones who are doing *some*thing, *any*thing at all, to stop the all-but-completed murder of our nation?

It can't possibly be people like Howard Zinn, or like my hypothetical antagonist on the matter of *Hamlet*. It seems perfectly reasonable—doesn't it?—to think of those two as representative of the many millions of people who, more likely than not, would consider themselves as being somewhere within or near the "progressive left." If true, how terrible a thing it is to recognize that *these people cannot help us.*

It's impossible to doubt that such people's thinking had its first roots in a commitment to the moral, the just, the right, and the fair. But—through the shaping of who knows how many other influences of whatever enormous a variety—the very strength of that commitment led them away from the historical and toward the a-historical; away from breadth, empiricism, and the organic and, as we've seen, toward the moral absolute. As a consequence of all this, their method of thinking is now narrow, rigid, fixed, moralistic, non-empirical, far more susceptible to fragmentation than unity, and *powerless*.

How shocked they would be, do you suppose, if someone were to point out to them that *their* way of thinking is the same as that of the Bush administration as described by the Downing Street Memo? Round pegs can go into square holes if one's zeal is sufficient to allow—or cause—a simple ignoring of squareness and of roundness, sort of like ignoring four-fifths of Enlightenment philosophy if the remaining one-fifth suits your agenda better. How did it go in the famous memo? War was wanted, so war there would be, with the result that "the intelligence and the facts were being fixed around the policy."[187]

How can it *be* that the political *and* intellectual depravity revealed by the Downing Street Memo failed to stir even a large enough proportion of the American population so as to generate at *least* a major showdown with the Bush administration and at *best* the early stage of an outright change in policy? "How Lethally Stupid Can One Country Be?" asks David Michael Green,[188] and I'm afraid the answer to his question may be more devastating than any of us has ever dared imagine. I do know, as far as the famous memo goes, that the holier-than-thou—or the "more-sophisticatedly-informed-and-above-the-hysterical-fray-than-thou"—preening, parading, and generally prissy-snooty airs of all the Michael Kinsleys of the land[189] has more to do with high neurosis than plain stupidity, but clearly there must be more than enough of the latter to make it obvious by now that *no* one is going to come forward to help us, that *no* one is going to do

---

[187] See http://www.afterdowningstreet.org/node/1

[188] "How Lethally Stupid Can One Country Be? Presidents and prime ministers will lie their countries into war—but why do We the People keep buying it?"(March 28, 2008, Alternet.org: http://www.alternet.org/world/80497/

[189] See "No Smoking Gun," *The Washington Post*, June 12, 2005: http://www.washingtonpost.com/wp-dyn/content/article/2005/06/10/AR2005061001705.html

anything at *all* to prevent the completion of the murder of the republic that began *before* 9/11, was triggered *on* 9/11, and that has been moving steadily forward step by death-dealing step ever since.[190]

Back at the start of this piece, on the subject of what the presidential candidates, professional liars-by-omission, *weren't* talking about in the campaign, we got only as far as Paul Krugman's saying that "We're now in the midst of an epic financial crisis, which ought to be at the center of the election debate. But it isn't."[191] It's doubtful that anyone reading these words—either those words of Paul Krugman or these of mine—needs a list of the candidates' lies-by-omission, although a simple list of words like "Antarctic ice," "famine," "depleted uranium,"[192] "genocide," "assassination,"[193] "police state,"[194] "treason,"[195] "dictatorship,"[196] "real ID," "torture," "Jose Padilla,"[197] "Bilderberg Group,"[198] "war crimes," "crimes against humanity,"[199] "the Geneva Accords," and "9/11"—a simple list of words and phrases along these lines could go far in exposing the criminal, treasonous, immoral *absence* of truth, content, and factual knowledge that is the only *really* significant thing that exists in the presidential campaign.

The *horror* of it.

Whether the horror of the things that the U.S. does, the atrocities it commits, whether that horror or the horror of how infinitesimal a part of the American people knows the least bit about it or *cares* to

190 See the invaluable and horrifying "Bill of Rights Under Attack: A Timeline," on "The Kick Them All Out Project" web site: http://www.kickthemallout.com/article.php/Story-Bill_of_Rights_Attack_Timeline

191 *The New York Times*, March 24, 2008: http://www.nytimes.com/2008/03/24/opinion/24krugman.html?_r=1&scp=1&sq=Taming+the+Beast&st=nyt&oref=slogin

192 Leuren Moret, "The Trojan Horse of Nuclear War," in *The Journal of International Issues* (July 1, 2004): http://www.mindfully.org/Nucs/2004/DU-Trojan-Horse1jul04.htm

193 James H. Fetzer and Four Arrows, *American Assassination: The Strange Death Of Senator Paul Wellstone* (Vox Pop, 2004): http://www.amazon.com/American-Assassination-Strange-Senator-Wellstone/dp/0975276301

194 Larry Chin, "New Presidential Directive Gives Bush Dictatorial Power, in Online Journal (June 8, 2007): http://onlinejournal.com/artman/publish/article_2063.shtml

195 Nov. 14, 2001, "A Coup Against the American Constitution An interview with Professor Francis A. Boyle": http://www.ratical.org/ratville/CAH/fab111401.htm

196 Lee Rogers, "Bush To Be Dictator In A Catastrophic Emergency," in *Global Research* (May 21, 2007): http://www.globalresearch.ca/index.php?context=viewArticle&code=ROG20070521&articleId=5721

197 Andy Worthington, "Why Jose Padilla's 17-Year Prison Sentence Should Shock and Disgust All Americans," in *Information Clearing House* (Jan. 23, 2008): http://www.informationclearinghouse.info/article19146.htm

198 See Daniel Estulin, *The True Story of the Bilderberg Group* (Trine Day, 2007): http://www.amazon.com/True-Story-Bilderberg-Group/dp/0977795349/ref=pd_bbs_sr_1?ie=UTF8&s=books&qid=1206806062&sr=1-1

199 Jan. 20, 2010, "Francis A. Boyle: Crimes Against Humanity Complaint Filed Against Bush, Cheney, Rumsfeld at the ICC": http://www.rayservers.com/blog/francis-a-boyle-crimes-against-humanity-complaint-filed-against-bush-cheney-rumsfeld-at-the-icc

know the least bit about it—which of these horrors is the greater is almost a moot point. Either way, the United States and its people now together constitute a nation that is—unqualifiedly—shameful, depraved, ruinous, heinous, genocidal, treasonous, inhuman, unfeeling, and criminal both nationally and globally to a degree never before matched in its far, far from clean, fair, and just history.

And so we've got to talk about what to do.

First, don't vote—and, in emulation of Carolyn Baker, don't feel guilty or ashamed about it, but *talk* about it, explain to anyone who will listen why it is you're doing what you're doing—in other words, make *them* feel like the guilty ones for being stooges, patsies, pushovers, and fools and voting for the very same corpo-fascists whom the voters undoubtedly *claim* to be opposed to and even *believe* they are opposed to. If you need some help and strength to follow through in this act of not voting, go back and read—and then re-read—Carolyn Baker's powerful essay from 2/14/08, "Celebrating Un-President's Day: Why I Will Not Vote for a President in 2008."[200]

•

Not voting will be hard enough a thing to do, so deeply and powerfully engrained in almost every American—certainly in me—is the fundamental idea that the vote is no trifling thing, but that the vote is sacred, that the vote *is* democracy.

Now, though, on the lip of the abyss where we stand, looking down, the presidential vote is neither democracy nor does it have the least thing to do either with democracy or with the democratic project. In truth, it has far more to do with treason and crime than with anything even faintly related to democracy. To vote, now, is to be a patsy, used and exploited, who never quite "gets" what it is that's being done to him, or certainly doesn't "get" it until it's too late. To participate in the election fraud and sideshow, in this enormous diversion, is, both pitiably and tragically, to live out Einstein's well known definition of insanity.[201]

Not voting is a good start, but there are other important things to do that will feel, at least in the beginning, just as awkward, unnatural, backward, and wrongheaded as not voting is going to feel.

It's time, for example—far *past* time—to revolt against the fraudulence of the putative and pseudo "progressive left." It's time to

---

[200] In *Dandelion Salad* (Feb. 14, 2008): http://dandelionsalad.wordpress.com/2008/02/14/celebrating-un-presidents-day-why-i-will-not-vote-for-a-president-in-2008-by-carolyn-baker/

[201] "The definition of insanity is doing the same thing over and over again and expecting different results."

revile and repudiate all that's *using* us while claiming to be *serving* us. Remember Sean Madden's "Open Letter to Amy Goodman"? Well, if you don't, now's the time to re-read it, and now's a good time also to memorize the excellent and revealing sentence in which Madden states the kernel of his accusation against Goodman: "You deign to give your goodhearted listener-viewer-readers the symptoms, never the fundamentals which would empower them."[202]

In an email back in December 2007, I said something similar: "Progressives like Amy Goodman," I wrote, "hide behind the good they do in order to escape censure for the bad."

The same is true of Howard Zinn. The same is true of Joe Conason.[203] The same is true, among many others, of David Corn, of Katrina vanden Heuvel, of Tom Engelhardt, Matthew Rothschild, Jacob Weisberg, Keith Olbermann, Michael Lerner, Christopher Hayes, Frank Rich, Arianna Huffington, Robert Silvers, Rodrigue Tremblay, Gene Lyons, Richard Posner, Leon Wieseltier, Thomas de Zengotita, and Noam Chomsky.

It's time to stop reading, or even being polite to, *any* of these people. It's time to stop reading, or tolerating, *any* of their publications, magazines, articles, or periodicals. It's time to stop watching *any* of their television appearances. It's time to declare all of these people to be what they *are* and to boycott and dismiss all of them *because* of what they are.

And what *are* they? The answer is that they all—wittingly or unwittingly is usually impossible to say—work for the corpo-fascist government that set about in earnest murdering the republic on 9/11 and that is now almost finished with the job it set out to do. They are all liars—again, whether wittingly or unwittingly is usually impossible to say—*primarily* but not only and by no means always, by omission. *All* of them—knowingly or unknowingly, intentionally or effectively, wittingly or unwittingly—stand in the way of 9/11 truth's being revealed. They all are standing in the way of that truth's being correctly, properly, openly, ethically, and responsibly revealed, publicized, described, and made known. And if *that* truth is not made known in *those* ways, the republic will die, and, furthermore, it *will* be dead by inauguration day of 2009.[204] On the other hand, if that truth is made known in those ways, and if it is made known soon enough, the republic, and we, the citizens of it, *may* survive.

202 "An Open Letter to Amy Goodman" (Friday, January 25, 2008): http://blog.inoodle. com/2008/01/open-letter-to-amy-goodman.html

203 *It Can Happen Here: Authoritarian Peril in the Age of Bush* (Thomas Dunne Books, 2007): http://www.amazon.com/Can-Happen-Here-Authoritarian-Peril/ dp/0312379307/ref=pd_bbs_sr_1?ie=UTF8&s=books&qid=1206817445&sr=1-1

204 Update: "An American Police State was inevitable once Americans let 'their' government get away with 9/11." Paul Craig Roberts, "It Is Official: The US Is a Police State," (September 25, 2010): http://www.lewrockwell.com/roberts/roberts283.html

Paul Craig Roberts recently pointed out that what Nancy Pelosi and her party colleagues did after the 2006 election in taking impeachment "off the table" is parallel to what the Enabling Act[205] accomplished for Hitler in 1933, releasing *him* from any accountability to or control by the Reichstag—just as Bush, as all who have eyes can see—has managed to escape control by congress.

It's an almost absolute certainty that *every one* of the people I listed three paragraphs above, if they were here in person, would immediately ridicule the very *idea* of there being the least validity to any analogy of this kind between Bush and Hitler. And they would be—wrong. Whether from criminal motives or motives of ignorance, they would be wrong. They would be like those of my students who, decade after decade, refused adamantly to accept the logic of any analogy unless it showed two things to be parallel not only in *kind* but also in *degree*. They would, for example, wholly reject my analogy that coming to class without remembering your textbook was like a soldier going into battle without remembering his rifle. Those students would not or *could* not—whether through refusal or inability was often impossible to say—see, understand, or accept any parallel between defending oneself against intellectual death and defending oneself against physical death. Period.

But they, too, were wrong. And to reject the Bush-Hitler analogy on the grounds that the two criminals, even if parallel in kind, are not parallel in degree is *also* wrong, both as a matter of logic and as a matter of morality. Ask William Butler Yeats whether it's "more wrong" to murder two people than one, or four than two, and he might well read back to you his famous lines, from "Lapis Lazuli," about dying:

> All men have aimed at, found and lost;
> Black out; Heaven blazing into the head:
> Tragedy wrought to its uttermost.
> Though Hamlet rambles and Lear rages,
> And all the drop-scenes drop at once
> Upon a hundred thousand stages,
> It cannot grow by an inch or an ounce.

Whatever her motives, whether she even knows them or not, Nancy Pelosi, precisely like the people I cited above, is, wittingly or unwittingly, an aider and abettor of the traitors and criminals engaged in the murder of the republic of the United States. Here, in its entirety, is what Paul Craig Roberts wrote on March 5, 2008, in "How Republicans Created Executive Branch Hegemony." I have put

---

[205] See "The History Place: Hitler's Enabling Act": http://www.historyplace.com/world-war2/timeline/enabling.htm

into bold type those passages that most immediately pertain to our discussion here:

Having made the mistake of confirming Michael Mukasey as US attorney general, the Democrats again find their efforts to hold Republican government officials accountable for illegal and unethical behavior stonewalled by the Department of Justice [sic] and blocked by the Brownshirt tactics for which the Bush Regime is now infamous.

White House Chief of Staff Josh Bolten and former White House counsel Harriet Miers were found in contempt of Congress for refusing to comply with subpoenas and refusing to cooperate with congressional committee investigations of the Bush Regime's political firings of eight Republican US attorneys. The eight fired US attorneys declined to politicize their offices by investigating only Democratic officials and ruining their election chances with leaks from "investigations" designed to smear their reputations.

Mukasey gave House Speaker Nancy Pelosi and the majority Democrats in Congress the finger and refused to refer the House of Representatives charges against the two Bush Regime operatives to a federal grand jury for investigation. Following the now established practice by the Bush Regime, Mukasey told the speaker of the House that members of the executive branch are above the law and are not accountable to the US Congress, formerly a co-equal branch of government under the US Constitution in the days now past when the executive branch felt obliged to abide by the Constitution.

Mukasey boldly asserted in his letter to Congress that Miers and Bolton are immune from congressional subpoenas and, thereby, their "noncompliance did not constitute a crime." According to Mukasey, "The contempt of Congress statute was not intended to apply and could not constitutionally be applied to an executive branch official who asserts the president's claim of executive privilege." [Dan Eggen, "Mukasey Refuses to Prosecute Bush Aides," *Washington Post*, March 1, 2008)]

The way matters stand in America today, the executive branch can falsely prosecute, frame-up, and imprison members of Congress and governors of states at will, but itself cannot be held accountable to law.

Pelosi herself was instrumental in making the executive branch unaccountable to Congress or to law when she declared impeachment of Bush to be "off the table." This declaration by the speaker of the House has effectively released the Bush Regime from any accountability, just as the Enabling Act released Hitler from any accountability to the Reichstag, the German constitution, or statutory law.

Moreover, the case for impeaching Bush and Cheney—indeed the entire administration—is by far the most powerful and necessary

case for impeachment that has ever existed. By declaring Bush unimpeachable, Pelosi is giving away Congress' only remaining power to prevent tyrannical rule by the executive branch. **If Bush is above impeachment, every future president will be as well.**

The Democrats naively believe that just one more year and the Bush Regime horror will be gone. But that is not the case. No matter who is the next president, the Bush Regime has established that the executive branch is no longer a co-equal branch of government. It is the primary branch, armed with unaccountability and the discretion to consult with other branches of government if it so wishes. The US Congress cannot give up the powers it has given up during the Bush years and ever expect to get them back.

The US Congress cannot conspire in Bush's destruction of US civil liberty and expect a future restoration of civil liberty.

Republican federal judges who have aided and abetted the rise of an executive branch dictatorship cannot expect the judiciary to continue as a check on the unconstitutional and illegal behavior of the executive branch.

The Bush Regime, with the complicity of Congress and the judiciary, has destroyed the American constitutional system. For the Brownshirt Republicans only THE AGENDA is important. Law, Constitution, separation of powers, truth, decency, honor—all of these things and any others in the way of THE AGENDA are dispensable.

While neoconservatives used 9/11 to pursue American and Israeli hegemony, Republicans used 9/11 to pursue executive branch hegemony. Whether or not Republicans can hold on to the executive branch through election theft or declaration of national emergency, the power that they have accumulated in the executive branch will remain. In the November 2006 congressional elections, voters gave Democrats control of Congress in order to rein in the Republican administration, but by then Congress had been reduced to an impotent branch of government and has proven to be incapable of reining in even an unpopular president with a 19 percent approval rating.

If a regime that has come to be despised and deplored by a majority of Americans and the world can ride roughshod over law and the Constitution, constitutional government obviously has no future in America.

Pelosi says the House of Representatives is going to file a civil suit against the Bush administration for refusing to help it enforce its subpoenas.

Who does Pelosi think is going to prosecute the suit—the politicized Republican US attorneys? The Republican federal judges who have helped to create the unaccountable executive?

The White House branded Pelosi's request for a federal grand jury to enforce the House subpoenas "truly contemptible." Pelosi's House Republican colleagues dismissed her request as "a partisan political stunt." White House spokesman Tony Fratto played the fear card and denounced Pelosi for trying to investigate loyal Americans instead of passing legislation that makes Americans safe by allowing the executive branch to spy without warrants. House GOP leader John Boehner's spokesperson accused Pelosi of making Americans unsafe by "pandering to the left-wing fever swamps of loony liberal activists."

The only power the House has left is impeachment, and Pelosi is too frightened to use it. Why is the speaker of the House afraid to use the power the Constitution gives her to remove from office a president who deceived Congress and the American people, who violated US and international law, and who is a clear and present danger to American liberty, to the US Constitution, and to peace and stability in the world?[205]

The especially pertinent—and ominous—phrase in any consideration of the Bush-Hitler analogy, of course, is the innocent-sounding "formerly a co-equal branch of government." Roberts emphasizes that "The way matters stand in America today, the executive branch can falsely prosecute, frame-up, and imprison members of Congress and governors of states at will, but itself cannot be held accountable to law."

How did—how *could*—such a situation come about? *Here?* In the United *States?*

Paul Craig Roberts again:

> Pelosi herself was instrumental in making the executive branch unaccountable to Congress or to law when she declared impeachment of Bush to be "off the table." This declaration by the speaker of the House has effectively released the Bush Regime from any accountability, just as the Enabling Act released Hitler from any accountability to the Reichstag, the German constitution, or statutory law.

Those who so choose are free to reject the analogy and to declare it invalid. It seems to me, however, that doing so is in effect to join the side of treason, to join those willing to allow the Constitution to be abandoned, and in fact to join those willing to *aid* in its abandonment.

How much more plainly can it be put, the sheer enormity of what's happening?

> The only power the House has left is impeachment, and Pelosi is too frightened to use it.

---

206 In *Online Journal*, March 5, 2008: http://onlinejournal.com/artman/publish/article_3027.shtml

If a regime that has come to be despised and deplored by a majority of Americans and the world can ride roughshod over law and the Constitution, constitutional government obviously has no future in America.

•

Even Roberts, this powerful, courageous, dedicated patriot, sometimes pulls back a little, wincing, as though he, too, can scarcely bear to see, describe, name—or *admit*—the treason and criminality that are right there, hidden in plain sight, out in the open. Maybe this is why he suggests first that Pelosi is "complicit" and later that she is "frightened." In murder, however, the crime is murder. It remains unchanged whether the murderer is frightened or not.

And murder it will be, of the republic, if something isn't done fast to prevent it—and at this point we return to the matter of the elections. What's all-important about the elections, once again, is that they will make no difference whatsoever in anything.

People want to believe, as we've seen all too well and all too clearly, that the elections have meaning. But they do not. They are empty. They are hollow. They are corporate-owned. They cannot make any difference.

Nothing can make any difference except taking back the power that has been stolen by the traitors and murderers who either constitute or govern the Bush administration.

Impeachment has got to happen—soon—or we're goners.

Roberts himself points out—the emphasis is mine—that "the case for impeaching Bush and Cheney—indeed the entire administration—is *by far the most powerful and necessary case for impeachment that has ever existed.*"[207]

One repeats to oneself the phrase, "that has ever existed."

Here's the rest of that sentence, again with my emphasis:

By declaring Bush unimpeachable, Pelosi is giving away Congress' only remaining power to prevent tyrannical rule by the executive branch. If Bush is above impeachment, *every future president will be as well.*

The phrase this time of greatest importance, or the sentence of greatest importance, is this true, and truly horrifying one:

If Bush is above impeachment, every future president will be as well.

---

[207] In *Online Journal*, March 5, 2008: http://onlinejournal.com/artman/publish/article_3027.shtml

4.

The End

Unless Congress—the branch of the people—is once again made "a co-equal branch of government" before the inauguration of 2009, the democratic republic of the United States of America will have ceased to exist forever. That means that impeachment must take place before then. And that means, as I said before, that, in order to start the impeachment movement and make it impossible to stop, the truth about the events of 9/11 must be correctly, properly, openly, ethically, and responsibly revealed, publicized, described, and made known.[208]

The truth about the events of 9/11 no longer has anything whatsoever to do with "conspiracy theory" or any other such fraudulent and diversionary red herring, but it has only to do with history.

So much scholarship has been done on 9/11, so much has been written, demonstrated, revealed, and shown about it, about the crucial and relevant events preceding it,[209] about the tactical and strategic origins of the plot,[210] about the precise manner of its execution,[211] about the long and causative *political* history preceding it,[212] and about the deliberate and intentional means by which the truth about

---

[208] Update: Anyone reading these words knows that impeachment did not come about. And that means, according to my own words, that "the democratic republic of the United States of America [has] ceased to exist forever." I suspect that this is true, even though it may not look like it to people going through their daily lives. But—democratic? Yesterday, Omar Khadr, was found guilty by a military tribunal on the charges of having, at age 15, committed "murder in violation of the law of war" and having failed to be wearing a uniform, another "[requirement] of the laws of war." [*New York Times*, Oct. 26, 2010, p. A-12] But, may I ask, WHAT war? No war has been declared. And how many of the civilian contractors fighting and killing on the U.S. "side" are wearing U.S. military uniforms? How democratic the hypocritical "thinking" is. Obama wants to beat back the law suit that might keep him from murdering an American citizen—be a pity, wouldn't it, if he couldn't do that—in "U.S. Weighs How to Block Suit on Targeted Killing" (New York Times, Sept. 16, 2010, p. A-10]. And then the "FBI raiding homes of int'l solidarity activists in Mpls, Michigan, NC, Chicago" on Sept. 24, 2010 (http://denverabc.wordpress.com/2010/09/24/breaking-fbi-raiding-homes-of-intl-solidarity-activists-in-mpls-michigan-nc-chicago/) led Paul Craig Roberts to write later in the day that "It's Official: The U.S. Is a Police State" (http://www.vdare.com/roberts/100924_police_state.htm). And see Roberts' "Death of the First Amendment: The 'Nazification of the United States" (*Global Research*, Aug. 26, 2010): http://www.globalresearch.ca/index.php?context=va&aid=20783 The signs, at best, are less than poor as to a good outcome for the survival of the republic. EL

[209] Peter Dale Scott, *The Road to 9/11: Wealth, Empire, and the Future of America* (The University of California Press, 2007) http://www.amazon.com/Road-11-Wealth-Empire-America/dp/0520237730/ref=pd_bbs_sr_1/105-4791811-3350040?ie=UTF8&s=books&qid=1191764020&sr=1-1

[210] Tarpley, Webster, *9/11 Synthetic Terror: Made in USA* (2005), http://www.amazon.com/11-Synthetic-Terror-Made-Fourth/dp/0930852370

[211] Ruppert, Michael C. *Crossing the Rubicon: The Decline of the American Empire at the End of the Age of Oil.* (2004)

[212] Nafeez Ahmed, *The War On Truth: 9/11, Disinformation and the Anatomy of Terrorism* http://www.amazon.com/War-Truth-Disinformation-Anatomy-Terrorism/dp/1566565960/sr=1-1/qid=1166125709/ref=pd_bbs_sr_1/104-4231058-189532?ie=UTF8&s=books

the events of that day has been and remains suppressed and covered up[213]—so much evidence has been accumulated and so much scholarship has been completed and written, including breath-takingly perceptive, thorough, and irrefutable *scientific* scholarship,[214] that *any* American citizen with the least iota of political conscience, with the least sense of civic responsibility, with the least possession of independence, free agency, and intellectual curiosity, and with the least desire to bequeath to their children and to their children's children a place and a way to live other than under torture, other than in chains, and other than in hunger—any such American citizen who still adheres to the government's seven-year-long chain of continuous and contemptible lies about what really happened on 9/11 is either a fool, a complete non-entity socio-politically, *or* a party to the cover-up and thus to treachery.

Or is unbelieving and scared to death.

Be strong, be courageous, and urge others to follow you. Carry around copies of Carolyn Baker's essay[215] about not voting so you can hand them out. Begin following *Online Journal*[216] all the time, and the same for *Information Clearing House*,[217] where you'll find reliable news and commentary, and do the same also with *CounterCurrents*[218] and Global Research.[219] You may even find yourself donating to those extraordinary online publications. And be sure also to read the powerfully truth-telling essay by Edward S. Herman and David Peterson, "There Is No 'War on Terror.'"[220]

They will all be tonic, I assure you.

Stick with the *real* real. Stick with the truth. Expose the lies.

Time has never been shorter.

Eric Larsen
March 30, 2008

---

213 Barry Zwicker, *Towers of Deception: The Media Cover-Up of 9/11* (New Society Publishers, 2006): http://www.amazon.com/Towers-Deception-Media-Cover-up-11/dp/0865715734/sr=1-1/qid=1167929084/ref=pd_bbs_sr_1/104-4231058-3189532?ie=UTF8&s=books

214 *Where Did the Towers Go? Evidence of Directed Free Energy Technology on 9/11*: http://wheredidthetowersgo.com/

215 http://dandelionsalad.wordpress.com/2008/02/14/celebrating-un-presidents-day-why-i-will-not-vote-for-a-president-in-2008-by-carolyn-baker/

216 http://www.onlinejournal.com/

217 http://www.informationclearinghouse.info/index.html

218 http://www.countercurrents.org/

219 http://www.globalresearch.ca/index.php?context=home

220 http://www.informationclearinghouse.info/article19117.htm

14.

THE "DEBATE" OVER 9/11
APRIL 28, 2008

To the Reader:
And what on earth *is* there to debate about 9/11?
Well, maybe you could debate the *results* of 9/11,
for example, whether or not this declamation is true:
"What a deeply, thoroughly, unremittingly, ruinously,
lamentably diseased, sickened, poisoned body the
United States is today! No one with eyes to see, no one
with ears to hear, no one with a conscience to live by, no
one with a knowledge of nations' histories, no one with
a sound or experienced mind to use in judgment of
what's before it can or could ever in a thousand years do
otherwise than diagnose the present United States as a
monster of depravity and ruin, as a disease unto its very
self, and, worse, as a disease intent on spreading itself in
a purposeful and deliberate carrying of its sickness onto
the nations and peoples of all the world."

Debate? Was *that* the word just used? Do you mean debate over
9/11?

A mad idea, completely pointless. The debate is long since over and
done with—that is, *if* it's a debate about whether the "official" theory
(nineteen guys with box-cutters, etc.) is the true one or whether the
"alternative" theory (inside job, long-planned strategic end, "false-
flag op") is the genuine article—*then* the notion of "debate" is absurd,
a waste of time, the issue settled a long, long time ago.

The fact is that 9/11 *was* an inside job. It's a fact. And it's a fact
by now so patently obvious that there wouldn't and couldn't be any
point—couldn't or wouldn't be even any substance—in a debate on
the question.

I'll make a qualification. Any such debate about the "two theories"
would be pointless and absurd for certain people. It would be pointless and absurd for those people, first, who have a genuine interest in
the truth about 9/11. And, second, it would be pointless and absurd
for those who have such an interest and who also can read, do read—

a surprisingly small percentage in our hollowed-out nation, even among intellectuals—and *have* read, intelligently, about 9/11.

These are the people who would find a debate of the "which theory" kind to be pointless. They would find it pointless because it's absolutely clear to them that the truth of the question is not merely already known but *well* known, and, further, that it has *been* well known for years. Not in a court of law, but in a "court of logic," it's even long since been *proven*.[221]

Is water wet or dry? *Hey*, let's *debate* it!

If we still had a "free press"; if the First Amendment were honored in the observance rather than in the breach; and if there'd been fair and open dissemination of 9/11-related thought, research, and ideas in the years since the attacks, everybody in America would have long ago agreed that a debate about the "two theories" would be just as stupid as the debate about whether water is wet or dry.

But that's not the way it has been,[222] and it's not the way it is now. True as the fact may be that enough authentic information has seeped through the sweating walls of the Ministry of Truth that today only

---

[221] Update: As for proof, anyone interested in the *actual* means by which the WTC buildings were destroyed should become familiar with the unique and vitally important research of Dr. Judy Wood. See her website at http://www.drjudywood.com/. Her newly published book, *Where Did the Towers Go? Evidence of Directed Free-Energy Technology* on 9/11, is at http://wheredidthetowersgo.com/

[222] Near the fifth "anniversary" of 9/11, Emanuel Sferios wrote a piece called "9/11 Five Years Later: What Have We Accomplished?" and ran it on the "9/11 Visibility Project" (the piece is available now at http://pilotsfor911truth.org/forum/index.php?showtopic=1191. It began like this:

> Five years ago—on my birthday—the shadow government of the United States murdered over 3,000 of its own citizens (and hundreds of others) in a "false flag" operation designed to galvanize public support behind a war for control of the world's last remaining energy reserves. Many of us quickly saw through the "big lie" of 9/11 and began a movement to expose it, to reveal the truth, in the hopes that this would bring an end to the War on Terror, a war destined—if it continues—to turn nuclear.

> And now, five years later, what have we accomplished?

> In short, everything and nothing. We began this movement to convince the American public and the world that the official story of 9/11 was a lie, and that ruling factions within our own government were the real perpetrators. This we accomplished. Opinion polls conducted over the last two years show that the majority of Americans believe the US government was complicit. We bombarded every mainstream and alternative medium available with information, from Air America to internet blogs. We handed out leaflets in cities and towns across the country, held signs on street corners, wrote letters to everyone we could think of. And you know what? It worked. Today it is rare that I talk to a person who doesn't believe the US government was involved in the attacks in some way. Compared to just two years ago, when people would look at us like we were crazy for suggesting such a thing, this is an amazing success.

So much for the "everything." Sferios now turns to the "nothing" side of the matter. "Or so it seems," he writes:

> For at the same time, not a single perpetrator of 9/11 has been prosecuted, and the War on Terror continues unabated, as does the endless stream of lies and propaganda

sixteen percent of Americans actually believe the "official" theory[223]—true as that may be, the *false* theory is still the *official* theory. The false theory is still the one that remains the fulcrum for launching every one of the murders and crimes the US goes on launching. The false theory is the one that made possible the invasions and then occupations of Afghanistan and Iraq. The false theory is the one that made possible the wholesale fraud of the entire non-existent "war on terror." And the false theory is the one that makes certain the neocon fruitcake plan continues not to die. That is, the neocon plan for a hegemonic takeover of the globe, its probable next step—it seems

---

designed to keep us fearful and compliant. . . In other words, why, in the midst of total success, have we failed?

This is the question I have been asking myself over the last few years. As co-founder of the first national activist organization for 9/11 truth, the 9/11 Visibility Project, I devoted two full years of my life to building this movement. And to see it grow from a handful of struggling yet dedicated individuals into the enormous yet ultimately ineffective movement it is today, saddens me to no end. Thus for me this is not merely an academic question. I mean it honestly: why, in the midst of a seeming total success, have we failed?

He goes on to acknowledge that "many have concluded" that "The answer to this question, . . . involves the lack of political will of the people of the United States," and yet for Sferios that conclusion isn't convincing. While it's absolutely true that such lack of political will is visible in "Amy Goodman and the other producers of Democracy Now," and that "Many other examples [can be found]. . . not only from the left media, but from senators, congressmen, Eliot Spitzer, etc. How many of these people know the truth, yet do nothing? (Cynthia McKinney may be the one notable exception)."

In spite of such examples of cowardice or opportunism, Sferios refuses to abandon his faith in the political courage of Americans generally:

But to blame the American people alone for their lack of courage in opposing US imperialism fails to ultimately answer the question, for we must also ask why such a lack of courage exists in the first place. Certainly it isn't a lack of courage in general. The American population regularly demonstrates great courage and political will when it comes to social and domestic issues.

And so *why has* the 9/11 truth movement failed? Well, because of lies, liars, and lying. Sferios makes it clear. "Here is my assessment," he writes:

The reason for the discrepancy between what people know about 9/11 and what they are willing to do to stop the War on Terror; the reason we have ultimately failed, in other words, has to do with the scope and sophistication of the political and social control mechanisms used against us; namely, disruption and disinformation. I have been an activist for 20 years, and I have seen and experienced COINTELPRO-style disruption many times in the past. Yet never before have I witnessed it used on such a scale and with such precision as I have within the 9/11 Truth Movement.

"There are thousands of examples, but let me give you just a few," he goes on, and those who want to hear them should of course go on to read his entire essay (http://pilotsfor911truth. org/forum/lofiversion/index.php?t1191.html). For our purposes here and now, though, it is enough to know that in Sferios' view, as in mine, we have become a land of liars like never before—for what are "disinformation" and "infiltration" and "disruption" and "division" if not variants, one and all, more or less fancy and complicated ones, of commonplace lying?— EL

223 Angus-Reid Public Opinion: http://www.angus-reid.com/polls/view/13469

just now—to be the fulfillment of six-year-old "Dick" Cheney's happy-birthday dream of atom-bombing Iran.[224]

Here's a question—an important one—that I'll ask now, even though we won't get around to answering it until later. It's a question worth holding in one's mind, and here it is, in four parts: 1) Since the official—that is, the false—theory of 9/11 is the launching device for all the worst murders and crimes against humanity that the US has committed since 9/11, and since it is also the launching device for those crimes it is *poised* to commit; and, 2) since the only way[225] to achieve a diversion of either the Bush-Cheney administration or of any *subsequent* administration from this or an identical course of murder and crime is by the impeachment of Bush, Cheney, and Rice;[226] and, 3) given that in order to get the impeachment process started *and* make it impossible to stop, the events of 9/11 must be correctly, properly, openly, ethically, and responsibly revealed, publicized, described, and made widely known; now, given these three facts, 4) what activist person or people of any truly liberal, progressive, and humanist tendencies of thought and view would conceivably favor either a) an ignoring of the crucially important true facts of 9/11, or b) the suppression of those true facts?

That, then is the question. To my way of thinking, in fact, it's the *only* question about 9/11 that in any way whatsoever is worth debating. I'll go farther: It is, to me, not only a question worth debating, but a question that *must* be debated, one that must be debated *now*, and one, through the means of this debate, that *must* be answered.

It's arguable whether average people, the person on the street, need be or ought to be occupied by the question I'm asking or by my implorings in regard to it—although they, like anyone else, by *not* being occupied by it, and by *not* being involved in it, stand to lose, and very probably *will* lose, their right to citizenship in a free republic, whether by loss of the right, by loss of the republic, or by loss of both.

The matter is entirely different, however, in the case of any person who in any way is or holds him- or herself *as* a leader, adviser, counselor, instructor, guide, interpreter, or public mentor *to* or *of* the people of the United States or a significant *part* of the people of the United States in matters having to do with the political, the sociopolitical, the cultural, or the politico-cultural affairs of the nation

---

224 See Paul Craig Roberts, "A Third American War Crime in the Making" (*Information Clearing House*, Mar. 31, 2008:)http://www.informationclearinghouse.info/article19658.htm

225 See Paul Craig Roberts, "How Republicans Created Executive Branch Hegemony," in *Online Journal* (March 5, 2008): http://onlinejournal.com/artman/publish/article_3027.shtml. Reprinted also in chapter 13 of this book.

226 Update: So far, this continuity of crime has clearly been well enough proven in the case of the Obama administration.

and/or of its people. For any person such as this to be unoccupied by the question or to remain uninvolved *in* it—let alone to be in any way involved in the *suppression of* it—is to be, whether wittingly or unwittingly, a traitor to the Constitution and to the republic.

This is equally true no matter where a person is placed—or where a person *considers* him- or herself to be placed—on the "political spectrum." It's as true of, say, such charlatans and right-wing bigots as might hold forth on Fox News as it is of figures like Amy Goodman, Noam Chomsky, Matthew Rothschild, Tom Engelhardt, Arianna Huffington, or even Howard Zinn, who are associated with or associate them*selves* with the liberal side of things or with the progressive left.

It's equally true of each of these two cases, but that doesn't mean that the two cases are the same. No one, after all, would ever expect Bill O'Reilly to have an interest in 9/11 truth or even to give the least sympathy to any who do have such an interest. That fact, however, makes him no less an enemy of the republic, no less treacherous whether wittingly or unwittingly, than anyone else who either ignores or suppresses 9/11 truth. Through O'Reilly's suppressing—whether deliberately or *per accidens*[227]—the truth about 9/11 for the purpose of defending, supporting, or maintaining criminal power, *his* treachery is merely placed, as expected, in the same category as the treason of people like George W. Bush, Dick Cheney, Condoleezza Rice, and General Richard B. Myers—that is, people who are *known* to be liars about what happened on 9/11. Whether O'Reilly is a knowing or an unknowing liar makes no difference to the result of his untruth, and, either way, his behavior is perfectly consistent with what we would expect of him, just as is the sheer mendacity in the behavior of Bush, Cheney, Rice, and Myers.

Now, however, we come to a matter far more difficult, as we turn away from the bullying O'Reillys and away from the transparent fraud of the Cheneys—and turn instead to person after person, to figure after figure, who also does not tell, see, acknowledge, or show any degree of concern with or for 9/11 truth, and yet who comes not from the pitbull right wing but from the left of center, from what by tradition is the putatively liberal position, in many cases positions even more to the left of center—progressive, progressive-liberal, populist.

In other words, when we turn to any figure who comes from positions such as these *and* is a person who, as I put it before, "in any way is or holds him or her self [to be] a leader, adviser, counselor, instructor, guide, interpreter, or public mentor to or of the people

---

[227] **Faustus:** Did not my conjuring raise thee? Speak.
Mephistophilis: That was the cause, but yet *per accidens* / For when we hear one rack the name of God, / Abjure the scriptures, and his Savior Christ, / We fly in hope to get his glorious soul… (Christopher Marlowe, *The Tragical History of Dr. Faustus*, I, iii, 44–48)

of the United States or a significant part of the people of the United States in matters having to do with the political, the socio-political, the cultural, or the politico-cultural affairs of the nation and/or of its people"—when *this* is the case of a visible or public figure hailing from the left, for what conceivable reason would it not be the case that we could and should rightly and justly expect the "counseling" or the "guidance" of and from that person to be such as would be more concerned with the well-being of the worker than with that of the plutocrat, more concerned with the well-being of the people than with that of the banks, and more concerned with the interests of the lower and middle classes than with those of the corporatocracy?

Clearly, there is every reason that we could and should expect the former kind of concern in each case from such a person as opposed to the latter. That being the case, we're brought to what's probably the essential question, if not for our entire discussion, certainly for this part of it.

Since January 2001, we have seen a historically unprecedented, virulent, brazen, and astonishingly successful effort by an unelected administration to make one radical incursion after another on the constitutionally guaranteed rights and privileges of the American people; on the economic security and well-being of the American people; on the respect due to the American people, as in, for example, the treating of them with honesty and candor instead of lies, trickery, and deceit; and on the democratically expressed will of the American people, who by means of their vote have expressed powerful opposition to a war that does not serve their interests either politically or economically, that perverts the reputation and prostitutes the values of their nation, that hastens its own transformation from democratic republic to martial tyranny, and that serves to bring only immeasurable extents of suffering, ill, and ruin upon other peoples of the world—all of this in the interests solely of the stability, growth, and profits of the corporatocracy.

From public guides, leaders, mentors, analysts, and instructors who come from left of center, or consider themselves to have come from left of center, or even from far left of center, we should rightly expect condemnation of the situation and policies I've just described, particularly since that situation and those policies entail and employ oppression of, cruelty to, and massive injustice toward not only the American people but also and more greatly of, to, and toward millions and millions of non-corporatized people *and* peoples elsewhere in the world, people whose only crime is that of having happened to have been existing, through no fault of their own, in the path that the American corporatocracy chose to follow *this* time in the ruthless pursuit of means by which to satisfy its *own*, and no other's, greed.

And, indeed, these kinds of condemnations, lamentations, discreditings, and censurings *are* heard from liberal or left-leaning commentators, guides, and analysts. One can listen to Keith Olbermann's high and remarkable rhetoric of denunciation when he takes on both the policies and the personalities of Bush-Cheneyism; or you can read incensed and critical pieces by Amy Goodman that denounce similar elements of Bush policy, like her "It's Bigotry that Should Be Silenced,"[228] or the plaintive and sorrow-filled columns of Bob Herbert in the *New York Times*, like "Losing Our Will,"[229] in which the columnist laments that "A country that used to act like Babe Ruth now swings like a minor-leaguer," adding that "It's both tragic and embarrassing."

But something absolutely vital is missing. This absolutely vital thing is missing not only here, in the work of Goodman, Olbermann, and Herbert, but in almost *all* liberal or "progressive" work, research, writing, or commentary, however critical of the status quo it may claim to be, from *The Nation* through *Progressive Magazine*, from *The Huffington Post* through the *Progressive Populist*, from Ted Rall through Joe Conason and Greg Palast, from Noam Chomsky through Katrina vanden Heuvel, from Tom Engelhardt and Matthew Rothschild and Jacob Weisberg and Rodrigue Tremblay and Gene Lyons on through David Corn and Thomas de Zengotita and *The New Republic*, and so on and so on and so on.

If any of these admittedly—and rightly—criticism-delivering "liberal," "left," "leftish," "leftist," "left-progressive," "progressive," "populist progressive," or even "intelligent-conservative" or "moderate-conservative" people or publications were to be compared, say, to medical doctors, something significant and remarkable would reveal itself as missing from their relationship with any typical patient.

Consider the parallel. Suppose that I, a medical practitioner in gastroenterology, took a patient's medical history and noted his or her present symptoms, examined the patient, found two duodenal ulcers in mid to advanced stages, said to the patient that everything looked just fine, that he or she ought to return in a year, and ended with a "thank you for stopping in. Goodbye."

The problem? The diagnosed disease is there, but the plan for treatment is not. The patient, unless he or she happens to go elsewhere for medical help, will suffer increasingly unendurable pain and then die a slow and miserable death.

And what would happen to such a *doctor* as this? Well, such a doctor, if this kind of malpractice were reported, if it were investigat-

---

228 In *The Seattle Post-Intelligencer* (Dec. 7, 2006): http://www.commondreams.org/views06/1207-33.htm

229 April 12, 2008: http://www.nytimes.com/2008/04/12/opinion/12herbert.html?_r=1&scp=1&sq=Bob%20Herbert%20%22Losing%20Our%20Will%22&st=cse

ed by the relevant and appropriate authorities, and if it were proven by them to have been, or to be, true—such a doctor would at the least be de-licensed and barred from practice, and, at the most, be tried for manslaughter and conceivably for murder.

Now, our hapless doctor is a rare breed, a rarity for which we all thank whatever deity or non-deity we do or don't believe in or worship. But, far less happily for us all, *parallels* to this miserable cur of a practitioner abound everywhere in our midst.

Consider. To examine, analyze, and report critically on the Bush administration during its years in office as having been and as being fascistic is a perfectly valid and verifiable "diagnosis" for any liberal-minded, observant, accurate, and conscience-driven commentator, writer, mentor, guide, or interpreter. The same would be true of any such person's reports on or diagnoses of the Bush administration as having been and as being thieves who programmatically steal from the poor and the very poor and give to the rich and the very rich; as being traitors to the Constitution and to the Bill of Rights; as being witting violators of the oaths of office that were sworn by each of the administration's members; as being destroyers of a Constitutionally mandated balance of powers through three-part government and traitorous creators of a single-arm government, in effect a dictatorship euphemized by them as a "unitary executive"; as being murderous and careless—that is, murderous, careless, and wasteful of lives *and* of the property of others; as being torturers and thereby making themselves both traitors to their own country *and* making them criminals under international law; as being deliberate, contemptuous, and repeated violators of international law, international treaty, international accord and convention, as well as of international laws of war, thus making themselves many times over the committers of the same crimes that *this* nation executed others, hanging them by the necks until dead, for committing; as being liars; as being without conscience; as being unconcerned with the well-being of the world's nations but only with the well-being of their own corporatocracy;[230] as being blind with greed for the profit of the few but unconcerned either with the poverty, the suffering, or the death of the many; as being committers of genocide through the massive and continued use of depleted uranium in military weaponry, armaments, ammunition, and explosives; and as being rigid and uncompromising adherents to desolate policies that hugely benefit the corporatocracy but that jeopardize the very existence not only of its people but of Earth itself as a continuingly healthy and health- and life-providing organism.

---

[230] Again, see Paul Craig Roberts, "A Third American War Crime in the Making," in *Information Clearing House* (March 31, 2008): http://www.informationclearinghouse.info/article19658.htm

But enough. Even though there's more, much more, we'll call this a sufficiency for now.

But *what a diagnosis it leads us to!* What a deeply, thoroughly, unremittingly, ruinously, lamentably diseased, sickened, poisoned body the United States is today! No one with eyes to see, no one with ears to hear, no one with a conscience to live by, no one with a knowledge of nations' histories, no one with a sound or experienced mind to use in judgment of what's before it can or could ever in a thousand years do otherwise than diagnose the present United States as a monster of depravity and ruin, as a disease unto its very self, and, worse, as a disease intent on spreading itself in a purposeful and deliberate carrying of its sickness onto the nations and peoples of all the world.

The betrayal. The enormity. The horror.

So much for the diagnosis. Let us now turn to the plan of treatment, since we don't want to be stripped of our licenses and barred from further practice. Do we?

The plan of treatment is impeachment. Swiftly. Followed by criminal trial. Who will be impeached, how many will be impeached, in what order they will be impeached, whether impeachment will continue from Cheney (first in line for reasons beyond count) down as far as complicitous oath-breakers and betrayers like Nancy Pelosi and beyond—these are questions of infinitesimal importance compared to resurrecting the Constitution, restoring the republic, and helping save Earth itself and its peoples and economies from the insane predations of criminal and nuclear-armed corpo-zealots—and so let's not even ask those questions yet.

Instead, let's figure out how to *launch* impeachment. So here goes: Impeachment can be launched by nailing the perpetrators with incontrovertible guilt for 9/11, for the biggest crime in American history, by labeling them boldly and clearly as the traitors, mass murderers, perjurers, and killers that they are, labeling them with ink that won't fade, paste that won't dry out, stickers that will never come off.

Justification for doing this exists in plentiful degree. The history of the crime and the method of its achievement are there, if not yet in their entirety,[231] in more than a sufficiency. The facts are there, also in far greater amount than a mere sufficiency. The evidence is there. In short, the truth is there, and all that need be done is that that truth be *told.* All that need be done is that it be told "correctly, properly, openly,

---

[231] Update: As for the *method* used to destroy the World Trade Center, however, more has been proven than is generally known, namely, that the buildings were destroyed by directed energy weaponry. This has been proven by Dr. Judy Wood's extraordinary research (http://www.drjudywood.com/), assembled in her new book, *Where Did the Towers Go? Evidence of Directed Free-Energy Technology on 9/11.* Find it at http://wheredidthetowersgo.com/

ethically, justly, and responsibly"—and in these ways be revealed, publicized, and made known to all the people of the nation and all the people of the world.

And that's all. That's all that needs to be done.

•

Simple. Except for one enormous question: *Who is going to do the telling?*

Simple, yes, but also most, most terrible. And it's most, most terrible for the reason that that one enormous question is not *really* the question that needs to be asked at all. It is in fact a *false and misleading* question. The true, essential, imperative question is not, "Who is going to do the telling?" The true, essential, imperative question is, "Who is going to *stop covering up* the telling?"

On April 17, the writer Rand Clifford ran a piece in *Countercurrents* under the title "Beyond the Speed of Lies."[232] Like Paul Craig Roberts, Clifford always dares to look straight into the eye of the beast, and, accordingly, his subject here is once again as awful as it is important. It has to do with such hidden, buried, or lied-about horrors as the attempted anthrax murders of Senators Daschle and Leahy in 2001, the assassination of Paul Wellstone in 2002,[233] and programs under way to ascertain whether GI's can be trusted to kill their fellow Americans,[234] or even their own families, should the trained monkey in the White House declare martial law when signaled by Dark Cheney and other of his caped and visored helpers.

"Omission is the ultimate, but lies remain the staple of CorpoMedia," writes Clifford, pointing out that CorpoMedia's purpose, as we all know only too well if we know it at all, is to "[whisk] the masses to ever greater heights of misunderstanding." And what is the single worst lie, or "misunderstanding," from among the many? Again, in Clifford's words:

> 9/11 is the one event that if left buried in lies and omission, untreated, could destroy our nation; a cancer that first embedded over ten years ago with a neocon lesion called The Project for the New American Century (PNAC). Euphemisms have since softened the original documentation, but the PNAC remains no less an absolute must-read for every American

---

232 See: http://www.countercurrents.org/clifford170408.htm

233 See James H. Fetzer and Four Arrows, *American Assassination: The Strange Death Of Senator Paul Wellstone* (Vox Pop, 2004): http://www.amazon.com/American-Assassination-Strange-Senator-Wellstone/dp/0975276301

234 Paul Joseph Watson, "U.S. Troops Asked If They Would Shoot American Citizens" (Feb. 4, 2008): http://www.prisonplanet.com/articles/february2008/020408_shoot_americans.htm

concerned about their nation's health. Along with the wish list that contained the new Pearl Harbor, don't miss the 2000 report: "Rebuilding America's Defenses"—foundational plans for pursuing "Global American Hegemony," a euphemism for taking over the world...

Clifford's concern, clearly, is the same as ours—or, if I *must* speak only for myself, it's clearly the same as *mine*. And one last gathering of words allows Clifford to express—with an exactness and simple eloquence so rare as to be almost non-existent in most of the writing of our time but not in his—precisely what the nature, the dangers, and the dimension of that concern are. Here it is, with my emphasis added:

> We are losing the battle for our nation largely because few even realize *our only real war is internal.*

•

Some questions. Is it a crime if a person sees a murder take place and does or says nothing about it? Let it go. Next question. Is it a crime if a person sees a murder taking place, makes an effort to prevent it by trying to wrest the weapon from the killer's hand, fails in that effort, sees the murder completed, then departs, doing or saying nothing further about it? Let it go. Next question. Is it a crime if a *police officer* sees a murder taking place and—whether or not he or she makes an effort to prevent it—turns away from it upon its completion, doing or saying nothing further about it?

In the first two questions there may well be considerable disagreement as to what the answer must, should, or ought to be. But on the third question—no one can disagree with the assertion that, yes, *that's* a crime.

Why? Because the policeman has a sworn duty to protect others and is thus bound to those others by a special tie. Dante considered this kind of relationship so important that he reserved the very bottom pit of Hell, its ninth circle and farthest removed from god's light, for the punishment specifically of those who had sinned by being treacherous toward "those to whom they were bound by special ties."[235]

We have various oaths—including the oaths sworn by those elected to high office—and of course everyone knows about the Hippocratic oath, regarding the practice of medicine. Oaths of all these kinds have a clear, real, concrete reason for existing: What they do, very simply, is acknowledge, create, and solemnize one kind or

---

[236] *The Inferno,* ed. John Ciardi, p. 266 (Mentor paper)

another of "special ties." And along with those special ties go something else. That something else is special *responsibilities*.

So now we know why, in our question about the three different people who witnessed an act of murder, there was no ambiguity in concluding that the person who *would* have been committing a crime by doing or saying nothing was the one who was under *oath* to do or say something—that is, the police officer, who, through his oath, was bound by special ties to all those in his jurisdiction.

Now, the murder we're actually concerned with isn't our hypothetical one with the three possible witnesses to it, but it's the very real one wherein roughly three *thousand* people were murdered, the murders' motive being to scare the general population into accepting the "war on terror" with all its own attendant and additional crimes.

In this true case of murder, just exactly who is the equivalent of the policeman in the hypothetical case? Who, in other words, is bound by special ties in any meaningful way to the victims of the real murder? Certainly the police and firemen are, and were, so bound, in addition to having been victims themselves. And also the medical teams, the rescue crews, and the doctors. But mention of these various people leads us to a subsequent question. It's this: In the case of a crime, what is the most important thing—*after* administering aid, help, or care in any ways possible, that is, *then* what is the most important thing? After the catastrophe is over, after the murders have been committed, after those surviving have been cared for, *then* what is the most important thing? Think of the detectives, the police investigators, the fire inspectors who will come to the scene of the crime—why do they come?

They come for one reason and one reason only: To find out, insofar as humanly possible, *the truth about what happened.*

Now we're getting close to home, don't you think? Who else is bound by special ties to the crime in the way the fire and police investigators are? One remembers Amy Goodman herself saying that "the Hippocratic oath of the media today" should be the motto of the White Rose Collective in Nazi Germany: "We will not be silent."

"The oath of the media today." The media—that would mean journalists, then, editors, reporters, columnists, commentators, and beyond just those, also magazines themselves, and newspapers, including the editors, writers, columnists, reporters, and commentators serving *them*, not to mention the entirety of the *non-print* media, television and radio newscasts, news organizations of differing kinds, news and wire services, along with all the personnel who serve *them*, keep *them* going, work for them and are paid by them—all of this without even mentioning the enormous "industry" of book publishing, itself a major part of the media.

So "the media," as all know, is a phrase that covers a whopping lot of ground and includes thousands upon thousands upon thousands of people. And so a very great question arises. If "We will not be silent" really should be, or maybe even is, "the Hippocratic oath of the media today," exactly why is it, then, that the media, the whole vast and monolithic enormity of it, remains more silent than the tombs of the Pharaohs on the subject of what actually happened on 9/11?

It can't be accidental, can it. It's as if suddenly every bird in the sky—sea gull, sparrow, swallow, finch, heron, eagle, humming bird, condor—were to fly in precisely the same direction across the skies. But that's absolutely out of the question. That's not something that ever will or would or could happen in nature, unattended, of and by itself. And where does that leave us? It leaves us with the fact that here must be a plan. If you're a novelist, a plan can be called a plot. And if you're a politician, a plot can be called a conspiracy. What we're left with, then, is a conspiracy.

But of course.

Here is a list of media outlets that I myself am familiar with either through following them closely, or from following them *fairly* closely, or from following them at least closely enough to keep an eye on what their contents do—or don't—include about 9/11 and about the all-important idea that "We are losing the battle for our nation largely because few even realize our only real war is internal." It is a list, in other words, however incomplete, of Gatekeeper publications:

ABC
BBC
CBS
CNN
Common Dreams.org
CounterPunch
Every Major American Publishing House
Free Inquiry
Harper's Magazine
MSNBC
NBC
NPR
Pacifica Radio
PBS
Progressive Magazine
The Atlantic Monthly
The Huffington Post
The Nation
The New Republic

The New York Times
The Progressive Populist
Tikkun
TomDispatch.com

And here is a list of *people* I'm aware of who are, first, a part of the "media" as publishers, editors, commentators, writers, analysts, elected leaders, frequent speakers, and the like; all with their primary beat or a major *part* of their primary beat being the current political-cultural scene; who are, second, conventionally identified with "liberal" positions of one degree or another; and who, third, either denigrate 9/11 truth, ignore it, suppress it, or do all three:

Alexander Cockburn, Editor, *CounterPunch*
Arianna Huffington, *The Huffington Post*
Bill Keller, Editor, *New York Times*
Bill Moyers, writer, commentator, television host
Bob Herbert, columnist, *New York Times*
Christopher Hayes, journalist
David Corn, Washington Editor, *The Nation*
Elliot Spitzer, ex-Governor, New York State
Frank Rich, columnist, *The New York Times*
Howard Zinn, writer, historian
Jacob Weisberg, editor, *Slate*
Katrina vanden Heuvel, editor, *The Nation*
Larry Silverstein, Developer, Liar, Profiteer
Matthew Rothschild, Editor, *Progressive Magazine*
Nicholas Lemann, Dean, Columbia Journalism School
Noam Chomsky, political scholar, writer, speaker
Paul Krugman, columnist, *New York Times*
Ted Rall, columnist, cartoonist
Tom Engelhardt, Tom Dispatch.com (The Nation Institute)

Neither list is complete nor is either list intended to be authoritative in any official way. But each includes people or publications I'm familiar with or follow with some degree of regularity, people or publications that present themselves as serious, and people or publications either in the mainstream or near it.

And every item on this list represents either a gatekeeping publication or a gatekeeping writer. What I'm interested in—a question about 9/11 that really *is* worth debating—is *why* they continue, now into the *seventh* year after the attacks, still routinely and programmatically to hide, obstruct, denigrate, or ignore the truth—in short, to continue to lie through their teeth.

Why?

Before we come to a close, however, by grappling with *that* all-important question, there's another question that had better be cleared up.

This one has to do, again, with the business of people saying that I'm "picking on" or "being mean to" the likes of Zinn or Goodman by criticizing them in the way I have. A number of people have said, "You say they're *wrong* just because someone else doesn't *agree* with you, and that's presumptuous nonsense." I've been told, too, that it's not just impermissible for me to criticize people (or publications) as I have, but that it's *doubly* impermissible to criticize them *harshly* just for being what I (following Barrie Zwicker) call "left Gatekeepers." The reason it's impermissible, I'm told, is that other people's not writing about what *I'm* interested in is no justifiable reason to criticize them— and *certainly* no reason to condemn them. After all, what if a scholar becomes a specialist in Sir Edmund Spenser? You certainly can't criticize him or her for not publishing papers on Sir Philip *Sidney*.

Indeed not. But neither that first nor this second criticism of what I've been arguing or how I've been arguing it is valid. To show why not, let's return for a minute, not to those hypothetical cases of different people witnessing acts of murder, but to something similar.

Let's go back to the First Amendment and freedom of speech— *and* let's go into a crowded theater. In 1919, in Schenck v. United States, the Supreme Court decided (though it was later overturned) that a person did *not* have the right to pamphleteer against the draft during WWI, "because it presented a 'clear and present danger' to the government's recruitment efforts for the war" (Wikipedia). In his supporting argument, Oliver Wendell Holmes wrote the famous sentence that "The most stringent protection of free speech would not protect a man falsely shouting fire in a theater and causing a panic." (Wikipedia again)

Nowadays, incitement to riot is the general standard governing protection of free speech, but that isn't really what concerns us here. What concerns us here is this: *Whether a person is or is not in the theater.*

If I or anyone else falsely shouts "Fire!" while standing alone in the middle of a rainy hundred-acre cornfield in central Iowa—well, that's no problem, legal or constitutional, to or for anyone, although it might suggest a psychological problem for the shouter. *Only when a person is in the crowded theater* or in some equivalent place is the false shout of "Fire!" unprotected.

Makes sense. Now, compare this notion to two literary scholars, one a Sir Philip Sidney specialist, the other a Jane Austen specialist. Clearly, neither of the two would or could criticize the other for writing or publishing the "wrong" papers, that is, papers on the "wrong" author. Why not? Again, Justice Holmes' metaphor is appropriate and useful: There'd be no criticism *because the two of them are in separate theaters*. One is in the Sir Philip Sidney Theater, the other in the Jane Austen Theater. If someone *in the Sir Philip Sidney theater* "fails" to write about Austen—well, no criticism can or will arise there, just as it can't or won't in the opposite case, that of a person in the Sidney Theater who insists that he or she *not* write about Jane Austen.

And so when I criticize people like Zinn or Goodman or Englehardt or Moyers or Olbermann or vanden Heuvel or Rich it isn't because I disagree with or disapprove of what they're speaking or writing or broadcasting *about*—or, if it is because of that, it's only so because of something else first, which is to say that it's so *because of the theater that they're in*.

Before I can explain this more clearly, one more First Amendment-related question has to be asked—about the right to be silent, as we mentioned before.

We've agreed that you can't yell "Fire!" in the crowded theater, whatever theater it is. But consider another situation. Suppose that you were indeed in a crowded theater and in fact there really *was* a fire. Imagine one other thing in addition. Imagine that by some unknown circumstance, you alone, of all the entire crowd of people, were able to *see* that fire, all the rest of them for some reason or other remaining wholly blind to it.

Now, *two* questions follow, really. First, would your deciding to *say nothing about the fire* be a First Amendment-protected right? And, second, by *saying nothing about the fire*, would you be committing a crime?

All right. Let the fire rest for a moment, and let's talk about theaters. There's a Tatting, Crocheting, and Knitting Theater—and no one who has chosen to be a part of the crowd in *that* theater is criticized or discredited for, say, not talking about venture capitalism. There's a Jane Austen Theater, and no who has chosen to be a part of *its* crowd or audience or membership will be criticized or discredited for *not* talking about Laurence Sterne.

A brief note, and then we turn to the theater that truly concerns us: *Would* any of those in the Jane Austen Theater (rightly) be criticized or discredited if, just say, they insisted that the subject of *marriage* be *ignored* in discussing the Austen novels? Or, would any of them undergo the same discredit or censure if they made it clear that *at the very basis* of their analytic approach to the Austen oeuvre was their *firm and unarguable conviction* that Jane Austen had actually *been married two times and was the mother of seven children, five of whom survived*?

Yes and yes. Criticism, discredit, and censure must follow in both cases. In the first case, the error committed would be parallel to—or would *be*—lying by omission: To leave *marriage* out of the work and out of the material in the Jane Austen theater would be to leave out a *central element* of Jane Austen's art and literary achievement.

In the second case, the error would be parallel to—or would *be*—lying by commission. It would be to argue something to be true that is *not* true. Or, just as relevant to our own point, it would be to assert something to have happened that did *not* happen.

Those people and publications in the two lists back a ways, the lists of those people and publications I'm criticizing—that I'm supposedly being "mean" and "unfair" to—what theater are *they* in? The answer is easy, clear, and *immeasurably* important. They have all made it very, very evident that they are each and every one of them a part of the huge crowd in a theater that is very important, very visible, and has a very long name. The theater they are a part of; the theater that they are in fact *dedicated to*; the theater without which they *couldn't exist* as commentators, guides, mentors, analysts, scholars, broadcasters, or writers *of the kind they are* is The Theater of Contemporary Events, Politics and Culture, American Foreign Affairs, and Collapsing Society in an Age of Late Capitalism.

Those who are crowded into this theater, being politically "liberal" or "left of center" or, as I've said, "progressive" or "progressive populist," conceivably sometimes "libertarian" or even "intelligent conservative" or "moderate conservative," are studiously and steadily critical of American imperialism and criminality, of American militarism and bullying, of American theft of resources, curtailing of human rights, betrayals of freedoms, and even of its stripping away of its *own* Constitution and freedoms, and its careful, step-by-step preparations for martial law and military rule inside its own sovereign boundaries.

There they are, in this theater, simultaneously producing and watching this show, despising what they can't help but see, lamenting and condemning and criticizing and speaking out against and excoriating the behavior of the play's central character, the United States—night after night, week after week, month after month, year after year. The run is a very, very long one, and with each passing season the story-line grows more ominous, the pain and death and destruction and suffering caused by the central character more and more ruinous, hateful, despicable, lamentable, horrible, the audience more despairing, ever louder in its condemnation.

But what does not a *single member* of the audience in this theater *do*? In this theater there is, in fact, a fire. It burns and burns, but until the audience-members in this theater *see* the fire, or *admit* to seeing it—this fire which is, purely and simply, the truth about 9/11—until they finally start crying out *"Fire!"*—until that happens, the play will go on, the show will continue, the depravity and killing and loss and suffering and pillaging and rapine will go on without end. Only if the members of the audience indeed do cry out *"Fire!"* will the show be stopped. It will be stopped then only for the very good reason that the members of the audience will flee for their lives, and for the very good reason that the theater itself—if luck be with us, and if the immensity of 9/11 truth, transformed now into justice, accomplishes its proper and purifying job—the theater itself will be burned to the ground along with the stage, the sets, the lighting, the curtains, and also along with every last one of the liars, murderers, traitors, rapists, and thieves who constituted the members of the cast.

Rand Clifford:

> 9/11 is the one event that if left buried in lies and omission, untreated, could destroy our nation; a cancer that first embedded over ten years ago with a neocon lesion called The Project for the New American Century (PNAC). Euphemisms have since softened the original documentation, but the PNAC remains no less an absolute must-read for every American concerned about their nation's health. Along with the wish list that contained the new Pearl Harbor, don't miss the 2000 report: "Rebuilding America's Defenses"—foundational plans for pursuing "Global American Hegemony," a euphemism for taking over the world…

And Rand Clifford again:

> We are losing the battle for our nation largely because few even realize our only real war is internal.

Clifford's meaning? He means two things. One is that our own "Corpo-Government" is our great enemy, intent upon using us only for *its* own ends and depriving us of any of the aspects of life that might work against our being used solely and only for those same Corpo-Government ends.

The second thing Clifford means is that the people and publications on my two lists, and every other person or publication like them in the nation and world—every person, from Noam Chomsky to Amy Goodman to Howard Zinn to Robert Silvers to Matthew Rothschild to David Corn to Bill Keller to Tom Engelhardt to Frank Rich to Katrina vanden Heuvel—every person who is *in the audience* at The Theater of Contemporary Events, Politics and Culture, American Foreign Affairs, and Collapsing Society in an Age of Late Capitalism and is *not* screaming out *"Fire!"*—every one of them is our mortal enemy, every one of them is complicit in the same crimes they so studiously and consistently lament and decry, or pretend to lament and decry.

We are losing the battle for our nation largely because few even realize our only real war is internal.

•

Here, now, a quiz. I provide it with the intention that every member—*every* member—of the audience in The Theater of Contemporary Events, Politics and Culture, American Foreign Affairs, and Collapsing Society in an Age of Late Capitalism who is *not* screaming *"Fire!"* about 9/11—with the intention that every single person who meets those conditions be required to take it.

It will be very simple. It will require only that the respondent choose whichever of the available "answers" is a *true* answer.

What could be simpler? To get an "A" on the quiz, one need do nothing but *tell the truth!*

None of those mentioned previously as being in the audience of The Theater of Contemporary Events, Politics and Culture, American Foreign Affairs, and Collapsing Society in an Age of Late Capitalism and *not* screaming out *"Fire!"* is exempt from taking the quiz.

I ask all readers to write, call, and email all of these people, and to insist, over and over if necessary, that they not only *really do take* and complete the quiz, but also that they not fail to email the results to me at ericlarsen@oliveropenpress.com in order that I can tabulate them and make the results known and available to the world.

A QUIZ

Instructions: Put a mark on the blank after "T" for any statement that is *true*. Put a mark on the blank after "F" for any statement that is *false*.

Example: **I stayed home from work today because**:
1) My car wouldn't start
2) I was on a deadline to finish a piece better concentrated on at home than at the office.
3) I was sick with the fever and flu
4) My pet parakeet died and I was in mourning

The Question:
I am a member of the conglomeration of publishing, broadcasting, speaking, writing, and research businesses and undertakings that Amy Goodman once referred to as "the media." Goodman noted that "the Hippocratic oath of the media today" should be the motto of Hans and Sophie Scholl,[236] who were executed by the Nazis for disseminating the words "We will not be silent."[237] Nevertheless, even though I understand that the greatest part of my professional obligation and responsibility is to inform citizens of the truth and all aspects of the truth in and of the institutions around them and under whose policies and influences they live their lives—in spite of this high responsibility, I have never, in the nearly seven *years* that have passed since 9/11, given, allowed, expressed, or conveyed any hint or suggestion that the government's version of what happened on 9/11 has in fact been said, shown, and proven by many serious scholars and analysts to be wholly fraudulent and untrue. The reason I have kept silent for nearly seven years about the truth of 9/11 is:

1) I know nothing whatsoever about 9/11 truth, have never heard of it before now, and have never read, seen, or heard of any books about it or scholars who have studied it.

True: _____
False: _____

2) I know that books have been written about 9/11 truth, but, in spite of my prestigious and nationally-visible reputation, I have never paid any attention to them or their authors for the simple reason that I know them to be worthless books and worthless authors, their interests being only in what's sensational, and the entire undertaking being the work of nothing more than a bunch of "conspiracy nuts."

True: _____
False: _____

3) I know of the 9/11 truth books and have even read two of them. But I have never mentioned them or *allowed them to be* mentioned in any of my pieces (if I'm a writer), broadcasts (if I'm a news host) or publications (if I'm an editor or publisher). The reason for this policy is that I have chosen to ignore my professional and ethical responsibility not

---

[236] For "Sophie Scholl," see http://en.wikipedia.org/wiki/Sophie_Scholl
[237] Amy Goodman, "It's Bigotry that Should Be Silenced," *Common Dreams:* http://www.commondreams.org/views06/1207-33.htm

to remain silent simply because I know that the Board of Directors of the media group I work for would react most negatively to any hint of 9/11 truth and would very likely work to have me demoted or possibly fired. My job, income, and title are more important to me than the truth, even if that truth might be instrumental in saving the future not only of our nation but of the world.

True: _____
False: _____

4) I know of the 9/11 truth books and have read widely in them, and I have remained a close follower of a great number of informative web sites on and about 9/11. I am convinced beyond any reasonable doubt that elements of our own government in fact did plan and perpetrate the events of 9/11, and also that these elements of, within, and above our own government—including a number of very specific figures such as Dick Cheney and General Richard B. Myers—along with what can be called "corpo-government," are responsible also for the extraordinarily successful (and criminal) co-opting and perverting of all major elements of the mass media in the United States in order to keep the truth of 9/11 and of its cover-up unknown to and by the general public. In spite of these powerful beliefs, I have never mentioned the basis for them or allowed the basis for them to be mentioned in any of my pieces (if I'm a writer), broadcasts (if I'm a news host) or publications (if I'm an editor or publisher). The reason for my complicitous and guilt-ridden silence is that I would be afraid for my life if I were to break ranks. I'm afraid I might be murdered, like Marvin Bush's nanny,[238] or Dennis Kucinich's brother,[239] or Senator Paul Wellstone[240] and much of his family. My life is more important to me than telling the truth to the fellow citizens of my country. I know I'll go to hell, but at least I'll go to hell alive.

True: _____
False: _____

5) I once wrote that "the central disease of President Bush and his cohorts. . .[is] the pathological refusal to accept reality" and also that "the relentless denial of reality perverts judgment and rots the

---

[238] See Wayne Madsen, "Marvin Bush Employee's mysterious death - connections to 9/11?" (Oct. 10, 2003): http://www.apfn.net/messageboard/10-16-03/discussion.cgi.16.html

[239] See *Dispatch Politics*, "Kucinich's brother, 52, found dead" (Dec. 20, 2007): http://www.dispatchpolitics.com/live/content/national_world/stories/2007/12/20/ap_perry_kucinich_1220.ART_ART_12-20-07_A5_MM8R2NV.html?sid=101

[240] See "The 'Plane Crash' of Senator Wellstone": http://www.oilempire.us/wellstone.html

soul."[241] But I wasn't talking about 9/11 truth. I don't know *anything* about 9/11 truth. Before now, I'd never even heard that there *were* any books about it (that is, assuming that *you're* telling the truth, you, the writer of this quiz). No, what the American public wants to know and *deserves* to know is the *truth* about this corrupt, criminally war-mongering, and murderous administration, not a bunch of endless claptrap about some cockamamie conspiracy theory that doesn't have anything to do with anything.

True: _____

False: _____

EXTRA CREDIT: Respond to each of the following statements by indicating whether it is True (" T") or False ("F"):

E-1)
"The fact that the term 'conspiracy theory' has no literal meaning is one of the many things that was firmly established by the events of 9/11. The official explanation of events of that day is unequivocally a theory of conspiracy. It's the ultimate conspiracy theory for the world's most spectacular crime, but it's not called a conspiracy theory. That term is reserved for any ideas that contradict the official story. This is a very important point. Conspiracy theories are not about conspiracies, they are about forbidden thought. The label 'conspiracy theory' is a stop sign on the avenues of rational thought and inquiry. It says, 'Stop here. Entrance forbidden.'"

True: _____

False: _____

(Source: David Cogswell, "See No Evil," *Online Journal*, Feb 27, 2008: http://onlinejournal.com/artman/publish/article_3001.shtml)

E-2)
"In fact, it has been the government, with the help of the corporate media, that has terrorized the citizenry in an open and continuous act of psychological warfare. It has been the government, along with the Ministry of Truth, that has instilled fear and insecurity into the population. It is they who, under any definition of terrorism, have become our terrorists, our real enemy, our internal bogeyman. Fear

---

[241] Arianna Huffington, "Haggard and the White House: Both Living in Denial" (Nov. 5, 2006) http://www.huffingtonpost.com/arianna-huffington/haggard-and-the-white-hou_b_33324.html

mongering has never been so easy and, when the collective trauma of 9/11 wears off, all that is needed to reinvigorate the senses of the masses are lies of further attack, more dehumanization of the enemy, propaganda of imminent threat and insecurity and, if all else fails, one more false flag event."

True: _____
False: _____

(Source: Manuel Valenzuela, "The Year of Living Dangerously: Part One of Two," *Valenzuela's Veritas*, Feb 4, 2008: http://www.thepeoplesvoice.org/cgi-bin/blogs/voices.php/2008/02/04/p23062#more23062)

E-3)
"All that separates America from Amerika is one shock, one event, one opportunity for those whose enemies are freedom and democracy to orchestrate the Amerika of their sinister dreams. Most do not know the seriousness of the threat, nor the perilous danger roaming among us, nor the sinister ideology of our so-called leaders, or how imminently close we are to a vastly different America. For this cabal, this domestic enemy, the people are the obstacle, the real, and true, enemy. It is this group that is our greatest threat, our real enemy.

"Until we realize that what we have been led to believe for the last seven years is but a charade, that the 'war on terror' is but yet one more method of control, that our pursuit of terror has led us in the wrong direction, that the real terrorist entity is domestic, not foreign, that we have been unleashing hell on Earth on the wrong, and innocent, people, and that it is this internal threat that hates us for our way of life, we will never stop the hemorrhaging of our freedoms, rights and liberties."

True:
False: _____

(Source: Manuel Valenzuela, "The Year of Living Dangerously: Part Two of Two," *Valenzuela's Veritas*, Feb 5, 2008: http://valenzuelasveritas.blogspot.com/2008/02/year-of-living-dangerously-part-two-of.html)

E-4)   "If the Congress does not impeach this president and vice president, who have nearly taken the country down as a result of their reckless, dangerous, incompetent, authoritarian behavior, then the rule of law stands for nothing. And future elected leaders can legitimately believe that they more or less can also get away with anything they wish to do."

True: _____
False: _____

(Source: Bernard Weiner, "Impeachment now or apocalypse later?," *Online Journal*,
Apr 23, 2008: http://onlinejournal.com/artman/publish/article_3205.shtml)

•

FOR IMMEDIATE RELEASE

TO: ALL MEMBERS OF THE NATIONAL MEDIA
RE: RESULTS OF REQUIRED QUIZ
FROM: ERIC LARSEN
DATE: APRIL 28, 2008

SUBMIT YOUR QUIZ RESPONSES TO ericlarsen@oliveropenpress.com
SO THAT, AFTER COMPILATION, THE RESULTS CAN BE SENT TO ALL
OF THE PEOPLE OF THE UNITED STATES, EUROPE, AND ESPECIALLY
TO ALL OF THE PEOPLE, VICTIMS OF WAR CRIMES AND CRIMES
AGAINST HUMANITY, IN THOSE NATIONS NOW ATTACKED,
INVADED, OR OCCUPIED BY UNITED STATES POWERS, FORCES,
AND CORPORATIONS.

Eric Larsen
April 28, 2008

15.

IS DWIGHT GARNER A DISSEMBER, DECEIVER, AND MALEFACTOR TO HIS NATION? JULY 26, 2008

To the Reader:
It may *look* as though this essay is about *New York Times* book reviewer Dwight Garner. But don't be deceived by the surface of things. It's really about Americans in general, saying that they're hollow and empty inside, and doing what it can to say why:
"We're in the grip of a mass, corporate-sanctioned, corporate-sponsored, corporate-fed, corporate-gratified, corporate-rewarded know-nothingism and ignorance." (Practice it this way, if you like: "Garner-sanctioned, Garner-sponsored, Garner-fed, Garner-gratified, Garner-rewarded.") We're in a situation where all the "best" and all the "published" novelists have, long since but *doubly so* in the aftermath of 9/11, either deliberately or in their happy and marketable ignorance, abandoned not only as useless but as worse, as things *being in the way* of getting published, all of the vital and true elements and aims and qualities that characterized and informed the genre of the modern novel when it really did achieve and express and embody significance: The novel, that is, from Joyce to Woolf, Ford to Conrad, Lawrence to Forster, Faulkner to Hemingway, Beckett to Waugh.
"American literature is dead because American thought-feeling is dead, and the Garnero-corpo-milito-governmento powers are doing and will do everything it/they possibly can to *keep* thought-feeling dead—to keep *everything* that has to do with true individual intellectual existence and perception in all of America as completely dead as dead can be kept."

A new and explicit boldness—a heavy-handedness that's both shameless and unscrupulous—in delivering the sheerest neocon propaganda has lately become a staple of much of the writing in the *New York Times*. Exactly how significant this phenomenon is, I can't say for sure, but I know that to me it's alarming and despicable, and I know also for a fact that it's fundamentally detrimental to the survival of a free republic. As a writer, teacher, professionally trained literary person *and* practitioner, I can't—cannot—imagine how anyone who is in possession of a working conscience, a thorough knowledge of cultural-political affairs, the least element of integrity, and of a functioning intellect could actually bring him- or herself to write the sort of fraudulent, misleading, disinformational, propagandistic dreck that has become very nearly a daily and, I'm sorry to say, seemingly unnoticed element in the *Times*.

I see no reason not to start with the front-page piece of the *New York Times Book Review* for May 18, 2008. Written by Dwight Garner ("senior editor of the Book Review"), it's a review of the Joseph O'Neill novel, *Netherland*, run under the title "The Ashes."[242]
Here is its opening paragraph:

> There have been good novels about living in the post-9/11 world (Ian McEwan's "Saturday"), pretentious ones (Don DeLillo's "Falling Man") and sentimental ones (Jonathan Safran Foer's "Extremely Loud and Incredibly Close"). But sorting through the pile of so-called 9/11 novels is a sad exercise, one that grows more pointless by the day. They're all 9/11 novels now.

Before looking at exactly what the content of this abysmal paragraph of pre-fab-non-think actually is, I think some further quoting would be helpful. Here's Garner's next paragraph:

> It's impossible, though, to stop scanning the horizon for something else—the bracing, wide-screen, many-angled novel that will leave a larger, more definitive intellectual and moral footprint on the new age of terror.

So we're almost ready to begin. But, before we do, let's first get another matter out of the way—namely, the matter of what Garner thinks of *Netherland* as a *novel*. This isn't important so much as it is merely appropriate, since we're going to be talking about Garner, not *Netherland*, and about Garner's own hidden mind-messages, not his judgment of the novel. Partly as a clearing of the field, then, and—all but inevitably—partly in search of more hidden messages, let's hear what he does think of the book:

> Joseph O'Neill's "Netherland" is not that novel. It's too urbane, too small-boned, too savvy to carry much Dreiserian sweep and swagger. But here's what "Netherland" surely is: the wittiest, angriest, most exacting and most desolate work of fiction we've yet had about life in New York and London after the World Trade Center fell.

Okay. Let's set aside the curious and questionable notion that "Dreiserian sweep and swagger" are the qualities needed to achieve whatever

242 *The New York Times Book Review*, May 18, 2008: http://www.nytimes.com/2008/05/18/books/review/Garner-t.html?_r=2&scp=1&sq=%22The%20Ashes,%22%20Dwight%20Garner&st=cse

it is Garner is looking for. And, at the same time, let's accept his notion that *Netherland* is on the smallish ("small-boned," that's good)[243] side, whether it's true or not—as only those who have read the book will know.

And now, those matters being acknowledged, let's start talking about Garner and what's on—and in—that mind of his.

As to his taste in novels, I can testify that he's bending over backwards with euphemism if not outright benevolence in calling *Falling Man* merely "pretentious," when the case against it (and against Frank Rich and the *New York Times Book Review*), as we'll see later, is a powerful and serious one.[244] DeLillo's is indeed a writers' workshop-level novel that fails to justify its own existence while at the same time groveling shamelessly in the service of establishment propaganda—all notwithstanding Rich's front page rave review of the book, a long string of falsehoods making that empty and penurious novel sound like the century's highest achievement.

Coming back to Garner, I don't know whether or not Ian McEwan's *Saturday* really is "good," but I know that *Amsterdam* really is bad. From what I know, and from the bits I've read, and have heard read, Garner has chosen an accurate word for *Extremely Loud and Incredibly Close.*

But none of these questions, really, has anything to do with what's truly important in Garner's paragraphs. *That* subject—the subject of Garner, member of the intellectual class, serving as propaganda lackey for the destroyers of the republic by working in their Ministry of Truth[245]—*that* subject is contained right there in plain sight for all who can see it, while for those who can't, it's merely hidden behind the costume-shop veils of the journalese "novels about living in the post-9/11 world."

What absolute nonsense Garner writes. Here's an offer: I defy any thinking, trained, experienced, perceptive, widely-read literary person on the surface of the globe to identify even *one* "good" novel written by an American that can genuinely be said to be "about living in the post 9/11 world." To the first finder of such a book, I will give two free, signed copies of *A Nation Gone Blind* and, as I offered once before, a juniper martini at the Picnic Café.

With prizes like that, the hunt will be on immediately, I'm sure. A word or two of warning, however. I won't accept Steven Alten's *The Shell Game*, on the grounds that the book is entertainment, not

<hr>

243 *Player:* 'But who (ah, woe!) had seen the mobled queen—'
Hamlet: 'The mobled queen'?
Polonius: That's good. 'Mobled queen' is good." (*Hamlet*, II, ii, 490-492)
244 See chapter 17.
245 See Paul Craig Roberts, "A Free Press or a Ministry of Truth?" in Lew Rockwell.com (July 18, 2007): http://www.lewrockwell.com/roberts/roberts217.html

novel, whatever its apparent "acceptance" of 9/11 truth. As for Mike Palecek's books, like *Iowa Terror*,[246]—well, they're politically open-eyed, but as graphic novels they're not the same as, well, the "other" kind.[247]

But Alten and Palecek aren't the point, and I don't want to continue making comments about them—these books aren't high art, these books are inferior, etc., etc., etc.—comments that will backfire on me and make everyone accuse me yet again of being an elitist, a snob, out of touch with "the "people" and out of touch with "simple, real feelings," and so on.[248]

Therefore, back to our real subject: The mind of Dwight Garner, who is either (we're not sure yet) an absolute ignoramus about 9/11 or a high-ranking section-director in the Ministry of Truth—that is, a hard-working malefactor to his own nation.

The next Garnerian sentence for analysis: "But sorting through the pile of so-called 9/11 novels is a sad exercise, one that grows more pointless by the day."

A *"sad"* exercise? And *"pointless"*? Why and how could a state such as this conceivably be? Certainly, if Garner means, however remotely, to associate the word "sad" with the facts and meaning of 9/11, well, one gasps at so grotesque a miscomprehension and diminishment. Certainly he means that what's "sad" is the task of "sorting through" the "9/11 novels," and—seemingly worse—that it's "pointless." But *why* sad and pointless? Garner himself provides the answer to that question, though he does it in careful obedience (or maybe in blind obedience; how can we ever be certain?) to the strictures of the *New York Times* and its code of silence. That is, he does it without telling the truth—except perhaps *in* code, and even then the corollary question must remain forever unanswered as to whether he himself does or doesn't understand the code. Anyway, there it is, the answer, in his casually tossed-out word, "so-called," in the phrase "so-called 9/11 novels."

So what does it mean, "so-called," and, further, what does *Garner* mean by it as he uses it here? Again, I'm taking no bets as to whether he knows what he means, though I've got my suspicions. Does "so-called" mean "poor," "dull," "inept," "hackneyed," or maybe plain

---

246 See Seth Sandrosky, "Reviewing 'Iowa Terror,' at http://www.mujca.com/iowaterror.htm
247   Anyone seriously interested in what my phrase "the 'other' kind" means can get some idea by reading my interview of myself at: http://www.ericlarsen.net/author.interview.1.html
248 And then I'd be stuck right back inside *A Nation Gone Blind*, fighting all over again a three-hundred-page battle for the right to say simple things that are also true, like "this book is intellectually and emotionally meager," or "this book is poor because it's media-driven and generic," without incurring, again, outraged accusations of my being anti-democratic, a snob, and an elitist. If anyone is still reading this essay, and if any of them really does want two free copies of *A Nation Gone Blind*, here, between you and me, is a hint for a "good" book "that can genuinely be said to be 'about living in the post 9/11 world.'" See *Timing*, by Rand Clifford. Information at http://www.starchiefpress.com/timing/index.html

old "crummy"? We'll get some very good hints later, but for the moment we'll have to let this question remain a mystery.

The *meaning*-meaning of it, however, in a world that's free of code and that allows truth both to be spoken and to be heard, is extremely simple. And this extremely simple meaning is that the 9/11 novels Garner sorts through are "so-called" for the very good reason that *there aren't any such novels*; the truth is that 9/11 novels don't *exist.*

Yes, there are plenty of novels that make *use* of 9/11 in one way or another—as an excuse for lovers to meet, unhappy marriages to be ended, foreboding atmospheres to be created—but no novels whose very materials, conception, meaning are made out of and thereby are *constituted* of the real truth of 9/11 and its meaning—no such novels exist, novels, that is, that really *would* be "9/11 novels," while veritable hosts of "so-called 9/11 novels" do indeed litter our unfertile land.

And so who knows what the truth is to Garner? Is he sick of all these novels for the good and simple reason that they're every bit as fake as the "official explanation" of 9/11, that it was an event pulled off by nineteen young jihadist Arabs with box cutters? In other words, is Garner sick of all these novels because to a one they're pallid lies and meretricious propaganda?

Maybe. Conceivably. Possibly. We'll never know, more likely than not. For a certainty, Garner himself is never going to tell us, at least not in the pages of the *New York Times*, with its truth-taboo. For better or for worse, then, Garner will have to continue reviewing—and reviewing and reviewing—such books *without* telling the truth about them (without telling us that they really *are* just "so-called" 9/11 books and without telling us *why*), and he's going to have to keep on doing this no matter how extreme the toll may be on his mind, conscience, and intellect.

Huck Finn said "you can't pray a lie." If you work at the *Times*, the rules are that you've got to *play* a lie all the way from start to stop.

As I've said before, I'm unable to imagine, for any serious or conscientious intellectual or genuinely thinking person, how leading this kind of double life can help but be destructive, corrosive, and ruinous to conscience, and perverting to the inner self, much in the ways that were portrayed by George Orwell in his now long-ago novel about people living *exactly* in this manner.

When the truth is taboo, out of bounds, forbidden, what does or can a thinking person *do*? Well, either such an individual must cease *being* a thinking person, remaining at very best a *half*-thinking person—a step so savagely destructive to any true, genuine, and whole thinker as to reduce him or her to the status of the walking wounded, destined only for deterioration, even madness. Not so? Too dramatic a statement to make? Too strong a thing to say? I myself don't think so. I think that varieties of madness from exactly this sort of cause are visible everywhere around us, far and away most often although not always in the form of self-delusion, self-delusion itself being something inevitably and necessarily destructive to any mind that may once have been whole.

Most of American popular culture, by no accident, explicitly encourages self-delusion and tirelessly rewards it, not only among intellectuals but among everyone. A rather simple example is the way that so large a part of the adult male population has been largely redefined over the past several decades as the American *boy*, complete with playground swagger, visored cap, and simian arms held out from the torso. Among intellectuals, much the same kind of thing, a parallel kind of *reduction* or *diminishment*, has also taken place, far, far more frequently than you might imagine. An example of this kind of "reduced," or you might say "child-ized," intellectual is Garner himself.

In the case of a rare few, the "reduced" state may actually be a deliberate pose or conscious act, a kind of very careful playing dumb and pretending to be "anti-elitist" in order not to be fingered as a true thinker. Pursuing this route requires maintaining a carefully sustained role, skilled but phony, that includes the apparent embrace of popular arts and ideas on the grounds that these are genuine, robust, and generated through the energies of "the people." That popular arts and ideas, in fact, are *none* of these things but are almost wholly pre-fabricated by the ruling powers—this is a rock-bottom truth, or rock-bottom falsehood, that the intellectual-in-disguise must pretend to accept as being not only natural and proper, but furthermore as being desirable.

Far more often, however—one might almost say infinitely more often—American intellectuals are in fact *not* playing any such role but are *genuinely* reduced and diminished in such ways as no longer to be capable of being whole thinkers while nevertheless still enjoying the prestige of being taken as such. Dwight Garner is an example of this latter and vastly more prevalent kind of intellectual.

The Garner-style intellectual is not acting, but it really *is* doing its thinking in ways that are minimized, diminished, content with old habits and forms, and, above all, happy to dwell in a thought-world from which every bit as much (or more) is *omitted* as is *included.*

We have already noted Garner's statement, after his use of the word "sad," that "sorting through the pile of so-called 9/11 novels" is an "exercise... that grows more pointless by the day."

Our idea of the reason it's pointless is one that Garner apparently misses by 180 degrees—giving as his *own* reason what may be one of the most astonishingly banal of all such statements ever made. His reason is that "They're all 9/11 novels now."

And there, unless Garner as an agent in the Ministry of Truth is holding his cards far closer to his chest that I think he is, we're given a glimpse of the true emptiness within him. That "They're all 9/11 novels now" is nonsense. As we have seen, the truth is precisely the opposite, with the ruinous, deadening truth being that *not a single one of them is a 9/11 novel.*

What Garner may or may not actually understand and see—we still don't *really* know—is that importing 9/11, in one way or another, into the machinery of your publishable ("generic; empty; tame; establishment-friendly") novel is a dime-a-dozen thing to do. *Every*body does it. It's no longer a mark of distinction for a tale that it include 9/11 as a part of its apparatus, whether in foreground or background, whether as plot-trigger or as cute-meet device, as an oozingly ominous faux-Conradian "theme" (à la DeLillo in *Falling Man*), or as something heard of distantly from another side of the world.

We're in the grip of a mass, corporate-sanctioned, corporate-sponsored, corporate-fed, corporate-gratified, corporate-rewarded know-nothingism and ignorance, and we can see evidence of it here, in Garner's thinking. We're in a situation where all the "best" and all the "published" novelists have, long since but *doubly so* in the aftermath of 9/11, either deliberately or in their happy and marketable ignorance, abandoned not only as useless but, much worse, as things *being in the way* of getting published, all of the vital and true elements, aims, and qualities that characterized and informed the genre of the modern novel when it really did achieve and express and embody significance: The novel, that is, from Joyce to Woolf, Ford to Conrad, Lawrence to Forster, Faulkner to Hemingway, Beckett to Waugh.

American literature is dead because American thought-feeling is dead, and the corpo-milito-governmento powers, visible in Garner's writing, are doing and will do everything it/they possibly can to *keep* thought-feeling dead—to keep *everything* that has to do with individual conscience, consciousness, and perception in all of America as completely dead as dead can be kept.

Just look, for example, at the language Garner chooses, placidly content with (or merely deaf *to*?) its damning and deceitful, its *disinforming* metaphors of mass-think and nation-destroying propaganda. You think I exaggerate. Well, have a look. Here's Garner declaring himself to be waiting not for Godot but for the Great American 9/11 novel:

> It's impossible, though, to stop scanning the horizon for something else—the bracing, wide-screen, many-angled novel that will leave a larger, more definitive intellectual and moral footprint on the new age of terror.

And are you as appalled and angry as I am? No? You're lucky, then—and maybe also you're not a writer. How about a simple cliché-check? Let's "scan the horizon," shall we? And shall we have some *real* literary talk? Hey, let's use words like "bracing, wide-screen, many-angled" to get at the unique and definitive nature of what the genre of the novel really is: Which is to say, in Garner-land, that the novel is not only itself a cliché, but it's a *derivative* one, coming into existence not just by imitating *movies* but imitating *crappy* movies: The "bracing" (whatever that means) and "wide-screen" (*there's* a junk-metaphor) kind, the "many-angled" (movie, movie, movie) and "larger" (yes, bigger is *always* better in America) kind of TV-on-the-page or movie-on-the-page book that all the publishers in Garnerland most love ("generic; user-friendly; empty; tame; *establishment*-friendly").

No wonder American literature today is cobbled together only by those in a tribe of centrist-polite know-nothingism, of pseudo-writers encouraged by pseudo-critics whose pseudo-ideas lead the tribe's members to believe that the greatest of novels are in fact overblown movies splashed onto the page—tribe-members who would never, *ever* be caught *dead* actually reading a perceptive, individual-voiced, clear-thinking, vitally important literary essay like, say—well, like this one. And for damn good reason: The simple truth of this absolutely excellent, brilliant, individually-minded, truth-seeing essay by David Cogswell,[249] he being a *non-citizen* of Garnerland, puts every single one of the tribalists of easy ignorance right out of business as makers of any *serious* literature at all.

Read it and see. Find out about "forbidden thought" as Cogswell explains its existence among us here and now ("forbidden thought," in a nutshell, is the *truth*). And find out how forbidden thought affects the nature of "publishing" in America today—how forbidden thought Garnerizes it, you might say.

And so for the moment we end, having sipped once again from the stale well of a dead literature, written by dead authors, urged into being by dead critics. The next sufficiently great contender in this contest of the non-beings, Garner sings, will be that trumpeted-one who "will leave a larger, more definitive intellectual and moral footprint on the new age of terror."

Holy *shit*, thinks me, did you hear what the deadman just *said?* I guess an "intellectual and moral footprint" is sort of like a carbon footprint, but oddly so, since with carbon footprints, it's the smaller the better, while *here* the deadman is looking *for big, big, big!* But let it go. The *true* death being spoken in the deadman's words comes through when he talks with such uplift and eagerness and anticipation about the great new *field* of potential material for deadnovelists: "*THE NEW AGE OF TERROR*"!

---

[249] "See No Evil," in *Online Review* (Feb. 27, 2008): http://onlinejournal.com/artman/publish/article_3001.shtml

Ah, *yes! yes! Yes, I said, yes!* The New Age of Terror![250] It's far, far greater than the New Age of the Enlightenment, or the New Jerusalem, or the New Frontier! It's *wonder*ful! It's *full* of promise and challenge for all the American deadwriters of the American deadfuture! And while *Netherland* is pretty much a small-boned and wimpy contender, it will just have to do for now, being

> the wittiest, angriest, most exacting and most desolate work of fiction we've yet had about life in New York and London after the World Trade Center fell.

Fell? In Garnerland, much as in Oceania, you see, having huge buildings spectacularly demolished by your own government and by agents, assets, and allies of your own government means that what happened is that those buildings "fell." In Garnerland, they "fell," but in the small, tiny, under populated country of Trueland, in the land, that is, of those still capable of depending—and being courageous enough *to* depend—on their own powers of observation and common sense, the buildings were demolished or brought down, "pulled,"[251] or *caused* to collapse.[252] And all of that effort was expended for *what*? Well, it was expended for the Disney-esque and cartoonish fabricating of what didn't exist before and still doesn't exist (except in the minds of deadmen or witting malefactors), the *Great New Age of Terror* that will make such *great* business for all the "defense" industries, will allow for the killing of the republic and the stripping away[253] of its people's rights and freedoms, *plus*—happy, happy be all those in Garnerland!—creating a vast deadland that will be built on lies that will in turn be swallowed *as truth*, most *especially* by the deadcritics and deadeditors who will sing the praises of the non-truth, the death-truth, and raise hymns of praise for that lucky, lucky deadwriter or deadnovelist who can write a deadbook that will "leave a larger, more definitive intellectual and moral footprint on the new age of terror" than *any other* deadman!

It's *brilliant*, it's *beautiful*, it's *wonderful*! It's full of promise, but

---

250 Please see Edward S. Herman and David Peterson, "There Is No 'War on Terror,'" from Znet (Jan. 8, 2008): http://www.informationclearinghouse.info/article19117.htm

251 See Larry Silverstein admitting on television that WT7 was in one way or another rigged to come down: http://www.youtube.com/watch?v=7WYdAJQV100

252 Update: We know now, thanks to the research of Dr. Judy Wood, that the buildings didn't "collapse" at all but were in fact turned into dust by a process of molecular dissociation brought about by the use of directed energy weaponry. Study it all for yourself via abundant and irrefutable scientific evidence in Dr. Wood's *Where Did the Towers Go? Evidence of Directed Free-Energy Technology on 9/11*: http://wheredidthetowersgo.com/

253 Again, see this indispensible timeline of Constitutional destruction so far: http://www.kickthemallout.com/article.php/Story-Bill_of_Rights_Attack_Timeline

it's *more* full of death, *more* full of emptiness, *more* full of deadmen, *more* full of deadsociety, *more* full of deadliterature, *more* full of dead-think, and *much, much, much* more full of treachery and traitorousness coming from just about every source of deadauthority that you can either name or imagine.

In tiny little Trueland, on the other hand, people are still capable of reading real books instead of the ersatz, generic, lie-filled, fraud-ulent, insignificant, establishment-friendly, betrayal-books that they're urged to read by the highest authorities in all of Garnerland, books by those deadwriters who tell, and re-tell, and then tell again the biggest of all possible lies, earning the highest praises from Gar-nercommittees, being listed on prestigious Garnerlists, and, above all, over and over proving themselves to be generic, empty, tame, establishment-friendly, and *dedicatedly* treacherous in their love of Garnerland and their *hatred* of that conspiracy-filled little dump of a place that's filled with nothing but "nut-cases," Trueland.

With mind-cancer and soul-cancer and perception-cancer so vir-ulent and overwhelmingly destructive as this, alive and sucking the blood and fiber and tissue out of the very center of the nation's literary, intellectual, and aesthetic life, how long can that nation *conceivably* endure, even in its present, dead-populated, condition?

The question is moot, I suppose, the place being dead already, as Jason Miller brilliantly and impassionedly shows us.[254]

Who the devil was Winston *Churchill*? Damned if I know. I do know, though, that in the Garner States today, it's much, much better *not* to know than it is *to* know almost anything. Much safer. Just ask Garner himself. He'll tell you. And I also know something else. I know that never before in the history of this nation and I suspect of any other has so great a lie been foisted so successfully on so many by so few.

There's far worse to come, but it will have to wait until next time. God help us all.

Eric Larsen
July 26, 2008

---

[254] See Jason Miller, "Murdering God: Of Shotguns, American Capitalism, and Moral Ex-pediency," in *Online Journal* (July 17, 2008): http://onlinejournal.com/artman/publish/article_3503.shtml

16.

HOWARD ZINN AND THE
TEA COZY
AUGUST 17, 2008

To the Reader:
And *this* essay may look as though it's about Howard
Zinn—but it's about Zinn only as much as the preceding
piece was about Dwight Garner. The essays in this book,
especially these closing ones, are about something far
more important than any individual, writer, or person.
They're about *what's happening to Americans.* Readers
will remember this passage from Rand Clifford:
"9/11 is the one event that if left buried in lies and
omission, untreated, could destroy our nation; a cancer
that first embedded over ten years ago with a neocon
lesion called The Project for the New American Century
(PNAC). Euphemisms have since softened the original
documentation, but the PNAC remains no less an absolute must-read for every American concerned about their
nation's health." As you'll remember, Clifford went on
to say that "We are losing the battle for our nation largely
because few even realize our *only real war is internal.*"
     That internal war is being lost. It is being lost first
because there is emptiness inside American minds, as
we saw last time and will see again this time. And the
internal war is being lost also, as we'll see most vividly
next time, because that emptiness is being replaced by
lethal poison—life-destroying, spirit-destroying toxins
that remain unseen and unperceived by a blind and
increasingly ignorant nation but that yet continue to be
produced by our national "leaders" both political and—
quotation marks again—"intellectual."

For close to three years, I have been writing essays that describe,
castigate, and lament the patent madness, especially since 9/11, of
American policy, leadership, and popular thinking and behavior.
These essays have described and cried out against the deadly effects
not just on the political nation but on the nation's entire culture that
have been produced by Americans' choosing to go on living—or

"living"—within the corrupting miasma of one of the greatest, most grotesque, most destructive lies ever told in the long and admittedly grim history of the human race.

I've received a certain, though not great, number of attacks for my efforts, one of the goofiest being from an old socialist friend in Canada who seems to have gone over the edge of something somewhere. His position, as he explained via email, is that I'm myself the demented one for keeping up the battle for 9/11 Truth—because in actuality "9/11 was a flyspeck on the dust-jacket of history for nearly everyone except those who live in the US and believe fervently that the US is an impregnable monument to all things good and true."

My old friend must indeed have lost his marbles—and memory— if he really means to put *me* in the company of those who "believe fervently that the US is an impregnable monument to all things good and true." After all, he himself declared, just before putting me in that ungodly company, that what I (that is, me, not him) really "think" (or hope) is "that the ripcord of truth on 9/11 might bring down Bush and corporate-imperialist conspiracy," hardly the aim of one who sees in the U.S. "all things good and true."

But there's something more sinister at work in my friend's thinking, and something more self-paralyzing than just tossing out false accusations that certain people—me— worship the U.S. as being all good if not in fact the world's only good. The kindling that set my friend's anger aflame was an essay I wrote attacking, among other things, Howard Zinn.[255] The kind of "thinking" I attacked in Zinn's case is repeated by my friend himself in his attack on *me* for *my* attack on *Zinn*. Here's my friend's first sally:

> So what is Zinn's sin, what is at the root of EL's extended attack on this man? Only that he doesn't join in with his clarion call to denounce 9/11 as a false-flag inside job.

Even my friend's first shot is mortally compromised by that little word, the adverb "only." Other little smear-words, like "clarion call," we can ignore. But truth is truth, and the question of Zinn's failure to show any interest in the 9/11 Truth movement was in actuality "only" a part of what I did attack him for.

On the specific matter of 9/11 truth, my friend begins delicately and ends grotesquely:

> Now, I am not for a moment going to suggest that the official explanations [of 9/11] are true, but I will suggest that there may be a number of reasons why one bites one's tongue on this issue, the foremost of which is that,

---

[255] See Chapter 13, "The Premeditated Murder of the United States of America"

given the horror that is Amerikan history, it's not really that big a deal. Just stack it up next to the assassinations of Jack Kennedy, Bobby Kennedy, Martin Luther [King], Malcolm X, John Lennon, and Jimmy Hoffa, all within a period of less than twenty years—most, if not all, of these... also [being] "inside jobs." And this only scratches the surface of malfeasance: Arbenz in Guatemala, Allende in Chile, the Dirty War in Argentina, the Contra war against the Sandinistas, and on and on. And that's only Latin America.

So if EL thinks that the ripcord of truth on 9/11 might bring down Bush and corporate-imperialist conspiracy, then I might ask, if that were true, why did not the exposures surrounding the Bay of Pigs or the Iran-Contra scandal have the same potential? I'm sorry, but 9/11 was a flyspeck on the dust-jacket of history for nearly everyone except those who live in the US and believe fervently that the US is an impregnable monument to all things good and true.

What on earth kind of argument, may I ask, is that? Actually, it's in a crucial way parallel to the argument that informed Zinn's own thinking in "Empire or Humanity? What the Classroom Didn't Teach Me About the American Empire,"[256] the essay that recently, after some time away, drew my attention back to Zinn. In that essay, as we saw in chapter 13, the historian says, first, that his school years hadn't let him in on the secret that the U.S. in fact had a long imperial history. And, second, he says, or lets it be implied, that that failure was *really bad*. Well, who couldn't agree? That failure was intolerable. What it means is that schools in the U.S. didn't, and doubtless still don't, provide education, at least not in history, but provide propaganda instead, just like the mass media does, and the often treacherous *New York Times*.[257]

The trouble is, though, that the matter doesn't end there—or, rather, the trouble is that in Zinn's hands and mind it *does* end there. That is, there's so much more remaining to be said after what he *does* say, and yet Zinn chooses to express—and do—virtually nothing. It's as though his essay is all body but no brain, or is all face and no vocal cords. The essay seems to have no *conclusion*. It seems to take us *nowhere*.

Let's look at what really happens in the essay. Zinn tells us that in school he didn't learn about the "Trail of Tears," or the "Sand Creek massacre," or the fraudulent seizing of half of Mexico, or "the inva-

---

256 Posted as a "Tomgram" on Tomdispatch.com (April 1, 2008): http://www.tomdispatch.com/post/174913
257 See "All the Propaganda That's Fit to Print: *The New York Times*, Again, Tells It Like It Ain't," by Sean Madden (August 14, 2008): http://blog.inoodle.com/2008/08/all-propaganda-thats-fit-to-print-new.html

sion of Cuba" (after the phony battleship *Maine* sinking), or the subsequent "invasion of the Philippines, halfway around the world." Fine. Good. He cites for us these ruinous, rapacious, brutishly opportunistic things and events that he didn't learn about until *after* school. Fine and good, but now what? What is the essay going to *say*? What is Zinn, now, going to tell us *about* what he's told us so far? And there lies the great trouble. The great trouble is that there's not going *to be* anything more. We're given the litany of the acts and deeds of brute imperialism that weren't taught in school—but then *there's no further step.*

So what, do I hear someone ask? And my answer is, so *everything.*

What do I mean? Well, we've looked at the essay. Now let's look at it closely.

As you can see for yourself by reading the entire piece, Zinn's essay is related to a new comic book he's bringing out called *A People's History of American Empire.*[258] I find this association—and this new marketing project—very interesting.

Just suppose something for a moment. Just suppose that you were a very, very successful salesman of—well, let's just say of *snake oil*, although I hasten to add that not for *a millionth of a nano-second* would we think of Howard *Zinn* as a salesman of snake oil. No, we must all clearly agree that the snake oil metaphor is for illustrative purposes only.

Now that that's cleared up, let's pursue the illustration. If you *were* a successful snake oil salesman, what's the last thing in the world you'd want to happen? Well, *that's* an easy question, isn't it! The last thing in the world you'd want to happen is that people would become aware that your snake oil actually had no curative effects whatsoever—in other words, that it *had no power.*

You wouldn't want the whistle blown on your snake oil. You wouldn't want snake oil *reform.* You wouldn't want the snake oil market to bottom out and disappear.

Now let's shift gears just a bit. If you had built a long career based on—just say—your having very successfully continued selling claims that a certain government, or a certain aspect of a government, or even a certain trait, element, or unit of a government was vile, inhumane, deceitful, self-interested, and perfidious—well, if you *were* in that situation, and if sales *were* still going well, what's the last thing in the world that you'd want to happen?

If you *were* a successful salesman such as the purely hypothetical one described above, the last thing in the world you'd want to hap-

---

[258] *A People's History of American Empire* (Metropolitan Books, 2008): http://www.amazon.com/dp/0805087443/ref=nosim/?tag=nationbooks08-20#_

pen would be that the government you were concerned with should stop being vile, inhumane, deceitful, self-interested, and perfidious.

Fair enough? We hear a lot about "fallible human nature," and isn't it generally thought to be true that most people will follow that fallible nature and seek—or create—ways to protect and preserve their own interests?

And, if you agree with that premise, wouldn't a corollary premise follow that in all likelihood Howard Zinn would hope and choose for his own interests *not* to be squandered, dissipated, and transformed into airy nothingness?

In other words, how could you possibly reject out of hand the working hypothesis that Howard Zinn, best-selling author, might very possibly or even powerfully wish that the United States *not* stop being vilely, inhumanely, deceitfully, self-interestedly, and perfidiously imperial?

The logic is probable and clear, you must agree. On the other hand, in case you don't agree, let's look further.

First, let's take a close look at the closing three paragraphs of Zinn's essay. Thus:

> The American Empire has always been a bipartisan project—Democrats and Republicans have taken turns extending it, extolling it, justifying it. President Woodrow Wilson told graduates of the Naval Academy in 1914 (the year he bombarded Mexico) that the U.S. used "her navy and her army... as the instruments of civilization, not as the instruments of aggression." And Bill Clinton, in 1992, told West Point graduates: "The values you learned here... will be able to spread throughout the country and throughout the world."
>
> For the people of the United States, and indeed for people all over the world, those claims sooner or later are revealed to be false. The rhetoric, often persuasive on first hearing, soon becomes overwhelmed by horrors that can no longer be concealed: the bloody corpses of Iraq, the torn limbs of American GIs, the millions of families driven from their homes—in the Middle East and in the Mississippi Delta.
>
> Have not the justifications for empire, embedded in our culture, assaulting our good sense—that war is necessary for security, that expansion is fundamental to civilization—begun to lose their hold on our minds? Have we reached a point in history where we are ready to embrace a new way of living in the world, expanding not our military power, but our humanity?

Three points, and then a pulling of the three together. First point, corresponding to the first paragraph: Here, Zinn compiles some more imperialist lies and crimes—and, indeed, they *are* imperialist lies and crimes, no doubt about it. These all are in keeping with the *earlier* sections of Zinn's essay, which compiled other imperialist criminalities that came, generally, from earlier years of U.S. history. Therefore, the essay would seem to be bringing its subject matter, its interest, and its purpose increasingly close to the present.

And, indeed, point two (corresponding to paragraph two) reinforces this idea by means of its references to the present carnage in Iraq—carnage brought about by lies and more crimes—and then to the displacement and destruction of populations both in New Orleans and in the Middle East.

At this point a sub-question arises: Let's call it Question 2 (b). Here it is: Why stop there? If—*if*—the essayist's wish is that imperialism be challenged, brought down, and ended, then why doesn't he keep going and stick his lance into the biggest, most visible, and most *vulnerable* chink in the imperialists' armor, namely its enormous imperialist lie and crime of 9/11?

But no dice. Zinn hits the brakes instead. And *then* he drinks down a huge draught of some kind of intellect-numbing agent, a cliché-inducing liquor, or a draught of Lethe-like make-me-a-plain-vanilla-hollow-man drug. I suspect it may, in fact, be the same stuff that Dwight Garner drinks each morning to keep *his* airy glibness-while-malefacting machinery so well oiled.

And so we come to point three. And point three brings us to this great question: The question of just what Zinn *does* with his subject, exactly what it is he's going to do to help us get *rid* of a criminal, pirating, inhumane, earth-destroying, treason-engendering, treason-requiring, ugly, vile, despised, genocidal, republic-destroying and Earth-destroying U.S. imperialism.

And the answer to this question?

Nuthin'.

Take a look. Here's firebrand anti-imperialist Zinn telling us—in subordinate phrases—first, that the lies and crimes he's cited are "justifications for empire"; second, that they are "embedded in our culture" (dammit, let's *un*-embed them, then, and while we're at it let's un-embed the propagandizing press, too); and, third—oh, *lordy!* oh, *me!* can we stand up under the power of such rhetoric?— Zinn tells us that these lies "assault our good sense"!

"Assault our good sense"?! God in heaven, it's as though Henry James himself had stepped in front of Zinn and taken over the keyboard. *Fiery* in prose! *Resolute* in tone! *Masculine* in stance! *Determined* in judgment! *Immediate* in impulse! How much *less* direct a call to summary and significant action could we possibly imagine?

How interesting it is—that *this* is what we get from the great progressive historian and well known public figure—*assault our good sense*—when the actuality is dire, overwhelming, and so extreme as soon to be almost beyond reach of *any* correction or repair whatsoever: When the actuality is that the repugnant American imperialists now in power are indeed assaulting us with things infinitely less subtle or delicate than Zinn's phrasing suggests with his "[assaults] our good sense." No, the repugnant American criminals, imperialists, and pirates now in power confront us each and every day with things *impossible* to ignore, with repeated acts of treason, with repeated breaches of international law (much of that now-broken law having originated from the *American-sponsored* Nuremberg Trials after WWII), with repeated crimes against humanity, against peace, against the republic, against the Constitution, against their sworn oaths of office, against their own countrymen and their own countrywomen and against the *children* and the *poor* of their own nation, against the very elements of decency itself, against Magna Carta, against the individual, against the future and the well-being of Earth, against the subtleties and highest accomplishments of all cultures whether ancient or modern, against truth, and, again and again and again, against the most basic notions of humanity or feeling or decency or generosity or compassion in dealings either between peoples or between nations or between men.

Those are the actualities, and why do you suppose it is that instead of touching on them, recognizing and confronting them, let *alone* taking or demanding action to repudiate or defeat them, Zinn offers us only the most wan and pale of rhetorical questions: Has the time come when all these criminal and imperial lies and crimes and atrocities have "begun to lose their hold on our minds"?

But why *should* they have begun to "lose their hold on our minds"? What has *Zinn* said or done to help bring about any semblance or likelihood of an end so desirable as that? Why, for one, single, glaring example—an exact parallel of Naomi Klein's extraordinary omission in *Shock Doctrine*[259]—did he stop short of 9/11, merely skip over it?

•

Well. Now that we know Zinn isn't going to tell anywhere near the whole truth, and that in fact, historian or not, he shows no interest in the whole truth, his vacant, bland language, something like the language of a Lotus-eater, begins to make perfect sense. Labeled "progressive," frequent contributor to the moribund *Progressive* magazine,

---

[259] See Caroline Baker's indispensably important essay, "*Naomi Klein's Shock Doctrine's* Shocking Short Shrift": http://ccun.org/Opinion%20Editorials/2007/November/12%20o/Naomi%20Klein's%20Shock%20Doctrine's%20Shocking%20Short%20Shrift%20By%20Carolyn%20Baker.htm

he shows no quality here of anything like the true progressive but, instead, every quality of the keeper of the status quo. Have you ever in your life heard words less rooted in the hard stones and packed earth of the *real* events, crimes, and atrocities that constitute the horrors of imperial policy under the Bushiscti? Words any more suitable to the Sunday pulpit than to the progressive reformer? Words more calculated to bring on self-referential swoons of complacency rather than calls to *fight* the bastards than Zinn's closing sentence?

> Have we reached a point in history where we are ready to embrace a new way of living in the world, expanding not our military power, but our humanity?[260]

I first became aware of this essay, ancillary to Zinn's new comic book (previously mentioned), when it appeared on Tom Englehardt's well known Tomdispatch.com. On that site, above each new "dispatch," you'll find a sentence designed to explain what the web site's purpose and intended audience are. That sentence is worth a close look:

> Tomdispatch.com is for anyone seeking a deeper understanding of our post-9/11 world and a clear sense of how our imperial globe actually works.

Am I alone among the throngs of all humanity in finding this an eminently foolish sentence—and at the same time one perfectly suited to what we've seen of the spirit and stance of Howard Zinn? Two things leap out, one of them a genuine shocker, the glib and simple phrase "our imperial globe." Good *god*, is it true? Is it a fact that now not only the U.S. but the entire *globe* is imperial (and who's the emperor?)? Zounds, *that's* growth that will up the ante for the extent and breadth of Howard Zinn's exhausting work: Now he'll have to slave away at scaring everyone in the *world*[261] instead of only those in the U.S. with the horrifying facts of imperialist behavior while at

---

260 Contrast the closing three paragraphs of Paul Craig Roberts' "There May Be Many Mushroom Clouds in Our Future," (August 14, 2008)

"The Ukraine, where a sick nationalism has taken hold funded by the neocon National Endowment for Democracy, will be the next conflict between American pretensions and Russia. Russia is being taught by the neocons that freeing the constituent parts of its empire has not resulted in their independence but in their absorption into the American Empire.

"Unless enough Americans can overcome their brainwashed state and the rigged Diebold voting machines, turn out the imbecilic Republicans and hold the neoconservatives accountable for their crimes against humanity, a crazed neocon US government will provoke nuclear war with Russia.

"The neoconservatives represent the greatest danger ever faced by the United States and the world. Humanity has no greater enemy." (http://www.opednews.com/articles/There-May-Be-Many-Mushroom-by-Paul-Craig-Roberts-080814-100.html)

261 *A People's History of American Empire*, with Mike Konopacki and Paul Buhle (Metropolitan Books, 2008): http://www.amazon.com/dp/0805087443/ref=nosim/?tag=natio nbooks08-20#_

the same time making sure he does all he can to allow that set and species of great crimes to continue.

A Herculean task, but not, apparently, Sisyphean.

The other phrase in the Tomdispatch sentence is a wretched cliché, a phrase that can be spoken only by those plunged in ignorance, victimized by indolence, or in the grip of egregiously harmful malignancy. I mean the phrase "our post-9/11 world."

This phrase is, of course, with *very* few exceptions, always a lie,[262] intentional or unintentional. Those ignorant enough to believe the "official" line that on 9/11 the U.S. really was "attacked" by nineteen Muslim young men with box-cutters are unintentional liars when they use the words "post-9/11 world," since what they mean is "the world after the U.S. was attacked by Al Qaeda and nineteen young members of militant Islam." But in truth, of course, there simply *is* no "post-9/11 world" of that kind, since no "attack" of that kind ever happened. On the other hand, the *actual* malignant and treasonous perpetrators of 9/11, those from within our own government or associated with our own government, or those covering up for our own government, are liars of another kind, witting ones, when *they* speak of "our post-9/11 world." The reason is obvious: They lie, first, in order to maintain the wholly false myth that the U.S. really was attacked by Al Qaeda and members of militant Islam and that the world really was changed thereby, and they lie, second, in order to keep the way clear for the committing of the international crimes, crimes against humanity and against the republic and against the Constitution that had been planned and intended all along, with 9/11 to be the door that, once opened, would clear the way, with neither punishment nor accountability a result, first for the initiation of such crimes and then for the perpetuation of them without end in sight.

Now, the really fascinating question is the question of which kind of dissembler liar Tom Englehardt is. He plays his cards very close to his chest, telling his considerable readership that he will give them, as I mentioned, "a deeper understanding of our post-9/11 world," though without tipping his hand in any way whatsoever as to what that phrase or term might possibly mean. At the same time, it becomes clear that TomDispatch.com won't so much as entertain the idea of touching the subject of the truth of 9/11 with a ten-foot—well, with a ten-foot fire hook or maybe with a ten-foot-long contract governing TomDispatch's relationship with The Nation Institute.

Let it go—TomDispatch.com, after all, though calling itself "A Regular Antidote to the Mainstream Media," *is also* "A Project of

---

262 It deserves very careful comparison, needless to say, with the phrase "9/11 novels" as used by Dwight Garner in chapter 15.

The Nation Institute" and therefore a project also of the mainstream media. We all know—and if we don't, we should—that *The Nation* is one of the most visible, complicit, and treacherous of "left-wing gatekeepers"[263] that our now-all-but-lost republic is burdened and diseased-unto-the-death by. It follows that so is TomDispatch.com.

But let that go, too. Our real subject here, after all, is, first, the thinking of Howard Zinn, and, second, the thinking of my old socialist friend in Canada.

After its appearance on TomDispatch, the Zinn essay appeared widely on various outlets across the internet. And what could possibly be wrong with that? Well, nothing at all—except that, like Zinn's essay itself, all that exposure led to nothing, and certainly to nothing good.

As a way of suggesting why it led to nothing good, allow me refer to a recent and worthwhile piece by Kieren McCarthy called "Why TV News in the US is Utter Rubbish."[264] McCarthy deftly shows how and why U.S. television news is indeed "utter rubbish," and then he asks a perfectly reasonable question: "So where do you get your news while living in the US?"

The Daily Show and the Colbert Report, he says, are two places (sort of), but his most interesting observation has to do with National Public Radio. It's this:

> News-starved Americans usually hold up National Public Radio, NPR, as the best option. But with interlude music fresh from the 1920s and a twee, kitchen-table-chat approach, this is news wrapped in a tea cosy [sic].

And there it is: McCarthy has hit precisely on what the relationship is between Howard Zinn and *his* audience—*he's* wrapped in the tea cozy, and his audience absolutely loves how warm and soft he is. Even my angry socialist friend from Canada criticized my attack on Zinn for the very reason that Zinn "truly is a warm-hearted and brilliant leftist." Now, the "brilliant" point aside, if anyone can tell me what in the name of the devil being "warm-hearted" could have to do with any of the intellectual questions at hand, I hope they'll write and let me in on it. But as far as I can tell, my friend has effectively put his own imprimatur on the tea-cozy concept of Zinn, while Kieren McCarthy has pointed *his* finger of accusation at the tea cozy nature of NPR.

It means, quite literally, that for his particular audience, Zinn is the tea cozy. He is nice and warm and reassuring and soothing—*exactly* the things the tea cozy is. And, oh, disgruntled reader, I hear you ask-

---

[263] See Christopher Hayes, "9/11: The Roots of Paranoia," in The Nation for Dec. 25, 2006: http://www.thenation.com/article/911-roots-paranoia

[264] See *Information Clearing House*, Aug. 8, 2008: http://www.informationclearing-house.info/article20464.htm

ing, "And what's wrong with *that?*" Well, what's wrong with it is that tea cozies may be cozy, but they don't think, and neither do they express thought. And Zinn, in his function as tea cozy (just like NPR in *its* function as tea cozy), has set out to make *absolutely certain* that his audience continue to think that it's thinking while at the same time, at whatever cost, he continues to keep it from actually doing so. If this weren't the case, both Howard Zinn *and* NPR would be out of business, *tout de suite* and *in toto*. Would it were so, since *then* they might each be able actually to do some real and whole truth-telling and therefore some *good*.

Let's just consider, together, the cases of Howard Zinn and Tom Englehardt. Let's think of each of them as tea cozies. And let's do so, specifically, in regard to the question of the truth about 9/11—who did it, why they did it, and how they got away with it.

Of course, how they got away with it is almost entirely through the complicity of a corrupt, controlled, and treasonous mass media— with the initial exception of now-fired Dan Rather, who was far enough out of the criminal loop that he naively and honestly put into words exactly what he saw in the "collapse" of the WTC buildings.[265] But not Howard Zinn, and not Tom Englehardt. God forbid that Zinn as tea cozy should ever do anything that's, let's say, discomfiting or jarring to his audience of loving and devoted followers, or harsh or unexpected or against the grain or counter-intuitive or unfamil-iar or—or *true* in some unexpected way that the tea-cozy-cuddlers hadn't previously thought of, been in the *habit* of thinking of, or had reason to be awake to at all.

What would happen to Tom Englehardt if *he* told or revealed the truth about 9/11? Well, he'd lose his job with The Nation Institute, naturally.

And so what should Tom Englehardt do? He should—if he's an American, a patriot, a citizen of the world, a humanist, an adherent of international law and of the Geneva Conventions and the Nuremberg Principles and a defender of the Universal Declaration of the Rights of Man—he should tell, announce, and reveal the truth about 9/11 at once, immediately, boldly, bravely, and informedly.

And Howard Zinn? What would happen to Howard Zinn if he told or revealed the truth about 9/11? Well, he'd lose his publishing opportunities with TomDispatch.com, and with *Progressive Maga-zine*, naturally, and he'd lose half or more, maybe all, of the audience for his new comic book,[266] also naturally.

---

265 Hear Rather's voice as he says one of the "collapses" on 9/11 looked like a building "de-liberately destroyed by well-placed dynamite to knock it down" : http://www.youtube.com/watch?v=Nvx904dAw0o

266 See footnote 261.

And so what should Howard Zinn do? He should—if he's an American, a patriot, a citizen of the world, a humanist, an adherent of international law and of the Geneva Conventions and the Nuremberg Principles and a defender of the Universal Declaration of the Rights of Man—he should tell, announce, and reveal the truth about 9/11 at once, immediately, boldly, bravely, and informedly.

That is what they should do—and it's what they *must* do if they hope in any way whatsoever to avoid the absolute certainty of history's declaring them at some later date—a date that I devoutly wish be soon—to be quislings, malefactors against the republic, against the republic's Constitution, against peace, against international law, against conscience, against the sovereignty of nations, and against the sanctity of the individual human self.

Exactly the same is true also of the following people, not to mention many, many, many others not listed here: Alexander Cockburn, Arianna Huffington, Bill Keller, Bill Moyers, Bob Herbert, Christopher Hayes, David Corn, Dwight Garner, Elliot Spitzer, Frank Rich, Jacob Weisberg, Katrina vanden Heuvel, Larry Silverstein, Matthew Rothschild, Nicholas Lemann, Noam Chomsky, Paul Krugman, and Ted Rall.

And what about my old socialist friend in Canada? Do you remember what he said?

Well, in case you don't, here's part of it:

> So if EL thinks that the ripcord of truth on 9/11 might bring down Bush and corporate-imperialist conspiracy, then I might ask, if that were true, then why did not the exposures surrounding the Bay of Pigs or the Iran-Contra scandal have the same potential? I'm sorry, but 9/11 was a flyspeck on the dust-jacket of history for nearly everyone except those who live in the US and believe fervently that the US is an impregnable monument to all things good and true.

Well, old friend, you who value Howard Zinn because he "truly is. . . warm-hearted," how much of "a flyspeck on the dust-jacket of history" do you really think 9/11 is to the million and a quarter Iraqis now dead *because* of it, or the four million Iraqis now displaced *because* of it, or the unnumbered dead and dying from radioactive depleted uranium *because* of it? And how much of "a flyspeck on the dust-jacket of history" do you think it will mean to Canadians themselves when the sovereignty of their own nation[267] is stolen

267   See Michel Chossudovsky, "Canada's Sovereignty in Jeopardy: The Militarization of North America," in *Global Research* (Aug. 17, 2007): http://www.globalresearch.ca/index.php?context=va&aid=6572

268   See Mike Whitney, "Putin Walks into a Trap," in *Information Clearing House* (Aug. 13, 2008): http://www.informationclearinghouse.info/article20508.htm

from them because of it? How much of "a flyspeck on the dust-jacket of history" does it seem to the South Ossetians who are dying[268] *because* of it? How much of "a flyspeck on the dust-jacket of history" will it seem to the Iranians if they are atom-bombed *because* of it? [269]

And, old friend, your notion that 9/11 is "a flyspeck on the dust-jacket of history" because it's historically preceded by so many *other* heinous crimes committed by the same "Amerikan" elements that committed 9/11—well, what you're saying is the equivalent of this: "There have been cases and cases of typhus ever since the earliest dawn of antiquity. Therefore, any new case of typhus is nothing more than 'a flyspeck on the history of infectious disease' and shouldn't be treated as anything special—in fact, shouldn't be treated at *all*," especially since all those much *earlier* cases went untreated.

Good god, old man. You're not one of *them*, are you? One of the *Zinnians?* One of the *Englehardts?* One of the Katrina vanden *Heuvels?* One of the Amy *Goodmans?*

One of the default *complicitors?*

One of the *tea cozies?*

Tell me not, I pray you. Tell me not.

—Eric Larsen
—August 17, 2008

---

[269] Update: And how much of "a flyspeck on the dust-jacket of history" does it seem now to the increasingly many who are suffering and dying in Yemen, Somalia, Pakistan, Waziristan, and Afghanistan because of it?

16.

CAN THE LITERARY LIFE
EXIST IN A POST-*1984* NATION?
NOVEMBER 16, 2009

To the Reader:
Nature abhors a vacuum. I said before that the empty
space in the American mind is being occupied by lethal
poison—by "life-destroying and spirit-destroying
toxins." In this essay, we see those toxins at work. The
covering up of the truth of what happened on 9/11 is
one thing. Worse and far more harmful, dangerous,
and malignant is the turn of mind, the perverse political
aesthetic, that comes into existence as a result of the
genuflections and reverences that are part and parcel of
that on-going and repugnant cover-up. Here, we see the
true malignancy of those poisoned seeds now actually
germinating and sprouting in the ruinously corrupted
soil of American intellectual-political life.

1.

A number of pieces written by me but not appearing in this book
have involved close looks at the *New York Times*—for the very good
reason that the gray lady is so important a part of the news blackout
inside the United States. The *Times* is a paper dedicated to falsifying
on behalf of its overlords, and concomitantly a paper dedicated also
to the finessing and cosmeticizing of its dissemblings on those occasions when by accident or oversight they may have become so obvious that they might backfire—when, that is to say, the falsehoods run
the risk of being perceived by the average reader for the very falsehoods that they really are.

At the end of a piece that again is not included in this book but is
an analysis of the *Times*, I recommended a number of readings that
seemed to me refreshing in their uncensored truth-telling, however
grim the real nature of that truth may have been. One piece of this
recommended reading was James Petras' "The US War against Iraq:

The Destruction of a Civilization."[270] This is a piece journalism unlike any that would run in the *Times* in that it describes what the U.S. really did *in* Iraq and what it really did—has done—*to* Iraq. Making it possible by means of massive lies perpetrated on a gullible and conveniently ignorant public, the leaders of our nation set out, successfully, to do nothing less than, as Petras shows, destroy a civilization. That is an immeasurably vast act of evil, and yet our country planned it, executed it, brought it to completion. If Americans knew the truth instead of the dissembling and euphemized *versions* of the truth propagated by the media in general and by papers like the *Times* in particular, they would know a great number of things that most now have not the *least* idea about. For example, if there were real news in the U.S., it would never have been possible *for eight years* to suppress the very clear truth that 9/11 was brought about not by foreign "terrorists," and not by Osama bin Laden, but by terrorists in our own government and working for and within our own government who planned, executed, and brought to completion all the events of that day,[271] doing so in order "to hijack a country from her people and [to place] the interests of the rich and the powerful above justice and truth."[272]

Americans, however, don't know that truth. Americans also don't know that the entirety of the fraudulent, illegal, and criminal "war on terror" is itself a lie made up of other lies, an immense fraud made possible only by the earlier great lie of 9/11.[273] They don't know that "Islamic terrorism" is something, insofar as it exists at all, created by Americans for America's own purposes, something that has been stirred up and kept most carefully in "existence" ever since 9/11 for the simple purpose of giving the impression that America really does face a dangerous and ruthless foreign enemy when in truth, fact, and actuality, it faces no such thing—except from within.

I think we can stop here rather than going on to list yet more lies that America in general now swallows and has swallowed for the past decade or so, largely due to the national news blackout that for its effectiveness depends mainly on the twin evils of omission and disinformation. The on-going breaches of international law commit-

---

[270] The US War against Iraq: The Destruction of a Civilization, in *Information Clearing House* (Aug. 21, 2009): http://www.informationclearinghouse.info/article23342.htm

[271] Not to mention prior events related to it and in preparation for it—from as early as the African embassy bombings and the USS Cole attack. On this subject, one of the very best works is Nafeez Mossadeq Ahmed's *The War on Truth: 9/11, Disinformation, and the Anatomy of Terrorism* (Olive Branch Press, 2005). http://www.amazon.com/War-Truth-Disinformation-Anatomy-Terrorism/dp/1566565960/sr=1-1/qid=1167587061/ref=pd_bbs_sr_1/104-4231058-3189532?ie=UTF8&s=books

[272] Quoted from "The Turning Point," on *NycCan*, at http://nyccan.org/The_Turning_Point.php

[273] Again, see Edward S. Herman and David Peterson, "There Is No 'War on Terror,'" from *Znet* (Jan. 8, 2008): http://www.informationclearinghouse.info/article19117.htm

ted in the name of the "war on terror" are neither widely nor well enough known to be taken as the monstrosities they are, as neither are the ongoing crimes against humanity through the uses of torture and murder, the continuing crimes against civilians, including women and children, nor the depravities in general that have come to be routine aspects of United States "military" operations[274] in whatever parts of the globe our "nation" decides to commit its crimes as motivated by convenience and greed.[275]

In a word, by merit of their being lied to so thoroughly, unceasingly, and well, Americans don't see and don't understand that it's no longer a "them" who are the Nazis of today, but that it's *us*. Americans don't understand, as people like Paul Craig Roberts[276] try to point out over and over, that it's *we* now who are the nation-raping forces, *we* who are the Napoleonic armies, we who are the destroyers not only of nations but, as James Petras shows, entire civilizations.

2.

Another piece of reading I recommended was Ray McGovern's article, "Blackwater's Unwritten Death Contract,"[277] a chilling and revelatory piece about assassination programs under Bush and Cheney, along with a pdf of the memo of assassination-authorization itself, dated Feb. 7, 2002, and signed by Bush,[278] declaring that rules of the Geneva Conventions don't apply to prisoners taken in the "war on terror." *Anything*, the memo makes clear, can be done to non-people like them. Can things conceivably get uglier than this? "I have the feeling," writes McGovern, that "we are in for many more chapters recording how the lawlessness and savagery of post-9/11 Washington played out during the last seven years of the Bush/Cheney administration."

If the news blackout weren't so seamless, sustained, and complete, these examples of poisonous, destructive criminality would *have* to have been exposed to sunlight and destroyed long since. Or think of it another way. If the blackout weren't so seamless, sustained, and complete—made all the more so by the participation also of "liberal" and "progressive" media, like Pacifica Radio, NPR, *The Nation*,

---

274 Update: See John Chuckman, "Aung San Suu Kyi, Omar Khadr and Barack Obama: A dreadful tale of what America has become," in *Online Journal* (Nov. 17, 2009): http://online-journal.com/artman/publish/article_5272.shtml

275 Update: For "what America has become" be sure to see also Karen Kwiatkowski, "War Is Murder," on *Lew Rockwell.com* (Sept. 21, 2010)

276 For Paul Craig Roberts, see http://www.vdare.com/roberts/index.htm

277 In *Information Clearing House* (Aug. 21, 2009), http://www.informationclearinghouse. info/article23341.htm

278 The memo is at: http://www.gwu.edu/~nsarchiv/NSAEBB/NSAEBB127/02.02.07.pdf

and *The Progressive*—if we actually had openness and a more greatly meaningful degree of access to the truth, just think of what kinds of things we might have been able to do by now that would have been positive, fruitful, and *good*. It's perfectly reasonable to think that by now we'd long since have impeached Bush, Cheney, Rice, Pelosi, Reid, and perhaps a gross or two of the other Cabinet and Congress members most centrally responsible for the towering lies and for the secrecy that alone made the "war on terror" possible in the first place, and ditto for our nation's criminal torture-policy. Further, we might actually have had real *elections* in 2004, 2006, and 2008. Or maybe we'd even have re-established a *two-party system of national government*.

But not so. No dice. Not *one* of these things, not one of many *other* toweringly desirable or achingly important things, has happened. Nor *will* they happen—the crimes alone will continue—until the news blackout is either lifted (fat chance) or out-flanked, something unlikely but not impossible (and also our only hope). For now, however, in a state of ignorance as profound as most Americans occupy in their waking and sleeping lives, the very *possibility* of their taking action to reclaim either their culture or their country is all but non-existent. The crimes continue without resistance. In the United States, "things remain generally quiet, since the blind don't rebel." [279]

Speaking of the blackout on truth and on certain matters of intellectual importance, a third piece I recommended for reading was Frank Rich's column from the *New York Times* of Sunday, August 23, 2009, "The Guns of August,"[280] the task here being to look for the falsehoods, the varieties of them, and the particular *kinds* that form the fabric of that piece.

But there's not always time for "class discussion of outside work," and that may be the case here. If we took time to analyze Rich's groaning packet of smells in the detail it deserves, I'm not sure we'd have room enough to get on with our own piece, *this* one—and we'd end up postponing it yet again. So let's let Frank Rich dangle in the wind for awhile, the way he likes to leave his own victims, like the "conspiracy nuts" he so graciously referred to now so long ago.[281]

As Rich dangles, let us, unlike him, move forward.

From all we've seen so far, one thing at least can be declared with near hundred-percent accuracy: That we do indeed, at the present

279 *A Nation Gone Blind: America in an Age of Simplification and Deceit* (2006).

280 "The Guns of August" (the *New York Times*, Aug. 23, 2009): http://www.nytimes.com/2009/08/23/opinion/23rich.html?_r=3&scp=1&sq=Frank%20Rich,%20The%20Guns%20of%20August&st=cse

281 In "The Longer the War, the Larger the Lies," (the *New York Times*, Sept. 17th, 2006): http://select.nytimes.com/2006/09/17/opinion/17rich.html?_r=2&scp=1&sq=The%20Longer%20the%20War,%20the%20Larger%20the%20Lies&st=cse .

moment, here and now, live in what I call "a post-*1984* nation," a nation where lies are truth[282] and war is perpetual,[283] or, in other words, in what Paul Craig Roberts recently called "a failed state."[284] Now, the question I'm asking in this series of pieces, as I first mentioned back in February,[285] is this one: "Can the literary life still exist in a post-1984 nation?"

When I first posed that question, here's the way my proposal ended:

> Let me put it this way: If it's a question that we in fact cannot honestly answer *in the affirmative*, then there's no question either but that we're doomed, both culturally and politically. What I plan is to do every conceivable thing in my power to show that it's a question that *can* be answered in the affirmative. And then what I plan to do is everything in my power to act accordingly.

> Stay tuned.

If it's true that a negative answer will lead to our being "doomed, both culturally and politically," I say let's abandon ignorance and begin the search immediately. What better place to begin than with the *New York Times*?

3.

Back on Friday, August 20, Dwight Garner reviewed a new Rebecca Solnit book entitled *A Paradise Built in Hell.*[286] The review itself was headlined "Delighted By the Joy of Bad Things."[287]

The title and headline drew my curiosity, as did seeing that Dwight Garner was the reviewer, since he is a writer who'd very powerfully drawn my interest on earlier occasions.[288] Let's follow him again this time as he provides a sense of Solnit as writer and offers a hint of the nature of this particular book:

---

282 See Paul Craig Roberts, "Warmonger Wins Nobel Peace Prize, in *Online Journal* (Oct. 14, 2009): http://onlinejournal.com/artman/publish/article_5195.shtml

283 Paul Craig Roberts, "Another War in the Works," in *Counterpunch* (Sept. 30, 2009): http://www.counterpunch.org/roberts09302009.html

284 Paul Craig Roberts, "The US as Failed State," in *Counterpunch* (Oct. 22, 2009): http://www.counterpunch.org/roberts10222009.html Roberts remarks, in this piece, that "An unmistakable sign of third world despotism is a police force that sees the public as the enemy." Another Orwellian characteristic increasingly present everywhere among us. EL

285 February 11, 2009, in an essay not included in this volume. EL

286 *A Paradise Built In Hell: The Extraordinary Communities That Arise in Disaster* (Viking, 2009)

287 The *New York Times*, Aug. 20, 2009: http://www.nytimes.com/2009/08/21/books/21book.html?scp=1&sq=delighted%20by%20the%20joy%20of%20bad%20things&st=cse

288 See chapter 15 in this book, "Is Dwight Garner a Dissembler, Deceiver, and Malefactor to the Nation?"

The West Coast essayist and social critic Rebecca Solnit is the kind of rugged, off-road public intellectual America doesn't produce often enough. It's been fascinating to watch her zigzagging career unfold.

In her previous 10 books she has written about disparate topics like Eadweard Muybridge's photography, San Francisco's urban landscapes, the history of walking and the nature of political dissent, always stalking her mental prey from oblique angles.

Ms. Solnit's writing, at its worst, can be dithering and self-serious, Joan Didion without the concision and laser-guided wit. At her best, however—and the best and worst in Ms. Solnit coexist in the same book and sometimes the same sentence—she has a rare gift: the ability to turn the act of cognition, of arriving at a coherent point of view, into compelling moral drama.

So far, so good. With a matador's skill, Garner ends his introductory passes with the delicate throwing up of a flag that's sure to engage the bull's, or the reader's, attention. No one can miss it: The phrase "compelling moral drama."

But if your eye is alert, you may consider the flag thrown to be a false one. "Compelling moral drama?" Look at the phrase and listen to it carefully. It's empty. Is there any drama other than "moral"? If there is—amoral or immoral drama—is *it* also "compelling"? If it's *not* compelling, is it even *drama*?

Picking nits, some might say, accusing me, as so often happened over the decades when I was a "prof," of splitting hairs and blaming a writer for flaws too minor to matter.

But words matter, and they matter greatly. The future of our civilization is held in the hands of writers like Dwight Garner—and, if I may—like Rebecca Solnit and like me. If we lie, or if we allow our words to lie, we are failures or even criminals—not in courts of law but in courts of morality, a word I choose here with great care.

When I was a near-adolescent and my parents were—for a time— chicken farmers, I learned the rule of thumb that if you saw one rat in the barn, you could assume there to be a hundred that you weren't seeing.

Extrapolate that rule to the case of nits in writing and you'll find it to pertain in the same ratio. A corollary is that just as all rats are worth being aware of, so are all nits.

And so, onward. For a bit of added interest, see if you can find a nit near the beginning of this next paragraph and a case of falsehood-by-vagueness near its middle:

[Solnit's] new book, "A Paradise Built in Hell," is an investigation not of a thought but of an emotion: the fleeting, purposeful joy that fills human beings in the face of disasters like hurricanes, earthquakes and even terrorist attacks. These are clearly not events to be wished for, Ms. Solnit writes, yet they bring out the best in us and provide common purpose. Everyday concerns and societal strictures vanish. A strange kind of liberation fills the air. People rise to the occasion. Social alienation seems to vanish.

Any luck? It's clear that the book will be about good things coming from bad things—but did anyone's nit-detector quiver even slightly at the words "an investigation not of a thought but of an emotion"? Interesting dichotomy, isn't it. I mean, if a person sets out to "investigate" an "emotion," what will the person use to do the investigating? Well, thoughts and thinking, of course. I wonder what holds Garner back from simply saying something along the lines that Solnit "is investigating disasters and some of the emotional responses people have to them"?

All right, you may find this one down around levels one or two out of a possible ten on the "nit-importance index," but I'll stand by it even if I must stand alone. Some readers may remember the days when copy editing still existed and when copy editors were the real McCoy. There's not a copy editor on earth—or wasn't, once—who wouldn't see the logical merits and greater accuracy of our nit as revised over the nit as written.

Let it go. But some readers, too, may remember when exactness, clarity, and accuracy were considered up there among the highest merits in writing—the days, one could say, of Strunk & White. There the defense rests.

But how about the example of falsehood-through-vagueness (if you'd be more comfortable, we could call it error-through-inaccuracy)? Nobody found it? How about that phrase "and even terrorist attacks"? Faint though it may be, the allusion is to 9/11, something that was not a terrorist attack.[289]

And now back to work. A few more words give another brush stroke or two as to what the exact nature is of this feeling of potentiality for *good* that Solnit observes in people during disastrous events:

> "What is this feeling that crops up during so many disasters?" Ms. Solnit asks. She describes it as "an emotion graver than happiness but deeply positive," worth studying because it provides "an extraordinary window into social desire and possibility." Our response to disaster gives us nothing less than "a glimpse of who else we ourselves may be and what else our society could become. . ."

The disasters themselves can vary, but even so, Garner explains,

> the altruistic human response to them [is] consistent, Ms. Solnit writes.

---

289 He who demands accuracy should in turn be accurate. It's true that 9/11 was a terrorist attack, but an attack neither by *foreign* terrorists nor by Muslim ones.

She compares the odd joy of living in their wake to existing in benign anarchies of the kind Thomas Paine described in "The Rights of Man."

All right. If good can rise from bad, or even if a sense of *future* good can arise from bad, how can a person object? Well, a person can't object, or shouldn't, so far as I can see. But as one goes more thoroughly into the review, certain things one finds there—or, more accurately, fails to find—become more and more deeply unsettling, even excruciatingly so.

4.

Exactly what catastrophes does Solnit choose to write about? We get that information from Garner:

> In "A Paradise Built in Hell" Ms. Solnit probes five disasters in depth: the 1906 earthquake and fires in San Francisco, the Halifax munitions cargo ship explosion of 1917, the Mexico City earthquake of 1985, the events of 9/11 and Hurricane Katrina. She also writes about the London blitz, Chernobyl and many other upheavals and examines the growing field of disaster studies.

That there *is* a "growing field of disaster studies"—a field growing, I assume, in colleges and universities—strikes me as bad news in itself. But let it go. Let's turn to Rebecca Solnit's selection of which disasters she finds deserving of her study. I wish I knew what others might make of her selection. I myself am called back to some of the words that Garner used earlier, and in fact I'm going to quote them again, now that we know more about which disasters Rebecca Solnit has in mind:

> These disasters differ, of course, in fundamental ways. But the altruistic human response to them was consistent, Ms. Solnit writes. She compares the odd joy of living in their wake to existing in benign anarchies of the kind Thomas Paine described in "The Rights of Man."

I know perfectly well what Solnit is talking about, just as *you* know perfectly well what she's talking about. In itself, it may be significant or it may not, but anyone who's been through even a mini-disaster—say, being on a street corner when a car accident takes place—knows it. Some people just gawk, sure. But lots of others do behave in certain other ways. It's true that "Everyday concerns and societal strictures vanish," or at least do so sometimes and partially. People from social ranks high and low may talk to one another as if they were old friends or acquaintances. Possibly even "a strange kind of liberation fills the air," though I'm a good bit less willing to go along entirely with exactly that Pollyanna choice of words. More undeniably true is that in such situations "Social alienation seems to vanish." Briefly, but, yes, vanish.

But what is it, then, that's bothering and troubling me so badly? Even though I might find it shallow or slight, still, if I can't wholly *denounce* Solnit's simple essential premise—that disasters tend to bring people together—then what in the devil is it that's driving me crazy and forcing me into all the miserable trouble and effort of slaving over this piece of writing?

Well, all right. What can I do other than just spill it?

It's this: It's that neither Garner nor Solnit have the least clue of what they're really talking about. Either that *or* the two of them are both actively engaged in some kind of extremely tricky Machiavellian plotting. That is to say, they are both actively and wittingly engaged in maintaining and keeping leak-proof the blackout that now governs the mainstream news and all mainstream publishing in the U.S. This is the blackout that now exists and that will prove, when the republic does die, to have been the single, most powerful, efficient, and deadly of all the weapons to have been used to bring that national death, unspeakable and ugly, about.

5.

As far as I can find or see, not one shred of the political or of political *consciousness* is revealed either in Garner's review or, assuming the review to be a reliable reflection of it, in Rebecca Solnit's book.

And so what, you ask? Does all writing, if it's going to be considered deserving, have to include in itself a "political consciousness"?

And the answer is, well, yes and no. The more complete and whole and conscious *any* work is, the more it will be superior to any other work.[290] The writing of figures as different as Emily Dickinson and A. J. Liebling has exactly that trait of consciousness and completeness in common: They both excel, have depth, and remain meaningful beyond the time of their origin by merit of the great degree in them of completeness, wholeness, and, as already said, of *consciousness.*

That consciousness may or may not be *overtly* political but still be there. On the other hand, if the very subject of a work itself is political and yet that work, or its creator, holds no overtone or vestige of

---

290 "I have never seen such gladness as there was on that Oxted night. They were very simple people really. All great authors are. If you are not simple, you are not observant. If you are not observant, you can not write. But you must observe simply. The first characteristic of great writing is a certain humility."—Ford Madox Ford, *Return to Yesterday: Reminiscences of James, Conrad, and Crane* (1932)

political consciousness whatsoever—what can we conclude other than that the work is thin, superficial, incomplete, possibly just plain and overtly *wrong*?

And that's the situation we have here. Few would argue that the San Francisco and Mexico City earthquakes were events brought about by political energies, or that the Halifax armaments explosion was either. More, however, might find there to be political origins in the Chernobyl failures, if only as a result of the very risks posed all along by the construction of plants for nuclear power, construction that was driven by and for political ends. Still, the *immediate* political cause perhaps does remain debatable. In the cases of 9/11 and Katrina, however, we have events that were solely, only, purely, completely, and absolutely political in their origins, political in their planning, political in their intent, and political in their outcomes and results. Yet even here we find that there seems not a shred of the political or of political consciousness to be evident in Solnit's book, and certainly none in the treatment given it by its reviewer.

Yes, a hurricane is a "natural phenomenon." Yet at the same time I know that I for one am light years from being ready to consider Katrina as a "natural" force—especially not one that had *anything* to do with a resulting "paradise" or "joy"—until I'm able to detect evidence *at the very least* that the person asking me to give such consideration to the big storm has shown awareness of HAARP,[291] of what HAARP is, of who supports and funds it,[292] of why they do so, of the kinds of purposes they're putting it to[293] or may put it to, and of the huge amount of material available[294] on the subjects of military and government research into control of the weather.

If Dwight Garner's review is accurate in reflecting its subject, Solnit's book is not only uninformed about the military and governmental politics that are intimately related to the subject of Katrina, but when the author *does* begin to touch on political matters, the result seems to be a mix of gibberish, shallowness, and contradiction—a mix that Garner seems as happy with as a kid with candy.

Catastrophes, presumably, bring out human good, bring out an "odd joy," and result in "altruistic. . . responses." Yet that's far

---

[291] See Michel Chossudovsky, "It's not only greenhouse gas emissions: Washington's new world order weapons have the ability to trigger climate change," at *Global Research* (Jan. 4, 2002): http://www.globalresearch.ca/articles/CHO201A.html

[292] See "HAARP: A Premier Facility for the Study of Ionospheric Physics and Radio Science": http://www.haarp.alaska.edu/

[293] See Michel Chossudovsky, "The Ultimate Weapon of Mass Destruction: 'Owning the Weather' for Military Use," at *Global Research* (Sept. 27, 2004): http://www.globalresearch.ca/index.php?context=va&aid=319

[294] See the results of googling "HAARP": http://www.google.com/search?domains=global research.ca&q=HAARP&sa . Also see *Angels Don't Play This HAARP*, Jeanne Manning and Dr. Nick Begich (Earth Pulse Press, 1995, 2002).

from all that happened in New Orleans, even though what Solnit does describe *did* happen. But the evidence of *other* occurrences is writ large in Garner's review. He tells us that Solnit's "book's most absorbing and eye-opening section" is not one devoted to "joy" or "altruism" or "delight" at all, but instead the part devoted to her "examination of elite panic in New Orleans after Katrina."

At least in this "most absorbing and eye-opening" *non-part* of the book, maybe *some* consciousness of the political is going to enter in to explain what's actually meant by the "elite panic" that brought about not joy and not altruism and not delight but that instead caused "New Orleans [to be] turned into a prison [where] . . . [people] were treated like animals."

Pardon me? Well, here's the explanation of how it is that the book's thesis isn't really the book's thesis. It seems, according to Garner's telling, that Solnit thinks that

> the news media and other factors have conditioned those in power to believe that people tend to behave badly in times of crisis and to believe the Hobbesian notion that "we are all easily activated antisocial bombs waiting to go off." Thus a mentality she calls "elite panic" sets in.

What "other factors" are, I'll have to go to my reward without knowing, but they do *seem* to be related to "the news media" (and thus to the *New York Times*, I should think). An equally unanswerable question is that of just who "those in power" are—especially if, even though they're "in power" they're also at the same time being "conditioned" by "other" influences, suggesting—to me, anyway— that those other influences and "factors" must be the ones that are *really* in power, since they have the strength to condition the ones *putatively* in power.

Well, however it happens, and whoever the "elite" may actually be, the argument goes that it was this "elite" that went into "panic," and that it was this "elite panic" that then made the *really* catastrophic stuff happen:

> The true disasters [in New Orleans, Solnit] suggests, happened large-ly because of fear and unexamined beliefs about human nature. Myths spread about things like the rape of children in the Louisiana Superdome, of mass looting, of black mobs menacing white property. Tape loops of the very worst behavior ran over and over on television, obscuring what life in the city was really like.

Who held those "unexamined beliefs"? And why did they hold them? Were these the "elite"? Were they the ones "in power"? Reading about Solnit's book by means of Garner's review, it seems as though *no one was responsible* for what happened. Of one of the most politically influenced, affected, charged, manipulated, and both purposely and ruinously handled events in recent history, the review gives no sense of who actually did what or of why they actually did it.

"Myths spread." Well, how? Via what agency? From what source or origin? These myths were about "things like" child-rape, looting, and mobs. But as to who originated and who perpetrated and who promulgated these myths—not a word.

Please look at this sentence and read it very carefully:

> Tape loops of the very worst behavior ran over and over on television, obscuring what life in the city was really like.

What do you notice? Well, at least part of what I notice is the evasive use of the passive voice, or of a construction that effectively creates the same effect as the passive voice: The true passive voice would go "Tape loops of the very worst behavior *were run*." But, insofar as the party that *should be* in the subject position of the sentence is replaced by "tape loops," the effect is the same: The "tape loops ran the tape loops." Who or what was actually responsible for running those tape loops "over and over on television" goes unnamed. Who or what *was* it? *No* one? An unknown agency or force, from outer space? The point is that politically speaking, the entire sentence— just like, it may seem, the entire book and the review of it—is politically naïve, unassertive, non-investigative, pallid, and ideologically acquiescent and un-alive to a point far, far past what common sense would allow as believable.

Yet there's worse to come. The "loops," even though they were "run" by powers unknown, did the absolutely most strange thing you can imagine: They "*[obscured] what life in the city was really like.*"

But please, wait just a moment. What *was* "life in the city" really like? I thought that life in New Orleans was like "a prison" where people "were treated like animals." And don't the "loops" portray "life in the city" as something much like that?

It would seem that both Rebecca Solnit and Dwight Garner are less than razor-sharp in their ability to distinguish between what's real and what's not. Here's something that Garner writes about Solnit:

> She notes that the British intellectual Timothy Garton Ash fed stereotypes after Katrina, saying that the storm's "big lesson is that the crust of civilization on which we tread is always wafer thin." Ms. Solnit's optimistic book advances just the opposite worldview.

Her *optimistic* book? How can it conceivably be optimistic if it can't even identify where the true causes lay that brought about the entire catastrophe? It can be *optimistic*, it would appear, because Dwight Garner says so.

But let's look at something else Dwight Garner says in the same review and *then* decide whether or not we can trust him on distinguishing between an optimistic or a pessimistic—or between a whole or a partial—book. The passage I'm thinking of is here, where Garner is citing what he takes as Solnit's weaknesses and flaws:

> "A Paradise Built in Hell" has its problems. Ms. Solnit occasionally falls into jargon. (Looting by citizens is, at one point, "improvised attempts to aggrandize their resources.") She has no feel for popular culture, and her analysis of disaster movies feels ham-handed. When she criticizes the television series "Survivor" for cynically setting people against one another in contradiction to how they would really behave, she's as guilty of underestimating average citizens as any government. We know it's just a TV show.

A person reads such reviews as this one, such passages as this one, and sinks into horror and despair. Solnit is confused by what she thinks is the difference between how people "really behave" and the way they "behave" on "reality shows." Garner pooh-poohs her confusion, declaring that in her naïveté she fails to see and understand what other and more astute observers see and understand ever so clearly. Says he, *"We know it's just a TV show."*

Those italics aren't Garner's. They're mine. I'm the one who added them. And I added them because I was shocked that a major reviewer at the *New York Times*, a person of presumably good education, wide experience, and broad reading, *could say such a thing as that*. What does Dwight Garner think? Does he really not know that he's absolutely, dead wrong in the idea he hopes to express when he says *"We know it's just a TV show"*? Has he read nothing of Orwell, Marshall McLuhan, or Samuel Beckett, and has he so few powers of individual observation left that he actually is able to say that what's on TV isn't every bit as "real" as every other aspect of the environment we live in, and, in fact, that what's on television may very well be taken as *more* real—or possibly more "real"—that what's *not* on TV?

It may be a fault of my own, but I can't believe that the disingenuous "thinking" that Garner shows in his review, along with the "thinking" that he attributes to Solnit in her book, can them*selves* be real. Neither of them is *authentic*. And this inauthenticity—a result in great part of an incompleteness, an emptiness—is a thing of overwhelming importance. I think that these two writers are lying. Whether they are lying to us or to themselves, and whether they know that they are lying or don't know it—neither of these questions makes the least difference whatsoever. They may very well believe they are telling the truth. But they are not. Consequently, they are dangers to us, our nation, our nation's intellectual well-being, and therefore our nation's survival.

6.

We turn to 9/11, another of the "disasters" helping nudge people toward "paradise" that Solnit includes in her book. And here we come to the realm of what seems to be extremely clear incorrectness, to the realm where truth is abused so egregiously and in the context of such enormous importance—that any reader who has tried to find a way or has succeeded in finding a way[295] to penetrate the massive blackout of news and information—such a reader will be overwhelmed at the degree of ignorance shown here, if that be what it is, or at the degree of misprision and dissembling, if *that* be what it is.

That Solnit can use 9/11 as a subject in which to find *any*thing of positive value is shocking to a reader of conscience who knows the history of 9/11. And that Garner can blithely remain silent about so absurd a misdirection as Solnit's shows him only, once again,[296] to be a deadman, a wrongman, either a stooge for treacherous figures and forces, or a treacherous figure himself.

Strong talk? Yes. But the plainest truth can sound like the thunder of Armageddon if the untruths covering it up have accumulated into something heavy, deep, and thick enough to have *themselves* come to be taken as the "truth."

War is peace. Freedom is slavery. Ignorance is strength. We have devolved into a condition closely enough parallel to the Oceania of Orwell's great novel that the three famous statements from the façade of the Ministry of Truth have become as "true" for us as they were "true" for the people of Oceania. So far as I can tell, there remain only three *essential* differences between the United States and Oceania. The first is that life inside the United States still appears to us in Technicolor, or in "living color," whereas life in Oceania, to readers of *1984*, seems entirely monochrome and drab.[297] The second difference is that in the United States the *means* of creating and maintaining the people's ignorance are technically far, far more subtle and also far more powerful than was Orwell's conception of the technical side of Big Brother's surveillance system. And third, at this point unquestionably the most important remaining difference between the United States and Oceania, is that incarceration and torture are *not*

---

295 That is, primarily, by means of reading. See Appendix.
296 See chapter 15, "Is Dwight Garner a Liar, Deceiver, and Malefactor to his Nation?"
297 The same is true, of course, also of photography from World War Two.

yet used widely and routinely on ordinary citizens as means either of punishing them for or of preventing them from the speaking or writing of *actual* truth as opposed to "state truth."[298]

As of now, it seems unlikely that writers will soon be jailed or tortured for saying that "state truth," or "Big Brother truth," is false while "true truth" is not. The probable reason for this is that, at least now, so very few people would even *believe* such a writer or so few people would *hear* about her that her views would be nothing more than "a flyspeck on the cover of the great book of state truth" and would be considered of no danger *to* that state. In fact, given the indoctrinating, blinding, and propagandizing of the American public that have taken place even over just the past seven years, it may already be impossible to gain *any* ear that's still capable of hearing true truth. "State truth" is *so enormously* pervasive, state truth is *so widely* unquestioned, that *most people*, when they hear me say or write, for example, that Rebecca Solnit and Dwight Garner are malefactors to the republic by merit of thinking in falsehoods and writing in falsehoods, *most people* would immediately consider the falsehood to be on *my* side rather than on *theirs*. The layers of "state truth" are so deep and have come for so long and by so many to be taken as "true truth" that, plain and simple, it's shocking for people to hear me say that others—especially others in prestigious positions—are dissembling, telling untruths, or being malefactors. The burden of proof, immediately, is put on the accuser, the speaker of "true truth" rather than on the accused, the speakers of "false truth" or "state truth." As this situation worsens, the use or presentation of *evidence* itself fails to be taken seriously or even to be accepted at all as part of what at one time constituted the foundational processes of argumentation or of thinking itself. [299]

For the teller of true truth, if in a situation like the one I'm now in, the defensive tack perhaps most commonly taken would be to euphemize, meliorate, palliate. For example, I could concede that a person can't be a liar if they're not being one on purpose or with forethought— a concession that would have *some* truth in it but legally speaking not a whole one. It *would* have the effect of euphemizing—but it would also make *me* a liar for the simple reason that if someone is speaking state-truth, they *are* telling untruth, and whether they know it or not can't and doesn't change that fact. Then, too, someone in my position could turn to the palliative of suggesting that *certainly* Rebecca Solnit and Dwight Garner are doing what they're doing unwittingly rather

---

298 Update: Alarmingly, the incarceration and torture of Pfc. Bradley Manning in Quantico, Virginia, where he is held without charge, necessitate a reconsideration of this third "difference" between the US and Oceania.

299 Update: Hence, among other things, the rise of the Tea Party.

than wittingly—that is, out of ignorance rather than out of a knowing will. But taking *that* course would make me just as significantly a liar as would the earlier course—for the simple reason that I would be claiming to know something that I *don't* know.[300] After all, I have no conceivable idea whatsoever whether Solnit and Garner are writing their untruths out of ignorance and insufficient thinking on the one hand or in order to please the boss on the other.

Ignorance is strength. Orwell's invented slogan is right and correct—but, as he himself very well knew, it is right and correct *only* if a person *already* lives under a tyranny where speaking, writing, or thinking the truth is a crime. That is not, *so far*, the case in the United States.[301] I pray that it will never become so and, meanwhile, I will abstain from making *myself* a liar in order to allow people to feel less shocked at hearing me say that Dwight Garner and Rebecca Solnit are dissemblers and malefactors. I will abstain also from saying they are ignorant, even though personally speaking I would prefer that over their being *witting* malefactors. As a very early teen, I was once, with two others, breaking a law that none of us knew *was* a law. The sheriff who stumbled on us doing this explained in the clearest of terms that ignorance of the law was no excuse for the breaking of it. Since that time, when I suppose I was thirteen or fourteen, I have become aware of Thomas Jefferson, whom I knew nothing of then:

> If a Nation expects to be ignorant and free in a state of civilization, it expects what never was and never will be. . . . If we are to guard against ignorance and remain free, it is the responsibility of every American to be informed.[302]

For another example of the great question of ignorance versus malefaction or treachery, the reader could read this piece from November 2007 by Carolyn Baker entitled "Naomi Klein's *Shock Doctrine*'s[303] Shocking Short Shrift."[304] Here's the essence of Carolyn Baker's reason for being shocked:

---

300 In *The Republic*, Socrates explains that those who fear death are liars in this way, since no living person has ever experienced death and therefore none can possibly know whether it is fearsome or not.

301 Jane Harmon, representative from California, however, hoped to make it so through HR 1955, named the "Violent Radicalization and Homegrown Terrorism Prevention Act." Harmon introduced the bill on April 19, 2007. It passed in the House but was never voted on by the Senate. See http://www.govtrack.us/congress/bill.xpd?bill=h110-1955

302 Identified as taken from a "letter to Col. Charles Yancey, January 6, 1816," at this site: http://quotes.liberty-tree.ca/quote/thomas_jefferson_quote_9b77

303 *The Shock Doctrine: The Rise of Disaster Capitalism* (Henry Holt, 2007): http://www.amazon.com/Shock-Doctrine-Rise-Disaster-Capitalism/dp/0805079831

304 Find the essay at http://ccun.org/Opinion%20Editorials/2007/November/12%20o/Naomi%20Klein's%20Shock%20Doctrine's%20Shocking%20Short%20Shrift%20By%20Carolyn%20Baker.htm

With respect to 9/11, Klein's incisive grasp of disaster capitalism's brilliantly devised, superbly-engineered machinations alongside her stochastic insistence that the administration did not deviously plot the catastrophe defies all logic. By page 400, the reader has digested an encyclopedia of conspiracies carried out by a series of U.S. administrations of both political parties, but on page 426 is nevertheless asked to believe that 9/11 "just happened".

On that page comes the most breathtaking statement of all—that quote to which I promised to return. Arguing that the U.S. government did not have a hand in the attacks, Klein states:

> The truth is at once less sinister and more dangerous. An economic system that requires constant growth, while bucking almost all serious attempts at environmental regulation, generates a steady stream of disasters all on its own, whether military, ecological or financial.

I could not agree with Klein more in terms of economies based on growth generating a steady stream of disasters, but 9/11 is a bit more than a few molecules in a "steady stream." It was and is the defining moment in the history of disaster capitalism.

The truth of 9/11, says Klein, is "less sinister, and more dangerous"? What could be more dangerous than the U.S. government orchestrating the attacks in order to achieve all of the motivations that Klein has so incisively and painstakingly explained? After 425 pages of unrelenting recitations of bona fide conspiracy, I am asked to swallow the stochastic non-analysis of a steady stream in which 9/11 just happened to rear its ugly head?

Clearly enough, all of the same questions pertain here, in the case of Naomi Klein, as pertain in the cases of Rebecca Solnit and Dwight Garner, albeit on a seemingly diminished scale.

7.

Now, an extremely serious question and one that's absolutely essential to the matter of our republic's survival. Here it is: Just *how deeply* corrupted, soiled, perverted, criminalized, anti-educated, de-intellectualized, infected, diseased, infantilized, deprived of both conscience and of consciousness, made self-deceptive, delusional, and driven crazy *have* the United States and its people been made since 9/11?

The answer is: Widely, profoundly, and devastatingly. The republic may be lost already, having been reduced to a condition so stupefied and enfeebled as to allow it no longer means of being *able* to recover from the forms of tyranny that have, even now, eaten away great pieces of its most vital elements and are poised in readiness to devour the entirety, digest it, then pass it on, pass it through, and pass it out again in the form of a perfected police state.

And all of this is happening *why*?

All of this is happening because too many—because *so* many—people in positions of authority, responsibility, and power have betrayed their own consciences and have betrayed also the people to whom they *should have* remained responsible, by choosing to honor and follow the lies of a murderous, plotting tyranny and refusing to follow instead the simple truth—for, no matter how horrendous or frightening or intimidating it may be, that truth *is* simple, the truth that our own leadership inside our own executive, our own intelligence agencies, our own military, and our own wider government was responsible for planning, plotting, and executing the events of 9/11 as a means to seize and centralize power, strip the nation of its civil and Constitutional rights, freedoms, and liberties, and engage in a global military undertaking aimed at achieving world hegemony.

The people who have shut their eyes in order to reject this truth and in its place accept and celebrate *as truth* the many, feeble, fraudulent, and scientifically jejune lies put in place to cover up and putatively deny the true truth include journalists, writers, editors, broadcasters, teachers, professors, college presidents, administrative officers, deans, sub-deans, and mini-deans, counselors, corporate managers, directors, and heads, figures in and throughout government at every level from the White House down to the most junior member of the least significant committee in congress. People who have turned from the adult truth and have embraced the infantile falsehoods that will allow the destruction of the nation at best, and do even greater harm than that at worst, include people working in every capacity not only in the so-called "mainstream" media but also throughout the even *more* so-called "liberal" or "progressive" media, including those at NPR, Pacifica Radio, *The Progressive Magazine*, and *The Nation*, and they include also writers, bloggers, and journalists working under the auspices of The Nation Institute. They include owners, board members, editors, columnists, journalists, and writers at all major newspapers like, for example, the *New York Times*, where the rejection of the truth, the embrace of the lies, and the busy activity of proselytizing *about* the lies in order to pass them off as the real truth begin with those towering corporate figures who direct and control chief editor Bill Keller, extend through Keller himself and on down to the many names you're familiar with if you're either a reader of the *Times*, say, or a reader of commentaries *on* the *Times*.

You will remember that I began section seven of this present essay with a list of emotional and intellectual deficiencies, perversions, and corruptions now endemic in the nation and attributable in very great part to the corruption and perversion of thought, honor, and social, ethical, and moral responsibility that have burgeoned in the wake of 9/11 and, in addition, that have been brought about and nurtured by the countless dismal, corrupting, pernicious, infantilizing influences that have come into play in a nation where, as in *1984*, lies are truth, war is peace, silence is patriotism, and the individual conscience brings ostracism and sometimes death. Ours is now a nation, you might say, where TV has won and reality has lost. That victory has been helped, aided, and abetted by our leaders and advisors of each and every type I listed a moment ago. Every single one of them, every last type, position, title, or office-holder among them, is treacherous and a malefactor.

One of the perversions I mentioned at the outset of this section of this essay was "self-deception." Another was "infantilization." There are overlaps between these two, doubtless, as there are among many of the other insufficiencies, corruptions, and inadequacies on the list. But I propose looking at an example of each of these particular two, self-deception and infantilization, before we begin drawing this piece of writing to its poor, dreary, and grievous close.

It happens that the two examples I have in mind, first an example of self-deception and then one of infantilization, are, again, found in the *New York Times*. It happens also that both derive from Thomas L. Friedman.

On October 13 of this year, Patrick Martin published a piece called "Thomas Friedman Glorifies American Militarism."[305] In it, Martin refers to Friedman's *Times* column of Sunday, October 11, saying that Friedman there "devotes his entire column to a grotesque celebration of the role of the American military, presenting its operations, particularly in Afghanistan and Iraq, as humanitarian and liberating."

Martin continues:

He takes the occasion of the Nobel Peace Prize awarded to Barack Obama to suggest the US president go to Oslo in December, decline the award for himself, and then declare, "I will accept it on behalf of the most important peacekeepers in the world for the last century—the men and women of the US Army, Navy, Air Force and Marine Corps."

Friedman mentions a series of actions by the American military, including the Normandy landing of June 1944, the Berlin Airlift of 1948, the stationing of US troops in Europe throughout the Cold War, the troop

---

305 October 13, 2009, in *Information Clearing House*: http://www.informationclearinghouse. info/article23712.htm

presence in South Korea, and the ongoing operations in Iraq and Afghanistan. The very length of this list might give a reader pause—there is no other country whose military actions over the last 70 years would require a full column merely to name.

The recital, in Martin's view, is not merely incomplete but also made false by merit of its omissions. "Friedman's account of the 'last century,'" he writes,

> is highly selective. He leaves out more American wars than he includes. Left off his list are World War I, the Korean War, the Vietnam War and the first Gulf War. He makes no mention of the dozens of US military interventions in Central America and the Caribbean, including invasions and occupations of Haiti, the Dominican Republic, Grenada, Nicaragua, Panama and Mexico.

> Nor does he make reference to the use of American military, paramilitary and intelligence forces to overthrow governments, suppress popular revolts and establish dictatorships around the world. A partial list would include Iran, Indonesia, Pakistan, Brazil, Chile, Argentina, Peru, Venezuela, Paraguay, Bolivia, Uruguay, Guatemala, El Salvador, Greece, Turkey, and numerous African countries.

"Even in the wars Friedman does mention," Martin continues, "his account is one-sided and false."

> He refers to Normandy and the liberation of Buchenwald, but not Hiroshima, Nagasaki, or the firebombing of Tokyo, Dresden and Hamburg. He describes the role of US forces today in Iraq and Afghanistan as "peacekeeping," without noting the sea of blood that accompanied the invasion and conquest of those countries.

In Martin's view, the most egregious omission, however, is that Friedman fails to mention Vietnam. This is "the most telling exposure of Friedman's attempt to dress up American imperialism in 'democratic' and 'humanitarian' garb."

Martin is unsurprised by Friedman's dodge, since he finds the columnist to be now and to have been in the past less correspondent than propagandist:

> Friedman's column is only the latest effort to banish the "Vietnam syndrome" and revive a democratic façade for US military operations. His role is predictable, as the *Times* foreign affairs columnist has long been an apologist for American militarism.

Martin's piece functions as an accurate and just condemnation of the *Times*, or its columnist, as betrayer of the truth, in this case not about 9/11 directly but about the military consequences *of* 9/11. Still, of greater interest right now, or of greater interest for the purposes of this particular essay, are this writer's last two paragraphs. The interest these hold is due in part to their muted passion, and in part also to their clarity as they describe the extent to which "news media" like the *Times* have been corrupted, or have allowed themselves to be corrupted, or have corrupted *themselves* into purveyors of propaganda, of a "product" intended, in the case of the *Times*, for a very particular readership, a readership for whom the *Times* has become a purveyor of falsehoods built on a foundation of lies. Here are the two paragraphs:

> The *New York Times* speaks in particular for a social layer, a generation of the upper-middle-class that has enriched itself over the past three decades and dropped any previous association with perspectives of social reform, let alone opposition to American militarism. Ex-radical or ex-liberal, they recognize that it is impossible to present Vietnam as a great humanitarian effort, so they seek to pass over this seminal experience of their youth in guilty silence.

> But Vietnam was no aberration. It was the template for the current wars in Iraq and Afghanistan. The historical balance sheet is the direct opposite of the claims made by Friedman about a democratic and humanitarian role for the US military. Vietnam, Korea, Iraq, Latin America—the victims mount into the millions. In the half century since Hitler and Stalin, no institution has killed more people in wars and other acts of barbarism than the government of the United States and its military-intelligence apparatus.

8.

And so there's our example of "self-deception." Does Friedman *know* what he's saying (and not saying)? Does he actually believe that he's representing one truth when in fact he's representing something wholly divergent from it? Is he *conscious* of what he's doing and saying? Is he *not* conscious of it? Assuming that self-deception—being delusional—is a form or aspect of instability, we're forced by logic to ask whether Thomas Friedman is stable or unstable. Whether he's crazy or sane. Delusional or not.

Now, what would it do to help us answer this question if we were to find that Friedman *definitely* is infantilized? Certainty is a hard thing to come by in such matters, but my own sense of it in Friedman was strengthened by my reading of his column a week after the one Martin wrote about. As an aid to maintaining my own mental and intellectual hygiene, I had stopped reading Friedman, as I have stopped reading certain other of the *Times* columnists. It often feels intellectually and also spiritually *cleaner* to skip them. But on October 18, not only was my eye caught by the Friedman headline—"The Power in 11/9"[306]—but I saw the familiar "9/11" in the column's first line.

Whenever I happen to see a well-known mainstreamer *directly* addressing the great lie of 9/11, I tend to take a look, since it's on such occasions that writers of this sort are most likely to expose the truth about themselves. The truth? I mean the truth of whether they're telling untruth purposely and outright—shamelessly—or whether they're actually infantilized and thus lying out of deep, fawning, delusional, perhaps even obedient ignorance. In the latter case, not shamelessly but shame*fully*.

And, indeed, Friedman passed—that is, he failed—the test brilliantly. It's a while since I've seen a more infantile piece of writing in so public a place.

Here are the first two paragraphs:

> A few weeks ago, Americans "observed" the eighth anniversary of 9/11—that day in 2001 when the Twin Towers were brought down by Al Qaeda. In a few weeks, Germans will "celebrate" the 20th anniversary of 11/9—that day in 1989 when the Berlin Wall was brought down by one of the greatest manifestations of people power ever seen.

> As the Obama team tries to figure out how to proceed vis-à-vis Afghanistan, Pakistan and Iran, it is worth reflecting for a moment on why Germans are celebrating 11/9 and we are reliving 9/11—basically debating whether to re-invade Afghanistan to prevent it again from becoming an Al Qaeda haven and to prevent Pakistan from tipping into civil war.

It's so obvious, the infantile phrase, that it's like being poked in the eye with a stick. Not only is it an untruth, but it makes you feel you're being treated like a kindergartner—as indeed you are, with this phrase out of a child's primer: "that day in 2001 when the Twin Towers were brought down by Al Qaeda." It's *conceivable*, I suppose, that Friedman is so profoundly uninformed about *any* of the truth of 9/11 and *any* of the history of Al Qaeda that he imagines he's telling the "true truth" instead of "state truth." *Conceivable.* But as any capable writing critic or analyst can see, it's *more* likely, not provable but more likely, that he's dissembling through his teeth. And that's where the infantilism comes in. We're infantilized by the way *he's* treating *us*, but *he's* infantilized by the toy-dog-tricks—sit up! shake! speak!—he performs, without the least hint of adult embarrassment, for his masters.

---

[306] "The Power in 11/09" (the *New York Times*, Oct. 18, 2009): http://www.nytimes.com/2009/10/18/opinion/18friedman.html

Adult version: "that day in 2001 when the Twin Towers came down."

Adult version: "that day in 2001 when the Twin Towers were brought down."

Adult version: "that day in 2001 when the Twin Towers were brought down by our own leaders in government, the intelligence agencies, and the military in order that they could blame the disaster, falsely, on Osama bin Laden and nineteen young Arabs with box cutters (who really weren't even on the planes at all, if there even were planes) and begin a global war for profit, power, and plunder, claiming it to be a war of defense against the imaginary jihadist enemy and meanwhile, having sufficiently terrified the American people by means of these enormous lies and this huge murder, making use of this fear as an excuse for programmatically stripping away Constitutional rights and liberties in the name of providing ever-greater and ever-more necessary 'national security.'"

Now the infantilized version: "that day in 2001 when the Twin Towers were brought down by Al Qaeda."

Nothing can explain the presence here of the phrase "*by Al Qaeda*" except two possible things. First, Friedman is *so* uninformed, *so* ill-read, and *so* isolated from any and all sophisticated people in power or positions of political or diplomatic authority around the world that he actually believes his own words, that "Al Qaeda" *did* do 9/11.

The second possibility is worse. It shows him to be a lackey, a shill at work for his owners—and, *if* it's true, it shows him to be without the least presence or vestige of dignity, decency, conscience or fidelity to himself, to his people, to his country, or to the Constitution under which they are governed.

The second possibility, that is, shows him doing what he's told to do by his owners, however embarrassing and simple-minded it may be. And what his owners tell him to do is, pure and simple, write what's untrue. And he does so. But he's so bad at it—and the untruth is *so* far-fetched for anyone the least bit informed—that as he's doing his duty for his owners, his behavior is telegraphed immediately far and wide through an example of extraordinarily childish language.

It is quite absurd. No fewer than eight years have passed, and he's still "reminding" his readers that "Al Qaeda did it"![307]

The exercise is almost beyond the contemptible and falls into the comic, pathetic, dark, and absurd: So much time has passed that Friedman's owners are now frightened that his readers may have forgotten the untruth! Thus part of his job is to remind them of it. And he does, a bit like a circus-dog, on command, dancing around in a tutu.

---

[307] Even though, of course, they didn't. EL

The column's general idea is that the fall of the Berlin wall—11/9—is different from 9/11. The Germans *got* something from their 11/9 because *their* event was brought about and driven by "people power." Friedman writes:

> Germans showed the world how good ideas about expanding human freedom—amplified by people power—can bring down a wall and an entire autocratic power structure, without a shot. There is now a Dunkin' Donuts on Paris Square adjacent to the Brandenburg Gate, where all that people power was concentrated. Normally, I am horrified by American fast-food brands near iconic sites, but in the case of this once open sore between East and West, I find it something of a balm. The war over Europe is indeed over. People power won. We can stand down—pass the donuts.

The thinking in "The Power of 11/9" seems to be the "thinking" of a child—a treacherous little child, but child either way. Friedman's next paragraph:

> The events of 9/11, by contrast, demonstrated how bad ideas—amplified by a willingness of just a few people to commit suicide—can bring down skyscrapers and tie a great country in knots.

And that paragraph is an example of baby-talk, or perhaps one should say an example of baby-thinking. *This* is what Friedman's owners pay him to say and to write. *This* is the language of untruth, of ignorance, *or* of delusion. It is *not the language of an adult, informed mind.* It is, however, the language of tyranny, the language of hollowness and "state truth," the language that America has been manipulated into doing its speaking in, and manipulated into doing its *thinking* in. But that doesn't remove it from being the language of children—children kept indoors, away from experience, window shades drawn, watching cartoons.

9.

And so we come toward our end by returning to the great question that caused all of this searching—Can there be a literary life in a post-*1984* nation? Can there be a literary life in a nation of the kind the United States has become over the past few decades, and especially since 9/11? The answer is very clear. No, there can't and won't be a literary life in such a time and place, *nor* will there be the production of a *literature* of depth, complexity, authenticity, significance, or durability.

Why not? Because the creation of a true, real, or significant literature is impossible when a people lives or is forced to live in ignorance of the whole truth of their own lives, of their nation's life, and of the lives of those they live among. For so long as America remains a nation straitened, encumbered, and diminished by its idiotically determined dedication to a cheap lie—every bit as cheap as the lie under which Nazi Germany suffered, dwelled, and died—neither it nor its people can or will be productive in the arts in any way except in that same way as they live: Cheaply and falsely. For so long as Americans continue to be deprived of, or continue to be conditioned *into* an inability to see and know at *least* half of the truth of what their own lives *are*, and at *least* half of the truth of what their own nation *is* and is *doing*, they will remain at the very best halfpeople living halflives in halfblindness and thinking in halfthought. In this, in the condition that Americans and American intellectuals now exist, they aren't any different from the wretches chained into their seats in the bottom of Plato's cave, believing falsehood to be reality, shadows to be substance, lies to be truth.

Any art that isn't inclusive of the whole of life, or any art that lacks a *consciousness* of the whole of life, or that lacks even the *potential for* a consciousness of the whole of life, will fail to rise to the level either of significance or durability. We said something about this earlier, in the cases of Emily Dickinson and A. J. Liebling, and it remains a great and essential truth about the arts.[308] As I mentioned in the foreword to this book, Marilynne Robinson once put forth, in an interview, something very close to the same idea:

> Any writer, or any moment in writing, when the imagination seems to be as alert as possible to everything that can be understood out of a moment or situation, seems to me to be when that impulse is being made into art.[309]

Throughout this essay, example after example has come up of writers in one way or another, wittingly or unwittingly, intentionally or through self-delusion or through an ignorance that they've been encouraged to cultivate, maintain, and take pride in—examples have come up of writers *failing* to be "as alert as possible to everything that can be understood out of a moment or situation."

All writing holds the potential for reaching the level of art, but *no* writing, if it takes place under limitations like those just described, or if it is undertaken by *writers* with limitations like those just described—no such writing can or will ever reach the level of art, and all such writing will be feeble, diseased, impure, partial, and incomplete. All such writing, in and because of its incompleteness, will

---

308 Anyone interested in this idea might see the author's "interview with himself" (2006): http://www.ericlarsen.net/author.interview.1.html .

309 *Iowa Writers' Workshop Newsletter*, Fall 2001. Emphasis mine.

hold in itself a debilitating essence of falsehood, untruth, and non-life, flaws and absences that will destine it to live only briefly, weakly, and without dignity or strength. And so will those who write it.

Examples are everywhere of writing (and of thought) that's unable to rise above the cheap, the feeble, and the conventional, even the phony, since it itself, the writers of it, and even the publishers and reviewers of it—all of them, being residents of a malevolent, blind, and deceitful nation where lies are truth, fail to be imbued with life in any true degree of wholeness or completeness.

Cheap, phony, and feeble literature is the best that America will produce until such time as the nation will or can admit its citizens again into a full and free consciousness of the entirety and therefore the truth of the lives they lead as citizens of a nation comprised of flesh and blood men and women possessed of fully capable minds and hearts of their own—rather than in a nation of childlike talk and half-minded speakers like Frank Rich, Dwight Garner, Thomas Friedman, Rebecca Solnit and the manifold number of others here unnamed.

On May 27, 2007, the *New York Times* gave over the front page of its book review to the opening paragraphs of Frank Rich's hyper-laudatory piece on *Falling Man*,[310] the Don DeLillo novel ostensibly "about" 9/11. Rich's review was so wrong in so many ways—and at the same time so giddy, so positively silly in its praise, that, my deceit-detector on alert, I bought the book right away. As I'd expected, it was awful. It was terrible in almost every way a piece of today's "quality fiction" can *be* terrible. It was lazy in its way of lolling up against one old lamppost of "story" after another, shuffling over to a lamppost of "character," another of "setting," and so on, not a one of them in the least real but, instead, composed from a mixture of glue and perhaps ten or twenty compacted bushels of the sawdust that has gathered over the past hundred years on the floor of the Novel Workshop of the World. Even the book's central symbolic conceit—a performance artist who "hangs" from one point or another around the city in a supposed visual echo of the man photographed falling upside down from the north tower on 9/11—even this image is gimmicky, far-fetched, and not moving, nor, furthermore, is it any real way a part of the texture, fabric, or flesh of the rest of the novel.

Worst of all, though—and the thing, one suspects, that triggered Frank Rich into jumping and dancing for joy—was that DeLillo seems to have swallowed the entire phony story about 9/11 hook, line, and

---

[310] "The Clear Blue Sky," (the *New York Times*, May 27, 2007): http://www.nytimes.com/2007/05/27/books/review/Rich-t.html?_r=3&scp=3&sq=book+review%3A+%22falling+man%22&st=nyt

sinker. Not only did he swallow it, but, almost like a kid with a new toy, he set about to exploit and "celebrate" it, renting it out from this wonderful new "made in the USA" stock shop to use in setting up an ominous, ready-made atmosphere that was "morally-charged and dramatic" (the quotes are there to remind you of Dwight Garner's "compelling moral drama").

Astonishing, don't you think? Here's DeLillo, a writer who made himself very nearly king-of-the-hill in the realm of high paranoia, Pynchon-esque suspiciousness, certainty of there being ever-present cosmic trickery or a controlling "system" that looms balefully over everyone before coming down to seize them. Yet when the real thing comes about, he misses the truth of it totally, laps up the false version of it like a kitten laps milk, and lets it shake him around by the nape of the neck—all this even after he's had *five-and-a-half-years* to read about it and think it through!

How smart *are* we? How smart *are* our literary intellectuals? Who do they spend their time *talking* to? What do they *read? Do* they read?

And Frank Rich? His happy, happy dance of praise is positively intolerable. Don't read this next quote without a basin handy:

> If "Underworld" took its cues from the kinetic cinema of Eisenstein, "Falling Man," up until its remarkable final sequence, is all oblique silences and enigmatic close-ups reminiscent of the domestic anomie of the New Wave. In DeLillo's hands, this is not at all limiting or prosaic. There's a method to the Resnais-like fogginess. The cumulative effect is devastating, as DeLillo in exquisite increments lowers the reader into an inexorable rendezvous with raw terror.

That is a paragraph of *such tripe* as to offend any normal and moral person, if such a person were to pay attention closely to what it says.

To you, Mr. Frank Rich, I say not "raw terror," but *raw sewage.* How could *any* thinking, feeling, aesthetically (*and* politically) *complete* human being allow him or herself to celebrate such a thing as this, to wallow in the wondrous achievement of a mediocre novelist (at least this time around) spinning up out of *this* material a "cumulative effect" that is "devastating" (believe me, in truth the effect is claptrap and bunkum, but that makes no difference in a prevaricating-exercise of this kind) by merit of its using "exquisite increments" (there's not one "exquisite increment" in the entire book) that "lower" us "into an inexorable rendezvous with raw terror."

This is shameless, shameless junk. Whether Rich is dissembling first to himself and therefore only secondarily to us, or whether he's dissembling through his teeth *only* to us (and to DeLillo? Who knows?) hardly makes a difference. Just look at these words. "Inexorable" is conniving and cheap, implying that the 9/11 attacks *were* inexorable when in truth they were not in *any* way so, but were plotted and planned far in advance, with fore-knowledge aplenty, and could have been cancelled at any time the perpetrators chose.[311] So also with "rendezvous," a penurious, hollow bit of fakery plucked from the lines of cheap romances and thrillers ("*Oh, Raoul,*" she whispered, "*you and I have a rendezvous with destiny*") implying that the jihadists did every last thing in the attacks *all by themselves* and were not to be outwitted or stopped by any man or any force known to man—while in reality the chief guy who needed to be stopped was Cheney, commanding the entire horror-show from the screen of his monitor in the White House bunker room.[312]

Two things, both awful, both horrible, both deceitful, both abominable.

Rich's sixth paragraph:

> Bill Gray, the reclusive, Pynchonesque writer at the center of "Mao II," laments that terrorists, the bomb makers and gunmen, have annexed the territory that once belonged to the novelist: the ability to "alter the inner life of the culture." As he sees it, the "news of disaster is the only narrative people need," and "the darker the news, the grander the narrative." After 9/11, DeLillo picked up his fictional alter ego's point in an essay for Harper's, "In the Ruins of the Future," that grappled with how a novelist might respond to terror now that it had hit home. "The narrative ends in the rubble and it is left to us to create the counternarrative," DeLillo wrote. "People running for their lives are part of the story that is left to us" because "they take us beyond the hard numbers of dead and missing and give us a glimpse of elevated being." An event like 9/11 cannot be bent to "the mercies of analogy or simile." Primal terror—"the cellphones, the lost shoes, the handkerchiefs mashed in the faces of running men and women"—has to take precedence over politics, history and religion. "There is something empty in the sky," he wrote. "The writer tries to give memory, tenderness and meaning to all that howling space."

How can we not be doomed if minds like these really represent the minds of our literary intelligentsia? The sheer naïveté of it, the *silliness*, might be the most appalling thing, brought into existence through the prior embrace of a *truly wrong premise*. But the naïveté and silliness, whatever their origin, give way immediately to the

---

[311] Again, the foremost book to read on this particular aspect of 9/11 is Nafeez Ahmed, *The War on Truth*: http://www.amazon.com/War-Truth-Disinformation-Anatomy-Terrorism/dp/1566565960

[312] Full details of Cheney's role and behavior in the bunker aren't perfectly known, but many, many of them are—far in excess of what in a normal world would long before now have resulted in subpoenas, hearings, and *true* investigation followed doubtless by trial. Read Michael C. Ruppert, *Crossing the Rubicon* (2004).

greater horror of *the sheer atrocity* of what this midget-thinking and propaganda actually come to be celebratory of.

Let's go through it. Anyone who knows what literature really is, what it's for, what it's made of, and *why* it's made, will know instantly that DeLillo's "reclusive, Pynchonesque writer at the center of 'Mao II'" is a dim bulb and utterly preposterous in being poorly read. Here he is, disturbed because the evil, evil world is so busy co-opting the material that the *novelist* wants to use. Then and there, we see that he knows nothing whatsoever of the history of the novel. As for the things he wants to keep for *novel*-writing, they're really, really, really terrible and awful and ruthless and scary things, things done now by the "terrorists, the bomb makers and gunmen" (as if it hadn't been always thus).[313] So now the "Pynchonesque" Bill Gray is crying like a fifth-grader elbowed out of a marbles game. But what, really, is that game that he's been elbowed out of? Well, it's this one: It's the game where "the novelist alters the inner life of the culture."

Pah! *That's* a dumb game. It's not even a real one, but only a delusional one. And, for absolute sure, it's light years away from *any*thing having to do with novel-writing. *Comic* books, conceivably. But that's *it.*

DeLillo's pre-puberty, power-lusting, grade-school-level thinker, however, has no idea how foolish and misdirected his notion is. In fact, instead of being drawn to examining its obvious fallacies and limitations, as a grown-up thinker would (or a person who knew what literature was), all he does is make another braggadocio pronouncement trying to "explain" it. We've seen this passage already, but I'm going to repeat it, picking up right after the words that identified what Gray was afraid of losing, namely, "'the ability to 'alter the inner life of the culture.'" Read carefully and you will find the *truly* terrifying aspect of this short passage of terror-talk:

> As he sees it, the "news of disaster is the only narrative people need," and "the darker the news, the grander the narrative." After 9/11, DeLillo picked up his fictional alter ego's point in an essay for Harper's, "In the Ruins of the Future," that grappled with how a novelist might respond to terror now that it had hit home. "The narrative ends in the rubble and it is left to us to create the counternarrative," DeLillo wrote. "People running for their lives are part of the story that is left to us" because "they take us beyond the hard numbers of dead and missing and give us a glimpse of elevated being."

---

[313] Few better antidotes to the claptrap and mind-poisoning of Rich and DeLillo are available than a reading of Joseph Conrad's *The Secret Agent*, published in 1907 and set in 1886 London. EL http://www.abebooks.com/servlet/SearchResults?an=Joseph+Conrad&sts=t&tn=The+S ecret+Agent&x=43&y=13

Shall we talk about what's perverse, delusional, and infantile *now*, or shall we talk about it *later*?

Well, odious as it is, I suppose we'd better not put off the task. First, there's Gray's lie by omission, or, to put it another way, his lie-by-half-truth: "As he sees it, the 'news of disaster is the only narrative people need,' and 'the darker the news, the grander the narrative.'" In a single word, or in a single, two-syllable, compound word, we can evaluate Gray's "literary" pronouncement on its merits: Bullshit.

It's a staggeringly self-delusional half truth. It's wholly untrue that disaster-news "is the only narrative people need," even if they *do* rubber-neck at accident scenes on the highway or stand in sheep-flocks, reminiscent of audiences at the Roman Coliseum, waiting, hours if need be, for would-be suicides to jump from bridge-spans or high sills. Still, two things. People may be incorrigibly addicted to "disaster," but it's simply a blunt falsehood that that's "all they need." Please insert our compound word again at this point. The truth is that most people[314] feel tainted by self-disgust after having waited in *hopes* of seeing a "disaster." And even though most of us will ooh and aah at seeing a natural enormity—a St. Helen's or a Swiss avalanche—awe is quickly imbued with the same taint of disgust at oneself, though less piercing than it is after having watched the destruction of something *human* rather than merely something of *nature*. Often the two are mixed, I know, as in the Indian Ocean tsunamis of December 2006. And the result in the watcher, in one for whom the fascination of the abomination was irresistible, will be to suffer the taint of self-loathing afterward.

Only if Bill Gray is thinking of *all* "people" as amoral, sub-ethical, non-empathetic morons, only if he thinks of them as hordes of creatures *all* existing at a sixth-grader's comic-book level—only *then* can his half-truth hold even a modicum of validity. And at what cost, this "validity"? At the cost of stripping out of people everything that makes them human. And the truth is that for even the most ghoulish of us who do nevertheless remain human—my maternal grandmother, for example, who did indeed rise up to the least whiff of disaster—it's *still* an ugly, imperious, condescendingly dehumanizing falsehood to say that the "narrative" of disaster "is all they need."

Speak for yourself, John Galt.

Ditto for Gray's phrases "the darker the news, the grander the narrative." Here, DeLillo's character from *Mao II* is mixing even him-*self* up. Here again he's wrong in all the ways we've seen him wrong before, but this time he's even wrong in his word "grander." Let's

---

[314] So long as they are adult, in the least degree introspective and self-aware, and consequently empathetic—capable of being aware of what others feel. EL

suppose that "dark" means "gory" or "ghoulish" or "sadistic" (after all, what in the devil's name *does* it mean?). Well, a "dark" narrative could be a story of only one person, how*ever* well it might satiate and feed the grim lusts of Gray-DeLillo's imagined comic-book-level readers. But the gorier is *not* going to mean the "grander," certainly. All it could mean is the more piercingly or sharply or acutely satisfying to the sexual deviant that our writer-guys seem to want and imagine as audience—but never the more "grand." Scenes of Napoleonic suffering in the enormous grandeur of the Russian winter— these the dark and gory slice-em-up flicks will never equal.

There we are, then: We've looked at Bill Gray's lie-by-omission and at some of the concerns it raises. That means it's time to go on to our "second" matter, this one being "the *truly* terrifying aspect of this short passage of terror-talk" that I said you would find if you read carefully.

•

Awful, isn't it. After all, it looks as though DeLillo has done something that may be psychotic. It appears that he may have— has—*taken on as his own* the absurdities and limits of the tiny mind of his "Bill Gray" character from *Mao II*. I find this pitiful, appalling, and dangerous. Frank Rich, though—he *loves* it.

At first, it sounds harmless enough:

> After 9/11, DeLillo picked up his fictional alter ego's point in an essay for Harper's, "In the Ruins of the Future," that grappled with how a novelist might respond to terror now that it had hit home.

Well, from what we've seen of that "alter ego's" mind and thought, I'd strongly advise against even picking up "a point" from him, although if that's *all* it is, maybe no serious harm will be done. But we quickly learn the horrible truth that that's *far* from "all it is."

No, DeLillo puts on the whole suit and skin of his wrong-seeing and wrong-thinking alter-ego, and he trades his very brain for Gray's. And so we find ourselves following now the thinking not of DeLillo and not of Gray, but of DeLillo-Gray. We pick up after the phrase "now that [terror] had hit home":

> "The narrative ends in the rubble and it is left to us to create the counternarrative," DeLillo wrote. "People running for their lives are part of the story that is left to us" because "they take us beyond the hard numbers of dead and missing and give us a glimpse of elevated being."

If you haven't shivered or gotten goose bumps on your arms, or if the hairs on your nape haven't stirred—then you haven't read these words carefully enough. Go back, especially through the second half.

I feel much the way I imagine Paul Craig Roberts must have felt when he wrote that "Evidence that the US is a failed state is piling up faster than I can record it."[315]

I never, ever, imagined that in my lifetime I would see such ugliness, falsehood, propaganda, misprision, insensitivity, misdirection, and plain vileness woven into the very *fabric* of literary "thinking" or of literary "thought" as I have seen over the past decade or maybe fifteen years and that I see right here in Don DeLillo and Frank Rich. I know all the old stories of *political* failed-thinking among literary folk and of *literary* failed-thinking among *political* folk—Ezra Pound can be an example of the first, Grace Paley one of the many examples of the second. But I never, ever thought I would find myself having to say, in a piece of writing such as this one, to readers such as you, these particular words: "Imagine your way back to the middle or to the early-middle years of the Nazi period in Germany and ask yourself whether the notion that you've just read *here* would or wouldn't be the kind of thing you'd be likely to have read *there*.

Look at them, at *these words*:

> "People running for their lives are part of the story that is left to us" because "they take us beyond the hard numbers of dead and missing and give us a glimpse of elevated being."

We could be back in 1939, or 1942, when sacrifice of the mere individual, in the name of and for the sake of "the homeland," was not only an expected thing, but even a *desirable* thing—and why? Because a certain unexamined abstraction was held to be most important of all things, and, in dying for the sake of that abstraction, there would be the enormous reward, for those left behind, of their having been given "a glimpse of elevated being." The "hard numbers" of the dead give "us" the "elevation," the *meaning*—no, not the meaning, but *elevated* meaning. And what's that? What is this "elevated meaning"? How about trying out the word "glory" for the elevated meaning? How about the word "nation" as the thing one could be sacrificed for in order to reach elevated meaning? Or how about the word "*Homeland*"?

I can imagine readers, if they've come along this far, shaking their heads, disagreeing with me, then quickly growing adamant in that disagreement. *No*, they'd say. This isn't the same thing at all. Now isn't the same as then. This is *different* from Germany.

But I'm very much afraid it's not different. In *kind* it's not different. And even in degree and in severity, just exactly how differ-

---

[315] "Are You Ready for the Next Crisis?, in *Online Journal* (Nov. 4, 2009): http://onlinejournal.com/artman/publish/article_5224.shtml

ent *is* it, really, once you tally up *all* the numbers of *all* the mangled, ruined, poisoned, crippled, lost, or dead in the U.S., and in Iraq, and in Afghanistan, and in Pakistan,[316] and once you tally up *all* of the tortured and *all* of the grotesquely wounded, injured, and most, most pitiably ruined,[317] *all* of the imprisoned and *all* of the victims of extraordinary rendition, not to mention the changes inside our own state, the eliminations and disappearances of constitutional liberties and rights, the preparation of internment camps, the lifting of Posse Comitatus—how different is it, *really?*

As if, in any case, *numbers* were the only issue in questions of this kind.

Our nation, simply put, has turned inside out. We joined with allies in WW II to fight against the Axis, and now we *are* the axis. We were a nation of laws, not of men, and now our very "leaders" are criminals programmatically looting and robbing both the nation and its people blind. Take a look at Richard C. Cook's recent piece, "America the Betrayed."[318] Here's a sample, though I urge you to look at the whole thing for yourself:

> American family farming is practically dead and is under a new assault from speculators who are undercutting prices and forcing foreclosures. The local manufacturing sector never came back after the calamitous decline produced by the Paul Volcker recession of 1979-1983, when interest rates were deliberately raised to over 20 percent to kill off family-owned businesses so that global corporations could step in and take over. Since then we had the "Reagan Revolution" when the banks took over the economy, the Clinton dot.com bubble of the 1990s, which crashed in 2000, and the George W. Bush/Alan Greenspan housing bubble which blew up in 2008. Now Main Street lies shattered and shuttered as a result of the crimes and treacheries of the last 30 years.

This is the same argument as the one made by *A Nation Gone Blind*, except that my own book stays away from banking and bubbles

---

316 Update: And now also in Somalia and Yemen.

317 For some sense of the sheer scale of the destruction and suffering brought about among the non-combat population in Iraq alone, see this site, beginning with "New World Order Statistic." Begin reading, and then go on through the entire site. If you can bear it, look at the photographs. ("In September 2009, Fallujah General Hospital, Iraq, had 170 new born babies, 24% of whom were dead within the first seven days, a staggering 75% of the dead babies were classified as deformed. / This can be compared with data from the month of August in 2002 where there were 530 new born babies of whom six were dead within the first seven days and only one birth defect was reported. Doctors in Fallujah have specifically pointed out that not only are they witnessing unprecedented numbers of birth defects but what is more alarming is: 'a significant number of babies that do survive begin to develop severe disabilities at a later stage.'") http://www.thewe.cc/weplanet/news/depleted_uranium_iraq_afghanistan_balkans.html

318 "America The Betrayed: Walt Whitman, 'Poet of the People,'" in *Global Research* (Nov. 6, 2009): http://globalresearch.ca/index.php?context=va&aid=15952

and "legal" robbery of the people *by* the "government." But *A Nation Gone Blind* does zero in on the likes of Don DeLillo, Dwight Garner, Rebecca Solnit, and Frank Rich—the literati who are as blind as dead-men[319] to the actual truth of the very life right in front of their eyes.

Now, I'm still not convinced that Rich isn't an asset of some one or another of the huge handful of intelligence agencies the U.S. seems to grow the way dogs grow fleas, that he hasn't been planted to spew out disinformation from his bully pulpit in the *Times*. Either way, he's a quisling, whether he's spewing disinformation knowingly or out of an empty Grand Canyon's worth of non-information or disinformation. But DeLillo? Solnit? Garner? Shall we go on? Roth? Updike? Grisham? King? Koontz? Crichton? Shall we toss in Bill Keller? And, then, shall we rise up out of the cellar? Chabon? Marcus? Moore? Eggers? Foer? Readers of *A Nation Gone Blind* may remember Birkerts, Butler, Ford.

But there's no point in continuing. Bad enough is this awful fact: In all of America today there are *no* well-known literary—or even "literary"—writers either courageous enough, informed enough, or capable enough in the ability to see the *full* truth of life today—there are *none* sufficiently equipped in these ways so that they can or do use that full truth of our lives *as the material of their art.*

Fear, ignorance, hypocrisy, cowardice, treasonous criminality, or some lesser form of deceit—who knows the cause in each case? But we all know that in conditions like this, with writers like those we have now, nothing in our known, published, reviewed and acclaimed national literature is any longer true, but *all* of it is false. All of it is compromised. None of it can claim honesty,[320] and none of it can claim the stature either of art or of literature, let alone achieve perdurability.

We're washed up. Finished. Our "mainstream" writers, our recognizably "literary" writers, all of those who are now "known," who get visibly published, who get reviewed in visible places, *all* of them are either blind, blinded, half-blind, self-blinded, purblind, or blind through mere—no, *sheer*—obliviousness, lassitude, anti-educational conditioning, and ignorance. Perhaps fear—fear of the truth, and fear of being *associated* with the truth—plays a part in many, although fear of this kind, however understandable, is no more excuse in this case than is ignorance of the law in the case of a legal infraction *of* the law.

The situation is very, very near hopeless. How many writers may be like DeLillo in the aspects of DeLillo that we're now going to take a look at, I don't know, but it's essential that we take this look nev-

---

[319] See chapter 15, "Is Dwight Garner a Dissembler, Deceiver, and Malefactor to the Nation?"

[320] None of it can claim honesty insofar as none of it, to borrow a well-known comparison, tells the truth, the whole truth, and nothing but the truth.

ertheless. Almost as if merely in passing, Frank Rich, in his review of *Falling Man*, mentions a misconception of literary art that's so thunderously misconceived, so completely misguided and wrong, and so extraordinarily pernicious, that it demands correcting.

We've seen this passage already, but I'm not sure that everyone saw it—like a landmine that luckily got stepped *over* rather than *on* when we took this path before. The passage returns us to our good-buddy Bill Gray, who, as you'll remember, feels totally dissed and pissed because the "terrorists, the bomb makers and gunmen" have "annexed the territory that once belonged to the novelist"—those last are Frank Rich's words, and you'll notice that this now-stolen "territory," by a Richian bit of magic too devious and Mephistophelian to follow, somehow changes from a "territory" into an "*ability*," specifically, "the ability 'to alter the inner life of the culture.'" It's *this*, then—a "territory" that's been transmuted into an "*ability 'to alter the inner life of the culture*'"—that big novelist Bill is mad at having been cheated out of by the bad guys, the very same "*ability*" that we cannot help but take as being as desirable to Don DeLillo as it is to Bill Gray, since DeLillo does, after all, in his *Harper's* article, snuggle comfortably into the skin of big Bill and start talking out of big Bill's very mouth.

And what a travesty all of this Frank Rich-Bill Gray-Don DeLillo "territory" and "ability" and "inner life of the culture" stuff *is*. What a witch's brew of misbegotten, wrong-headed, non-literary, delusional, grandiose, under-educated, puff-brained false assumptions, erroneous purposes, fake powers and "abilities," curdled Romanticism, and essentially tyrant-minded stuff it is. Again, if *this* is an example of what America's literary intelligentsia is able to offer—well, as I said, we're finished. Washed up. And so is our literature.

What *is* "the inner life of the culture"? And where *does* it come from? And, above all, how does it get "altered"?

I pride myself that I do know at least something about these questions and the answers to them, since these are essentially the questions that make up the substance and subject of *A Nation Gone Blind*. That book reveals my own great fears about the inner life of the culture (that it's been starved to death, lied to, made blind, all but destroyed); my understanding of its origin (that it can come into existence, be kept in existence, and can thrive only within one indissoluble and essential individual self at a time, and never in more than one at a time, *ever*), that it can be harmed, sickened, poisoned, crippled, and made impotent or diseased with infinitely greater ease and simplicity of method than can conceivably be compared to the hard work, diligence, commitment, and complexity of effort that are required for it to be aided, nurtured, strengthened, deepened, made resilient, and generally kept alive, vibrant, whole, sensitive, rewarding, and fecund.

The good that exists in the "inner life of the culture" can be *learned* (by each single, indissoluble, individual self), but the good that exists in it *cannot, ever,* be dictated, forced, or compelled into existence.

It's infinitely easier to kill things than to bring them to life. This fact is as true of the "inner life of the culture" as it is of any other organic being or thing.

Over the past sixty years, America has done far more killing that creating. If that weren't the case, *A Nation Gone Blind* almost undoubtedly wouldn't have come into existence. But it did come into existence. When you're finished reading *it*, take a look at Richard C. Cook's recent short piece—we saw a bit from it a few minutes ago—"America the Betrayed."[321]

And then, if you *still* don't think we're finished, you're more of an optimist than I am. That doesn't mean, however, that I've given up, or that I'm *going* to give up. I'm a writer, and I'll go on writing until I die. Why? In part, because my definition of writing is this: It's the telling of the truth in a way that's itself also true.[322] And "truth" means truth the way we were talking about it earlier—truth that's not just true but that's the whole truth and nothing but. *And* it means, lest we forget, also being "as alert as possible to *everything that can be understood out of*" that truth.

Writing is a serious and significant thing. *Very* few people—including academics—any longer understand this fact, let alone care about it or believe it. If we can't increase the number who *do* understand it, and understand *why* it's both important and true—well, then I think we're finished.

The other part of the reason I'll keep on writing until I—or we all—die is that there's only one thing that can protect us from Frank Rich, Dwight Garner, Rebecca Solnit, Bill DeLillo, Don Gray and all the others who, by falsifying and lying, are, whether they know it or *not*, on the side of the people and the forces now prepared and determined to destroy our republic, bleed its people, and then, once bled, more likely than not imprison them, or imprison at least those who are still actually alive, including those who scream—and those who write.

The only thing that can prevent such loathsome and accursed things—along with the hateful, criminal, murderous, despicable events and undertakings that are *already* well under way—from being brought to completion once and for all is *truth*. As we've seen, there are very few examples of it around us these days. And even fewer practitioners *of* it.

---

[321] See chapter 15, "Is Dwight Garner a Dissembler, Deceiver, and Malefactor to the Nation?"

[322] For more on this idea, see my "Interview with Myself" at http://www.ericlarsen.net/author.interview.1.html

That's why the arts—not Frank Rich, not Dwight Garner, not Rebecca Solnit, not Bill DeLillo, not Don Gray, but the *arts*—are so fundamentally, radically, profoundly important: Because that's what the arts are *for*, to show, portray, tell, manifest, or be made up of the truth. That's the *only* thing the arts are for. Any "arts" that *fail* to be constituted in this way or *fail* to exist for the purpose of being, showing, manifesting, consisting of, or revealing truth—any "arts" failing in these ways are, in a word, phony; they're phony art. In fact, they're beyond phony. They're beyond despicable. Often, especially these days, they're traitorous as well. Nowadays, though, the failed kind is just about the only kind we've got.

•

So. If art really does exist to tell the truth in a way that's *also* true—well, the question will come up, the truth about *what?* The answer is this: The truth about the condition and nature of life *and* the condition and nature of our existence *in* it. Life, of course, includes *every aspect and element* of life.[323] This entirety—life and our existence inside it—provides and constitutes the subject, content, purpose, and form of all art.

That's what the arts are for. That's the *only* thing they're for.

The arts can't lie and be true. The arts can't be incomplete and be true—this means *all* arts, and *all* writing, *every* verbal and literary art, from Rich to Garner to Solnit to DeLillo to Birkerts to Butler to Friedman to Toni Morrison to A. Stephen Engel.[324]

Having come this far, it's much easier to see the real source of the cancer in Frank Rich's review, "The Clear Blue Sky," and to see the real source of the cancer in DeLillo's *Falling Man*.

---

323 Q: What truth? The truth about what?
A: Well, about existence, of course. About the nature of existence and of being alive in existence, which is the only subject there is for any art, ever. I mean, art doesn't have to be high, ponderous, or philosophical, doesn't have to be *The Magic Mountain*, say, or *The Death of Virgil*, though it certainly can be. It might take up only a tiny little piece of the one subject that nourishes all art—something akin to the glittery-eyed fox fur in "Miss Brill" or the lump of clay in James Joyce's story by that same title, "Clay." But if it's going to be art, if it's going to be literature, you can bet your boots that that's what it's got to be about, the fact of our existing, and the nature of our existing within existence. And it's got to tell the truth about that and do so in a way that's true. And both of those stories do exactly so, you can bet your boots again.
Q: Tall order, that definition of writing.
A: It's been done for centuries. It's been done for millennia.
Q: And today writing doesn't do that?
A: Writing today can't do it. It can't do it unless writers somehow become able, a thing I increasingly despair of, become able to regain control of their own true authentic selves and therefore their own true authority as individuals. (Read more from this self-interview at http://www.ericlarsen.net/author.interview.1.html)

324 See *Topiary: A Novel* (2009) at http://www.oliveropenpress.com/Oliver.003.topiary.html

The fact is that the chief task of the arts is *not* "to alter the inner life of the culture." The arts, after all, are themselves a *part* of that very "inner life." And their chief task—a task that, in any healthy culture, constitutes the highest of callings—is to tell, show, manifest, or reveal the truth, first, the truth about the nature *of* that life, and the truth, second, of the nature of existence *inside* that life.

Art becomes propaganda the instant it conceives of itself as a *separate thing* from the life, or the inner life, that it's *a part of* and can *only be* a part of. Bill Gray becomes a bully and a thug the instant he conceives of himself as one upon whom it's incumbent in the first place to "alter" the "inner life of the culture" or of anything else—just as every single writer becomes a bully and a thug, driven by ego and agenda, the instant he or she conceives of himself or herself as one upon whom it's incumbent, by means of novels, or of any other literary form, to "alter" the "inner life of the culture."

If you don't wholly, or quite, follow my meaning, try a word-substitution or two. Take that phrase I just used, "by means of novels," and substitute other words in place of "novels." Look at what you get:

the instant he or she conceives of himself or herself as one upon whom it's incumbent, by means of arguments, to "alter" the "inner life of the culture."

or

the instant he or she conceives of himself or herself as one upon whom it's incumbent, by means of knives, to "alter" the "inner life of the culture."

or

the instant he or she conceives of himself or herself as one upon whom it's incumbent, by means of bombs, to "alter" the "inner life of the culture."

or

the instant he or she conceives of himself or herself as one upon whom it's incumbent, by means of terrorism, to "alter" the "inner life of the culture."

Many, I know—very possibly most—will pooh-pooh the very idea that, within the bounds of reason, "by means of novels" can be declared comparable to "by means of knives" or "by means of bombs" or "by means of terrorism."

Well, I'll grant that I'd rather be "noveled" than knifed, bombed, or terrorized. On the other hand, if the phrase—as it must be—is expanded to "noveled to death," then the preferability of being "noveled" over being knifed or bombed disappears. Death is death. A corollary: Spiritual death is spiritual death.

It's crucial to keep in mind what our real subject is. And, while that subject is *death*, it's not *yet* necessarily *physical* death that we're talking about, however soon that may become the case.[325] For the moment, however, the subject is the death of conscience, the death of wholeness, the death of perceptiveness, and, corollary to all those, the death of art, truth, intellectual dignity, of the self, politics, freedom, liberty, of the republic; of America; and, if things continue unchecked in the direction they're now going, perhaps far more than only these.

When a culture collapses and proceeds to die, those living inside it may be among the least aware of what is happening. What people have become used to tends to be taken by them as "normal"[326]— thanks in part to "tyrant custom"[327] or simply to habit, the "great deadener."[328]

Habit—and six decades of powerful media persuasiveness encouraging people *to follow* habit—has led Americans to "believe" that elections are still honest and fair, to "believe" that a President would never lie openly in order to begin a transparently illegal invasion abroad, to "believe" that failure to bring relief to a major city struck by massive disaster could not conceivably be a failure by design

---

325 And of course it has *already* become the case for all those who have died in Katrina, or on 9/11, or in Iraq, in Afghanistan, in Somalia, in Pakistan, and in Gaza—*so far*. And it's important to stay current with the potential for more deaths as suggested by news pieces like this one ("H1N1: Police Hold Down WV During Forced Swine Flu Vaccination" [Nov. 11, 2009]: http://deathby1000papercuts.com/2009/11/h1n1-police-hold-down-wv-boy-during-forced-swine-flu-vaccination/) or this one ("Parents Must Immunize Their Children Or Go To Jail," in *Mark Century Truth News*, Wednesday November 14, 2007, Prince Georges County, MD: http://www.prisonplanet.com/articles/november2007/141107Immunize.htm).

326 "Non-empiricism is after all a form of blindness: there are certain things that, except through empiricism, can't be shown and thus can't be seen. Nor can they, therefore, be contested. A government that is non-empiricist will revert to, or, by definition *be*, a tyranny. A *people* that is non-empiricist will be governable only by appeal to desire, by appeal to the voluptuary or sensate, not by appeal to *idea*.

"In the United States today, we have both a non-empiricist government and a non-empiricist population. The situation, as Lewis Lapham put it, 'doesn't hold out much promise for the American future.' In the absence of essential change, stability can't be relied on for much longer, certainly not stability in any remaining context of liberty or freedom. As for revolt, it may no longer be possible for it ever to come. It *certainly* won't come in the immediate future, since most things still look normal. Most things still *look* regular and familiar. Things don't *look* unreal, so nothing's alarming.

"And that's *really* alarming." (*A Nation Gone Blind*, p. 195)

327 "The tyrant custom, most grave senators / Hath made the flinty and steel couch of war / My thrice-driven bed of down" (*Othello*, I, iii).

328 "But habit is a great deadener," *Waiting for Godot*, Act II.

but a failure only by "ineptitude," to "believe" that all vaccines are "good"[329] for you, that national and international health organizations must have the interests of the people at heart,[330] and that doctors and physicians, just like the *New York Times*, are *always* to be trusted. Habit led Americans to take as meaningful and "true" every glib phrase and empty platitude about "change" uttered by Obama throughout his campaign, even though *he himself* contradicted virtually everything he also claimed true.[331]

No news there, some may say—Americans have always been gullible, dumb, and behind the curve. Yes and no. Americans haven't *always* had television. Americans haven't *always* been non-readers to the extent they are now. Americans haven't *always* been as isolated from social and community institutions, meeting places, forums, and cultural places and events as they are now.[332]

And, importantly, those relatively few Americans who *do* still read have never been *so poor at it* as they've come to be now. Ditto for their writing. Poor at reading, poor at writing: Enormous audiences are pathetically unequipped—partly from their habitual reluctance to *become equipped*, partly from their being discouraged *from* becoming equipped, and partly from their *inability* to do so—to detect the lies both of omission and commission, the half-truths posing as whole ones, the ugly meanness and parochialism posing as the informed and fashionable, or to see for what they are the pure manglings and torturings of human feeling, common sense, morality, and simple truth when they're transmuted into the ugly, meretricious, vile, and propagandistic.

The arts, literature, intellectual wholeness, and with them political strength in*side* individuals, hence the individual ability to see the difference between smart and dumb, true and fake, real and unreal—all of these are weakened and to a great extent lost, leaving every single person who lacks them defenseless and exposed, helpless, possibly even the happy victim equally of fraud, folly, falsehood, and lies.

What in the name of all heaven's saints do Frank Rich and Don DeLillo mean when they put together, between them, a sentence like this one:

---

[329] See Robert F. Kennedy, Jr., "What you are doing to this generation of children," at *Global Research* (Nov. 10, 2009): http://globalresearch.ca/index.php?context=va&aid=16014

[330] See "The Jane Burgermeister Archive," http://www.theflucase.com/

[331] For much more on Obama's background and on the campaign, see Webster Griffin Tarpley, *Barack H. Obama: The Unauthorized Biography* (Progressive Press, 2008): http://www.amazon.com/Barack-H-Obama-Unauthorized-Biography/dp/0930852818/ref=sr_1_1?ie=UTF8&s=books&qid=1258127576&sr=1-1 .

[332] See Robert D. Putnam, *Bowling Alone: The Collapse and revival of American Community* (Simon & Schuster, 2000): http://www.amazon.com/Bowling-Alone-Collapse-American-Community/dp/0743203046/ref=sr_1_1?ie=UTF8&s=books&qid=1258127918&sr=1-1

An event like 9/11 cannot be bent to "the mercies of analogy or simile."

The stuff inside quotes is DeLillo's, the stuff outside is Rich's. What on earth does it mean that something can't be "bent" to analogy or simile? What does that metaphor of blacksmithing or iron-working *say* about Rich's assumptions regarding, first, the purposes and the uses and the nature of figures of speech; and, second, regarding the *nature* of those figures of speech in their relation to what—no matter *what* Rich cutely says or implies—can *still* be called *external reality*; and, third, regarding the work, role, and method of the artist in relation to those figures of speech, in relation to external reality, and in relation to the joining of the two?

Bent? Mercies? What are they *talking* about? Does "bent" mean that external reality is or must be falsified or changed in order for it to be expressed through figures of speech? On the other hand, does "mercies" mean that figures of speech do something *nice* to external reality—another way of suggesting that the external reality is to be *changed* by being expressed in figurative language?

These men, as we've already seen, are both grossly deceived in their apparent understanding of what the writing of narrative is, how it comes into being, and what it's traditionally and properly, in a *literary or artistic* way, intended for. We've seen already that what Rich and DeLillo seem to be is "reality bullies." One of them wants to "bend" reality, the other apparently wants to bequeath "mercy" upon it, while at the *same* time he wants to use it as a tool that will force things—including "inner life"—to be *different* from before.

If that's not *bullying* reality, I don't know the meanings of those two words, "bullying" and "reality."

How much one wishes that these two were better read, that they were more sensitively and widely *educated*, that they *knew more* about their own culture and its history, that they were more greatly experienced in the past and less reliant upon their experiences in and of the already-tawdry, falsified, meretricious simplifications of our present time.

How much would be gained if their understandings of art and narrative were drawn from sources more deeply seasoned by human thought, more threaded by consciousness of the past and of the arts of the past than can be provided to them by, say, comic books, thrillers, adventure escape, and television. Where else does big Bill Gray come from? The "bending" of reality to narrative? The use of art as a "tool" to "alter" a culture's "inner life"—something like putting art to its requisite uses under the likes of Hitler or Stalin.

How grateful all of us might be if DeLillo and Rich—let the classics go, let the middle ages go, let the Renaissance go, let Romanticism go—had merely read, and remembered, more Conrad, or more Ford Madox Ford, or more Virginia Woolf, these writers who showed the moderns (that is, until the moderns forgot it, started watching television, and themselves fell into being simple-minded reality-bullies) that the arts are powerful precisely because they show reality in *ways that are true to it* but in ways also that will allow people—who may never have seen or understood this before—to see or feel or understand *what reality really is.* After *that* kind of experience, people can and will awaken, change, look more fully at their world, be inquisitive, become more independent. *Then* the world might even get better. But after being reality-bullied, on the other hand, people simply feel hopeless, or emptied, or drained—or bitterly, or sadly, or numbly compliant to the false-real they've been caused to "consume" and thus accept as the best they can get, not even knowing there's any other.

Propaganda is loathsome. Art can*not* be loathsome, no matter how "shocking" or "ugly" it may be. Ford Madox Ford famously wrote that he and Joseph Conrad "considered a novel to be a rendering of an affair." It was a rendering, Ford went on,

> of one embroilment, one set of embarrassments, one human coil, one psychological progression. From this the novel got its unity. No doubt it might have its caesura—or even several; but. . . the whole novel was to be an exhaustion of aspects, was to proceed to one culmination, to reveal once and for all, in the last sentence—or the penultimate—in the last phrase, or the one before it, the psychological significance of the whole.

It doesn't "bend" that human significance, and it doesn't give it "mercy" and it doesn't "alter" it. Instead, it *shows it, reveals* it as only that particular artwork can. A few sentences further on, even more famously, Ford wrote this:

> For, in the end, Conrad and I found salvation not in any machined form, but in the sheer attempt to reproduce life as it presents itself to the intelligent observer. *I daresay, if we could only perceive it, life has a pattern.*[333]

The emphasis is mine, to draw attention to Ford's idea—to the profound simplicity of this one single aesthetic idea, or art-idea, the concept, and the one concept alone, that gives power and meaning and perdurability to art—*all* art—by merit of its being an idea, concept, or even an *act* that combines into a single thing the *material* of an art and the *material* of external reality; and that combines these two things in such a way that a previously unseen or unfelt truth

---

[333] Ford Madox Ford, *Return to Yesterday* (Liveright, 1932), pp. 203-204 (Liveright Paperbound Edition 1972): http://www.abebooks.com/servlet/SearchResults?an=Ford+Madox+Ford&sts=t&tn=Return+to+Yesterday&x=77&y=19.

about external reality, or *about* the capabilities of the art's material—
or about both—will be made perceptible.

How far is *that* from the undertakings of reality-bullies, or the
undertakings of liars, cover-up artists, or propagandists?

I'm sorry, but we've got to look yet again at some of the same
Rich-DeLillo conjurings that we've seen already but haven't seen as
deeply as we can now. Everyone will remember "An event like 9/11
cannot be bent to 'the mercies of analogy or simile.'" But here's the
sentence that follows it, again with what's inside the quotes coming
from DeLillo, what's outside them from Rich. Look closely at what's
being said. You can do this by looking for the bully-verb:

> Primal terror—"the cellphones, the lost shoes, the handkerchiefs mashed
> in the faces of running men and women"—has to take precedence over
> politics, history and religion.

I'm sure you saw it right away. And, may I ask, just *why* is it,
Mr. Rich, that "primal terror" *has* (bully-verb) "to take precedence
over politics, history and religion"? Those first two are your words,
"primal terror." But what you follow them with—DeLillo's words—
scarcely justifies your choice. "[The] cellphones, the lost shoes, the
handkerchiefs mashed in the faces of running men and women"—do
you mean also that we "*have*" to accept these details as "primal terror"? You're quite, quite wrong. What you've provided is simply a list
of three details of external reality. Now you're saying that we "have"
to accept them as "primal terror," which in simple fact they're *not*.
What *are* they? They're three details of external reality, and *you're*
insisting that they be taken as something else than that. No, you're
a bully-writer, and this is a classic example of bully-writing. You set
out not to convey external reality. Nor do you set out to reveal something previously unseen in external reality. No, *you* set out to weave
something *into* external reality that *isn't really there*. And then you
say that we *have* to follow along, and you play dirty tricks, dissemble,
and twist arms to "make" us do it.

Why? Why would you or any other writer wittingly *do* such
things? And look at the shameless extremes you go to in your dictatorial *making* us see things in external reality that aren't there—look
at everything that, according to you, we *have* to ignore, everything
we *have* to give up in order to follow your notion of what's *in* this
external reality:

> Primal terror—"the cellphones, the lost shoes, the handkerchiefs mashed
> in the faces of running men and women"—has to take precedence over
> politics, history and religion.

Quite a lot of external reality, isn't it, that you say we've "got" to ignore. We've *got* to ignore politics. We've *got* to ignore history. We've *got* to ignore religion.

"Ignore" means remain ignorant of. Pretty quickly, at the pace you set, we'll achieve a degree of ignorance that's positively American! We'll be right there in league with you yourself, for example, or maybe even with Rebecca Solnit, Thomas Friedman, and Dwight Garner.

Perhaps we can get jobs at the *Times*. Just look at you, Mr. *Times*-man. You seem to know even less about 9/11 than anybody with his or her own *eyes*. Let me address not you, any longer, but my own readers. Let me give you, *my* readers, another sentence from Frank Rich's breathless and idolatrous piece about DeLillo's lazy, inane, and truly ignorant novel. I'll propose a quiz, pass or fail. In this sentence about things that happen in the novel, find a single word showing that the writer of the sentence either *has no eyes* of his own or has *never used them* in looking at the external reality of 9/11. Whether he hasn't got them or has never used them doesn't really matter very much, since the result is the same—although of course it's possible that he *did* use his eyes and is now lying through his teeth. The sentence:

> Keith, a lawyer nearing 40, narrowly makes it out of one of the buckling towers, then turns up, "all blood and slag" and with "a gaze that had no focus in it," at the door of the wife, Lianne, from whom he has long been separated.

And yet again you got it in a trice! You're very, very good. Now, take a good long look at the website identified in this footnote[334] and see if you can find *any* justification whatsoever for using the word "buckling" in describing how any of the three towers fell. Take your time. Look around. Watch the videos. Then go to the page of that web site identified in *this* footnote,[335] the page that lists "Some of the principal data that must be explained" if the collapse of the three buildings is to be understood accurately and correctly rather than just blindly in accordance with "state truth." Here, too, just keep on looking.

If we were in freshman English, and if Frank Rich had submitted his "review" as an assignment, the instructor would have marked "WW" in the margin and drawn a circle around Rich's word "buckling." In case you don't remember, "WW" means "wrong word."

But what do you do in the case of a piece of writing so much bigger, so much more powerful, significant, and important—not to mention misleading, wrong, bullying, and untrue—than just another essay in introductory English?

---

[334] http://drjudywood.co.uk/wtc/
[335] http://drjudywood.co.uk/wtc/#AA2

What's the penalty for this "wrong word," the word "buckling" when no such thing as "buckling" ever took place?[336]

Two further points and we end. The first reveals merely fraudulence and two untruths. The second reveals the degradation and corruption, the poison replacing all the goodness that may once have existed in the hearts and minds of those who fabricate and choose to bully external reality, whether they do so from blindness and ignorance on the one hand, or from malice, self-interest, and deliberation on the other.

Let's take the easy one first, the simple fraudulence and two untruths.

Rich explains that DeLillo, in his novel, makes use of a

> mysterious, fictional[337] performance artist who starts to pop up around New York after the attacks. Falling Man's shtick is to appear unannounced and terrify onlookers with daredevil headfirst falls that in the end are broken by a safety harness.

If I may insert a small particle of truth here, these "appearances" by "Falling Man" are in no way terrifying to anyone, certainly not the reader. They are, as you'll find if you read the book, banal, anti-climactic, and silly. But let it go. Propaganda has certain requirements. About this "fictional" performance artist, Rich goes on to explain that

> A New School panel discussion can't decide whether he's a "Heartless Exhibitionist or Brave New Chronicler of the Age of Terror," but in any case he touches the third rail of 9/11 taboos.

No, he doesn't. The so-called "third rail of 9/11 taboos" has nothing to do with dangling in safety harnesses here and there. No, the "third rail" has to do with one thing and one thing only: That is, with telling the truth, all of it, about 9/11. No way does either DeLillo or his inane little dangling man do *that.*

Rich, in fact, is so powerfully smitten with starry-eyed love for this pet little propaganda-novel he's discovered that he walks right onto an open trapdoor of his own making and doesn't even notice the awful fall he takes. He's already told us that a "New School panel"— would that be a "fictional" panel, do you suppose?—can't decide which of two equal falsehoods about the dangling guy is "true." Now he tells us, right after that bit about the "third rail," this:

---

336 Except very briefly, when the top twenty floors or so of the south tower did begin falling sideways—before disappearing entirely and never hitting the ground.

337 Why on *earth* does Rich put in that superfluous word "fictional"? Just asking. But, please, think about it. Think hard.

In "Falling Man," as in life, no one wants to watch a re-enactment of the Associated Press photo of a man falling headfirst from the north tower— an image that was largely pulled from circulation after 9/12.

Interesting, isn't it. *And all wrong.* It makes me yearn for even a scintilla of truth. How *cleansing* it would be, even a *small bit* of that wondrous thing.

The first untruth, or error, lies in Rich's saying that "no one wants to watch a re-enactment of the Associated Press photo of a man falling headfirst," etc. He may be right in the "re-enactment" part (DeLillo's novel is tedious in the extreme), but he's absolutely dead wrong about the rest of it: *Every*body wanted, and *wants*, to stare and stare and stare and stare at that photo, the one that Rich with his professional's insider-dom reminds us is, or was, an AP image. "Was"? Yes, "was." Rich remains deadpan, being not even *conscious* of his second error, even though it both underscores his first one even as it introduces his second. The photo, he informs us, batting not an eyelash, was "largely pulled from circulation after 9/12."

Rich, the writer of propaganda that's aimed to control minds, alludes *obliviously* to the state apparatus that *also* controls minds by censorship either de jure or de facto. He therefore alludes also to the state apparatus that controls its own assets and agents. Now, why *really*, was that photo "pulled"? Well, I can tell you with a hundred-percent certainty that it was *not* because "no one [wanted]" to look at it. No. Frank Rich is dissembling like a rug when he tells you so, or when he even *hints* it. The photo was pulled because the real 9/11 perpetrators were afraid of it. They were afraid it might backfire on them, revealing plainly to everyone, by means of its pure and *utterly* riveting horror, exactly how they'd gone just a *little bit too far in doing what they did* to all those people who died in the towers. After all, instead of "pulling" the image, why didn't they, the way they did with *so very many* other things and details and atrocities, simply use it to "prove" yet again how unmercifully hate-filled, how monstrous, how murderous and cold-blooded the nineteen young jihadist hijackers really were, to have *done* such a thing, with the backing and direction of their big bearded boss, sneering and hissing back in his Afghan cave?

But such a ploy couldn't be used, not in this case. And that's because something about the image really, actually, *was* truly shocking. Not even the real 9/11 perps wanted anything to do with it. It was too strong. It was too hot. It showed *truth.* Too *much* truth. *This* one could backfire if it were ever discovered that the Bush-Cheneys and their agents and generals had been even remotely connected with having caused such a thing as *this.*

The truth about this image is that it was *too real.* This image *did* tell the truth. And it, therefore, had itself to be covered up.

The photo disappeared because Frank Rich's bosses and his boss's bosses told him and every other flunky throughout all of the media in all of the nation, whether explicitly or implicitly, that it was up to them to disappear it. And, as usual, Frank Rich and all the other quislings across the entire face of our great nation of self-reliant and independent professionals of all ranks did exactly as they were told.

•

And so we come to the end of this long journey, with two questions left to answer. The first: How can it be that Americans have become *so* thoroughly *evil*? There are those among us who lie, and there are those—most Americans, I suppose—among us who turn their backs on the lies, leaving them alone, just going along as though the lies were truth. But lying destroys you, even if you're not the one *doing* it. Turning your back on lies *also* destroys you. These two things together—lies and people's turning of their backs on lies— destroy entire nations, turning them evil first, as has happened to ours already, then bringing ruin to them, as is happening to ours now.

Just look at the madness. Don DeLillo, supposedly a literary man, is clearly *not* one and has been made crazy by turning his back on the lies, accepting them as truth. He is now working not for art, not for life, and not for truth, but he is working instead for our murderers.

Here's a place where it's revealed. We've already seen Frank Rich bullying us into accepting falsehoods and, along with them, happily welcoming greater and greater degrees of ignorance ("Primal terror. . . *has to take precedence* over politics, history and religion").

But we haven't seen DeLillo, in the two sentences following that one, reveal to us, all unwittingly, the degree of his *own* state of madness. Here are the two revealing sentences, with Frank Rich quoting DeLillo from *Harper's*:

"There is something empty in the sky," he wrote. "The writer tries to give memory, tenderness and meaning to all that howling space."

DeLillo still thinks, as he may have all his life, that the writer's job is to alter external reality (or psychological reality) rather than to explore and reveal it. Dangerous stuff. He doesn't *seem* dangerous, of course, since what he wants to "give" to reality are things that *sound* nice ("memory, tenderness and meaning"). The truth is that they may or may not be nice. But let it go, and look instead at what it is that he wants to change so that it *will* be nice: He wants to change emptiness ("something empty in the sky"), I *guess* so that it won't be empty any more; and he wants to change something else that sounds truly, truly dreadful ("all that howling space") so that *it* will be—well, nice, *too.*

And what exactly are those things that he wants to change, the empty thing and the howling thing? Well, in the context of his novel, and of his *Harper's* piece, and of Rich's review of his novel, it's clear that those things are 9/11. So what he wants to do is make 9/11 *nice.* He wants to give 9/11 tenderness, meaning, and memory.

He wants to propagandize, just like Rich, and *that* means, with his absurd tenderness and "meaning," that he's covering up the truth, protecting the real perpetrators and murderers, and that he's ignorantly doing their most devoutly wished-for bidding. He's working for Satan himself. No *wonder* Frank Rich thinks he's the greatest thing since zippers.

But, pardon me, they're outright loony, both of them. Near the end of his review, Rich writes that "Keith must descend back into the hell of 9/11 if DeLillo is to provide the counternarrative to terrorism he promised," whatever in the devil this "counternarrative" actually *is* that they both seem to understand so perfectly. Anyway, DeLillo promised it, and so he's "got" (god knows why) to give his readers the really, really juicy stuff, namely, a guided (whoo*pee!*) tour back into a soon-to-be-molecularly-dissociated tower. *Goodie! Goodie! Maybe we'll see it happen all over again! Oh, wow!*

This "counternarrative," explains Rich, is

> the story that takes us beyond the hard, anonymous numbers of the dead to retrieve what [DeLillo] called in Harper's "human beauty in the crush of meshed steel."

"Human beauty in the crush of meshed steel." Contemptible. Mad. Disgusting. Absolutely disgusting. Vile. Evil.

10.

The remaining question is the one I began this series of essays[338] in order to answer: "Can the literary life exist in a post-*1984* nation."

Or that I began this series of essays in order to *try* to answer.

It's not looking very good, is it. A nation composed entirely of prefabricators on the one hand and, on the other, of the self-deluded who either believe the prefabrications or accept them in an ever-expanding and endlessly adaptable ignorance—such a nation will never have a literature. How could it? None of the writers we've met

---

[338] Two of the three parts are not included in this volume. EL

in this essay would ever conceivably be able to provide even the barest rudiments of a literature. As for the "literary life," well, all that means is "literary person," isn't it? Same answer. So long as anyone is either lying to others or lying to him- or herself about the full and actual nature of the external reality they live within, such a person can't possibly be literary. Sure, they can write poems, stories, and novels—but those will be (as most already are) empty ones, shells, imitations of pieces that once may have been written for *real*, though these copies will be nothing more than copies, lacking the wholeness, the purpose, and the aesthetic drive of the originals. *These* won't be aesthetically meaningful, nor will they be aesthetically complete, and *these* won't be *intellectually* meaningful, nor will they be intellectually complete, since not only will they be imitations but they'll furthermore be born out of a false-world, or at best a half-world, with half-emotions, half-knowledge, half-feelings—a distant cry from Marilynne Robinson's true and indispensible notion that the readiness for art comes only "when the imagination seems to be as *alert as possible to everything that can be understood out of a moment or situation.*" Ignorance, self-delusion, and a life's diet of falsehood are no recipe for this kind of completeness and wholeness.

As far as the nation's present path indicates, if we continue on it as we are now, we're destined to become a nation only more and more ignorant, more and more empty, more and more insane. All of these developments are well advanced already, the spread and growth of ignorance, emptiness, and insanity. I know of no *public* literary figure of an eminence sufficient to make him or her generally recognizable who is doing anything whatsoever to prevent or slow our descent into an empty and ignorant madness. On the other hand, I know many—a great, great many, indeed—literary, near-literary, or semi-literary figures, who are doing everything possible, some wittingly and others not, to accelerate that same descent. These extend from the DeLillos and Riches on through the tribes of Philip Roths and Dwight Garners, further through the millions of soulless and ignorant academics, on to publishers and editors of every sort, from Robert Silvers and Sam Tanenhaus through, shall we say, Matthew Rothschild, Jonathan Galassi, Jacob Weisberg, going from these and their like to the thousands of others, including librarians, publishers, professors, agents, authors, booksellers, journalists, reviewers.

The literary establishment, in this way parallel to the political establishment, has become the enemy of literature itself, and certainly the enemy of what I've been calling the literary life. Those dwelling in this establishment destroy what's alive and then live off its ashes, doing their best to deceive everyone (and very likely also themselves) into believing that the ashes are honeysuckle, brightness, and morning dew. But the whole enterprise is built out of nothing other than lies: Lies driving ever more people ever more deeply into mediocrity and ignorance and hopeless delusion.

I've decided that these establishments as they have come to exist now in this country—establishments literary, political, commercial, and intellectual—are capable of nothing other than the destruction of those who may attempt to work within them—whether working in an effort to oppose them, or in an effort to improve them, or in an effort to gain from them, or simply in the desperate effort to find *some* affirmative means of addressing, enhancing, protecting, and enriching life from inside them.

All such efforts are doomed if one either chooses or tries to work from within these establishments. They have evolved increasingly into death-machines. As The Manager of The CityPlex comments in A. Stephen Engel's excellent *Topiary: A Novel*,[339] "The CityPlex is a slaughter house of entertainment." And so it is, a slaughterhouse of the mind, intellect, and also of the spirit. So are *all* of our corporatized "establishments." Nothing is left to do—at least for the time being—except to escape from them if at all possible and seek out small patches and areas of life, unnoticed places on the north sides of hills or in anonymous back bedrooms in distant cities and towns where *some*thing real has survived, however small, something still authentic, complete, thoughtful, and whole that the establishments haven't yet found, bled, trampled, and killed.

Instead of surrendering, therefore, instead of capitulating to this universe of lies, madness, profits, and delusion that I have been describing, I have decided to hold out, insofar as possible, by turning to the secret rear-guard activity of searching for bits of life that the great-booted thunderers, hypocrites, and destroyers haven't yet succeeded in eliminating.

In my case, it's literary life that I'm after. I'm in search of pieces of work that have the truth in them up to the bursting point, that are themselves *made out of* the truth, that are unique in having found a way to combine themselves *with* the truth to the detriment of neither the truth nor the art and to the enhanced and revelatory capacity of both. Such works as these, in our dying nation now, are very, very few. Quite often they are either hidden or actually *in* hiding, and usually they are quiet. But they're well worth looking for.

Without them we won't survive. Not a chance.

Eric Larsen
November 16, 2009

---

[339] The Oliver Arts & Open Press, 2009.

APPENDIX

This list of books is not complete and is not intended to be taken as complete. It is a partial list of 9/11 books that I myself know, have read, and think might be useful or enlightening to others who want to know more about 9/11 and its implications. As for the merit, quality, and validity of each (and of others not on this list), readers will have to judge for themselves.

In *The Skull of Yorick*, though, I do make reference to certain of the titles (and not others), sometimes frequently. That frequency can be taken as an indicator of the degree of value I place on them—and the degree of trust I have *in* them. Some of the books are dated in one way or another, but none has become irrelevant, and all still contain valid information and useful insight. In my own view, Nafeez Ahmed's *The War on Truth* remains absolutely essential and, if anything, has been strengthened by the time that has passed and the events that have occurred since its publication. I still recommend without hesitation or qualification Michel Chossudovsky's *America's 'War on Terrorism,'* Webster Tarpley's *9/11 Synthetic Terror: Made in USA*, and Barry Zwicker's *Towers of Deception: The Media Cover-Up of 9/11*. Michael C. Ruppert wrote the first significant 9/11 book to appear in the U.S., and there is still a very great deal in it of utmost importance to an understanding of 9/11, especially in regard to the exact chronology and nature of the events that took place (and that were deliberately prevented from taking place) throughout the "chain of command" on the morning of 9/11 itself.

As for the several David Ray Griffin books (not only those listed here), nothing has changed about them and yet in an important sense everything has changed. To me, it's not wholly clear who Griffin sees himself as working for or what he aims, in the end, to accomplish or hope to accomplish. In chapter 14 of *The Skull of Yorick* ("The Debate over 9/11), I cite the piece that Emanuel Sferios wrote on the fifth anniversary of 9/11, "9/11 Five Years Later: What Have We Accomplished?" In that chapter, in footnote 221, I quote considerable portions of Sferios' essay, and readers of that material may more readily understand my question now about David Ray Griffin's books.[1] Equally—or more— pertinent to the question is a piece by Matthew D. Jarvie, on his web site "Dissecting the New Age," called "9/11 Truth and its role in the game" (July 14, 2009).[2]

No longer missing from this list, thanks to the great event of its recent publication, is the most important volume of all those written on 9/11, a volume that I in fact consider—as I wrote in a Foreword that I composed for it—the most important book of the twenty-first century. This is *Where Did the Towers Go? The Evidence of Directed Energy Technology on 9/11*, by Judy Wood, B.S., M.S., Ph.D. Waste no time in finding extraordinarily important book, along with information about it, at http://wheredidthetowersgo.com.

EL
November 2, 2010

Ahmed, Nafeez Mosaddeq. *The War on Freedom: How and Why America Was Attacked September 11, 2001* (Tree of Life Publications, 2002)

Ahmed, Nafeez Mosaddeq. *The War On Truth: 9/11, Disinformation And The Anatomy Of Terrorism* (Olive Branch Press, 2005)

Barrett, Kevin, John Cobb, and Sandra Lubarsky. *9/11 and Amer-*

---

[1] The entire Sferios piece is now available at http://pilotsfor911truth.org/forum/index. php?showtopic=1191
[2] Jarvie writes:
"While I have found much of Griffin's information on 9/11 to be quite good, I found it suspicious that he was so adamant on placing the blame for an inside job almost entirely on the Bush administration. Certainly anyone who has even slight knowledge regarding government black-ops knows they go much higher than the puppetocracy of the White House.
"My suspicions about Griffin were further confirmed when I stumbled upon this YouTube clip of him (http://www.youtube.com/watch?v=m-TZypcH9eg) saying we need global governance to solve our problems." The entire Jarvie essay is available at http://sovereignsentience. blogspot.com/2009/07/911-truth-and-its-role-in-game.html

ican Empire: Christians, Jews, and Muslims Speak Out (Olive Branch Press, 2007)

Barrett, Kevin. *Truth Jihad: My Epic Struggle Against the 9/11 Big Lie.* (Progressive Press, 2007)

Chossudovsky, Michel. *America's "War on Terrorism"* (Global Research, 2005)

Griffin, David Ray, and Peter Dale Scott. *9/11 and American Empire: Intellectuals Speak Out* (Olive Branch Press, 2006)

Griffin, David Ray. *Christian Faith and the Truth Behind 9/11: A Call to Reflection and Action* (Westminster John Knox Press, 2006)

Griffin, David Ray. *The 9/11 Commission Report: Omissions and Distortions* (Olive Branch Press, 2005)

Griffin, David Ray. *The New Pearl Harbor: Disturbing Questions About the Bush Administration and 9/11* (Olive Branch Press, 2004)

Griffin, David Ray. *Debunking 9/11 Debunking: An Answer to Popular Mechanics and Other Defenders of the Official Conspiracy Theory* (Olive Branch Press, 2007)

Hicks, Sander. *The Big Wedding: 9/11, the Whistle-Blowers, & the Cover-Up* (Vox Pop, 2005)

Larsen, Eric. *A Nation Gone Blind: America in an Age of Simplification and Deceit* (Shoemaker & Hoard, 2006)

Marrs, Jim. *The Terror Conspiracy: Deception, 9/11, and the Loss of Liberty* (The Disinformation Company, Ltd., 2006)

Morgan, Rowland, and Ian Henshall. *9/11 Revealed* (Carroll & Graf, 2005)

Ruppert, Michael C. *Crossing the Rubicon: The Decline of the American Empire at the End of the Age of Oil* (New Society Publishers, 2004)

Scott, Peter Dale. *Wealth, Empire, and the Future of America* (The University of California Press, 2007)

Tarpley, Webster Griffin. *9/11 Synthetic Terror: Made in USA* (Progressive Press, 2006)

Wood, Judy. *Where Did the Towers Go? Evidence of Directed Free-Energy Technology on 9/11.* (The New Investigation, 2011, http://wheredidthetowersgo.com)

Zwicker, Barry. *Towers of Deception: The Media Cover-up of 9/11* (New Society Publishers, 2006)

www.ingramcontent.com/pod-product-compliance
Lightning Source LLC
Chambersburg PA
CBHW052032090426
42739CB00010B/1876